THE GEBUSI

*Lives Transformed
in a Rainforest World*

D1015192

THE GEBUSI

Lives Transformed in a Rainforest World

THIRD EDITION

Bruce Knauft

Emory University

The Gebusi: Lives Transformed in a Rainforest World, Third Edition

Published by McGraw-Hill, a business unit of The McGraw-Hill Companies, Inc., 1221 Avenue of the Americas, New York, NY 10020. Copyright © 2013 by The McGraw-Hill Companies, Inc. All rights reserved. Previous editions © 2010 and 2008. Printed in the United States of America. No part of this publication may be reproduced or distributed in any form or by any means, or stored in a database or retrieval system, without the prior written consent of The McGraw-Hill Companies, Inc., including, but not limited to, in any network or other electronic storage or transmission, or broadcast for distance learning.

Some ancillaries, including electronic and print components, may not be available to customers outside the United States.

This book is printed on acid-free paper

2 3 4 5 6 7 8 9 0 DOC/DOC 1 0 9 8 7 6 5 4 3

ISBN 978-0-07-803492-3
MHID 0-07-803492-2

Vice President & Editor-in-Chief: *Michael Ryan*
Vice President of Specialized Publishing: *Janice M. Roerig-Blong*
Editorial Director: *William Glass*
Sponsoring Editor: *Gina Boedeker*
Marketing Manager: *Patrick Brown*
Project Manager: *Melissa Leick*
Design Coordinator: *Margarite Reynolds*
Cover Image: *Courtesy of Bruce Knauft*
Buyer: *Louis Swaim*
Media Project Manager: *Sridevi Palani*
Compositor: *Aptara®, Inc.*
Typeface: *10/12 Janson Text Lt Std*
Printer: *R. R. Donnelley*

All credits appearing on page or at the end of the book are considered to be an extension of the copyright page.

Library of Congress Cataloging-in-Publication Data

Knauft, Bruce M.
    The Gebusi: lives transformed in a rainforest world/Bruce Knauft.—3rd ed.
        p. cm.
    Includes index.
    ISBN 978-0-07-803492-3 (alk. paper)
    1. Gebusi (Papua New Guinean people)—Social conditions. 2. Gebusi (Papua New Guinean people)—Cultural assimilation. 3. Gebusi (Papua New Guinean people)—Social life and customs. 4. Social change—Papua New Guinea. 5. Acculturation—Papua New Guinea. 6. Papua New Guinea—Social life and customs. I. Title.
DU740.42.K524 2012
305.89'912—dc23
                                                                2011049230

www.mhhe.com

To the memory of Yuway (c. 1961–2009)
May his decent spirit and good nature endure among the Gebusi

About the Author

Bruce Knauft is Samuel C. Dobbs Professor of Anthropology and director of the States at Regional Risk Project at Emory University in Atlanta. He has published numerous journal articles and two large ethnographies concerning the Gebusi of Papua New Guinea: *Good Company and Violence* (University of California Press, 1985) and *Exchanging the Past* (The University of Chicago Press, 2002). Dr. Knauft has also published extensively about contemporary analytic and theoretical issues in cultural anthropology and in relation to modern development, including his books *Genealogies for the Present in Cultural Anthropology* (Routledge Press, 1996), and *Critically Modern* (edited, University of Indiana Press, 2002). He is an accomplished scholar of Melanesia, as reflected in his books *From Primitive to Post-colonial in Melanesia and Anthropology* (University of Michigan Press, 1998) and *South Coast New Guinea Cultures* (Cambridge University Press, 1993).

During the past decade, Professor Knauft has become active in engaged or practical anthropology, including project activities that he has directed in West Africa, East Africa, the northern Andes, Inner Asia, and the Himalayas (see http://sarr.emory.edu). He has taught a broad range of undergraduates and also graduate students who have conducted fieldwork in diverse world areas and who are now professional anthropologists in their own right. He regularly teaches freshman seminars and introductory courses in cultural anthropology at Emory. The present book was written with an undergraduate and educated general audience in mind. Professor Knauft has continued his association with the Gebusi people of Papua New Guinea since his first fieldwork among them in 1980–82.

Professor Knauft's CV, selected papers and publications, photos, and flash video presentations, including concerning the Gebusi, are available on his university website (google "Bruce Knauft").

Contents

List of Map, Figures, and Photographs

Map

Figures

Photographs

Preface

BACKGROUND

Anthropology is little without powerful portrayals of peoples and their cultures across the world. For beginning students as well as advanced professionals, the wonder of learning about different ways of life can be both thrilling and provocative. We are pushed to stretch our envelope of understanding and to reconsider our own beliefs and practices. Over the years, a number of short books have exposed students to the richness of cultural variety and human experience. These typically take the form of short ethnographies—summary book-length descriptions of the people and culture considered. The present book follows in this same vein but is distinctive—at least so I hope—in two connected ways. First, I have written this book without the formality and jargon of technical scholarship. This is not to dismiss scholarly writing; I have published more than 1,500 pages of scholarly description and analysis concerning the Gebusi and related peoples in Melanesia, as well as books concerning general theory and analysis in cultural anthropology (see About the Author). In the present thin volume, by contrast, I have taken the liberty to write more lyrically and personally for a larger and more general audience. This book is based on substantial scholarship, but it portrays and humanizes Gebusi, and my experience among them, in ways that are hopefully engaging and evocative.

Second, as a teacher of both beginning undergraduates and graduate students, I have enjoyed writing this book to dovetail with topics and issues covered in introductory cultural anthropology courses and textbooks. This aspect of *The Gebusi* was important to me from the start but has evolved further in the book's present third edition.

Who are the Gebusi? When I first lived among them, they were a small ethnic group of some 450 horticultural foragers living in longhouses in the deep recesses of the interior rainforest of Papua New Guinea, just north of Australia in the South Pacific. At that time, Gebusi society was rife with amazing and seemingly long-standing practices of sorcery and ritual, body art and divination, feasting and camaraderie, violence, and alternative sex practices. When I studied with the Gebusi again sixteen years later, in 1998, they had largely transformed. They were now a Christian people of about 615 who frequented the local market, attended government development meetings, played in the regional sports league, and attended the local church. Their children went to government school five days a week. In the mix, they had become engaged with other ethnic groups in a regional process of nation-building, and they had given up many of their previous beliefs and practices. In 2008, and more recently, Gebusi, now numbering more than 900 people, have weathered an economic recession and near-collapse of the local cash economy. In the bargain, they have rediscovered and resuscitated many aspects of their previous culture. Now, the linchpin of their Province's regional political economy—the large Ok Tedi copper and gold mine, 100 miles to their northwest—is slated for downsizing or closure.

In all, Gebusi have spanned a sizable arc of social and cultural transformation—from their remote isolation in the early 1980s to their active engagement with national and global lifestyles, and then to the resurgence of many of their previous practices. As such, their development illustrates a range of key issues in the understanding of social development, globalization, inequity and marginalization, and also of cultural change and vitality over time.

THE GEBUSI, 3E

In this third edition of *The Gebusi*, I have gently drawn out comparative and general themes. In the process, I have attempted to carefully and selectively revise all the book's chapters without compromising their liveliness and occasional drama. General points, concepts, and themes are then separately summarized and listed in **Broader Connections** segments that are formatted separately at each chapter's end. These can be drawn upon by instructors for presentations in introductory anthropology courses as well by students for purposes of review and linkage to issues otherwise presented in the course. In the book's Table of Contents, the **Broader Connections** topics for each chapter are listed in italics beneath each main chapter title. In all, I have tried to enrich the evocative accounts and experiences related in *The Gebusi* by delineating their connection to themes and concepts taught in beginning anthropology courses. On the other hand, more advanced students can benefit from new Advanced Student Study Questions that link the main text of each chapter to deeper theoretical, analytic, and conceptual issues in anthropology.

In association with the above changes, Chapters 7 and 8 from the second edition are now combined into a new Chapter 7, and former Chapters 9 through 12 are now revised, respectively, as Chapters 8 through 11. The former "Conclusions" are now substantially expanded and reconfigured as a **new Chapter 12, "2012 and Beyond,"** that brings the Gebusi up to date and considers larger issues of political economy, globalization, and engaged anthropology. These changes have allowed me to expand broader contemporary implications at the end of the work.

For purposes of teaching in class, my **flash photo narration** concerning the Gebusi is now available on my academic website (68 minutes in total, in three segments) at http://www.anthropology.emory.edu/FACULTY/ANTBK (or google "Bruce Knauft"). Sound clips of Gebusi music past and present, PDFs of my recent academic papers on the Gebusi, my academic curriculum vitae, and narrated photo presentations of some of my experiences in other world areas are also available on my university website. Information about the States at Regional Risk project that I presently direct can be found at http://sarr.emory.edu.

For this third edition, **a test bank of objective multiple-choice and true/false examination questions** concerning the Gebusi is available for instructors online (see further below). Chapter-by-chapter **Study Questions** have been expanded and are now posted on "The Gebusi Information Center" McGraw-Hill website, and also on my university website, rather than printed in the book itself. A separate set of study questions especially **For Advanced Students** have been configured and posted for each chapter of the book's third edition. These questions relate the revised chapters of *The Gebusi* to issues that students often address in intermediate and upper division courses, including both advanced topical matters and issues pertaining to the narrative and rhetorical structure of the book and the subject position/s of the author within it. The **Advanced Student Study Questions** can be productively used to frame or stimulate essay writing assignments concerning the book—in addition to the use of the "regular" study questions for this purpose in lower division courses and for use in shorter or more descriptive student assignments.

As in the second edition of the book, personal names are in most cases actual names, used with permission, and in a few cases pseudonyms, including when a depiction is potentially unflattering or embarrassing in a modern context and the person is still alive. Increasingly, however, names are original and actual. Quotations taken from my Gebusi field notes have often been edited from the original to make them clearer or more succinct for a general audience.

KEY FEATURES

Broader Connections segments at the end of the chapters summarize the chapter's main points and relate them to general themes and concepts in cultural anthropology. Students can use **Broader Connections** sections to review the chapter and link it to concepts and themes in their larger course and/or their textbook. Instructors can also use these sections to link *The Gebusi* to their presentations on a range of topics and concepts in introductory courses—and to quickly see the substantive changes between the second and third editions of the book.

A full-length photo narration of The Gebusi—in three segments—is publicly available on the author's academic website.

An updated List of Persons printed in the book's end matter provides an alphabetical listing of persons mentioned in the book, including their changed status over time.

A test bank of **30 Objective Examination Questions** concerning *The Gebusi, 3e*, is available for instructors via the McGraw-Hill EZ Test Online website. Instructors can easily request and receive a login. This also allows instructors to access the entire library of questions from McGraw-Hill, including from other of their textbooks, and to combine these as desired with examination questions concerning the Gebusi specifically. The Gebusi exam questions are also available for instructors at The Gebusi Information Center website for the third edition under Instructor Edition.

Newly formulated **Study Questions for Advanced Students**, for use in intermediate and upper-division courses, are available on the McGraw-Hill Gebusi Information Center website for the third edition of the book and also on the author's academic website. **Regular Study Questions** for use in introductory classes and for shorter student assignments are also available at these websites.

Sound clips of Gebusi music past and present are available on the author's academic website.

An **Image Library of 350 color photographs of Gebusi, organized by chapter and cross-indexed by topic** can be used for student interest, projects, or extra-credit assignments. Photos can be copied and used by instructors in their own classroom teaching and presentations. Photos are accessed by chapter under the "choose one" tab on the student edition section of the McGraw-Hill Gebusi Information Center website for the third edition of the book.

Notes keyed to Gebusi, 3e link the text to further information and larger issues and topics, as well as references for further reading, that provide deeper understanding as well as material and guidance for student essays and research projects. **Notes** are available on the McGraw-Hill Gebusi Information Center website and also on the author's academic website. These sites also contain a full **Reference List and Citations** of scholarly sources.

The author's recent academic papers on Gebusi and the author's full Gebusi reference list are available on the author's academic website.

The Gebusi Information Center website for the third edition can be found at www.mhhe.com/knauft3e.

ACKNOWLEDGMENTS

It is hard to express the personal and professional gratitude that I have for my Gebusi friends and acquaintances. Deepest thanks go to Sayu, Didiga, Keda, Yamdaw, Mosomiay, Abi, and Father Aloi. I gratefully acknowledge help throughout from officials and staff at Nomad and Kiunga and the Catholic Church in both of these locations.

Especially in remote regions, field research is difficult if not impossible to complete without financial assistance from funding and granting agencies. I gratefully acknowledge funding for my Gebusi field research from the U.S. National Science Foundation, the U.S. National Institutes of Mental Health, the Rackham Graduate School at the University of Michigan, the U.S. Department of Education, the Wenner-Gren Foundation, the Harry Frank Guggenheim Foundation, and Emory University. Major support for my States at Regional Risk Project (SARR), described in Chapter 12, is gratefully acknowledged from the Carnegie Corporation of New York.

Thanks go to numerous persons who have read and commented on various drafts of this book, including anonymous reviewers, Stuart Kirsch, and the McGraw-Hill editors. Kathryn Bennett helped edit and proof the second edition manuscript, and attentive assistance in proofing and correcting this third edition of *The Gebusi* is very gratefully acknowledged from Helen Simmons at Emory University. I thank Eileen Knauft for her photos of Gebusi during 1980–82 and her information about women's lives and experiences during that time. Small parts of *The Gebusi* overlap with my book *Exchanging the Past*, published by the University of Chicago Press in 2002. I owe a special debt to my undergraduate and graduate students at Emory University. They have given me the courage not simply to teach anthropology from the heart but to go back to the field and learn it all over again!

This book is dedicated to the memory of Yuway. Yuway befriended me when I first arrived and was learning the Gebusi language, and he was my stalwart friend since that time. He was one of the most decent, thoughtful, and pleasant people I have ever met. Born about 1961, Yuway died after a major illness, about 48 years of age, in June 2009. Amid the ailments and short life span that continue to afflict Gebusi, Yuway embraced the full potentials of the precolonial, colonial, and the modern post-colonial eras—all during a span of less than five decades. He did so with grace, good humor, and perseverance. May the memory of him remain bright, and may his children, his family, and his broader community prosper in their own rich ways.

Entry

IT LOOKS SO GRAND from a thousand feet up, the forest glowing deep, green, and vast. The broccoli tops of the trees form an endless carpet, an emerald skin shielding worlds of life within. You look down to see two blue-brown ribbons of water etching the forest canopy. You follow them through the window of your tiny plane as they snake toward each other and merge in gentle delight. Below, in the nestled crook of these two rivers, you look closer, to where the green shifts from dark to bright, from old forest to new growth that has repeatedly been cut down but always sprouts anew. Inside this lime-green patch, you see a score of white squares arranged neatly in two rows. Ten line up evenly on one side and their partners face them across a broad lawn, metal roofs glinting in the strong sun. You recall how these structures were built as homes by early Australian patrol officers, so colonial and rugged, trekking in across swamps and rivers. Beside the houses is a rectangle laid out long and flat, its grass kept short and trim. Your plane will swoop down on it now, the gilded spine of that book you have come so far to read. But its content is not what you thought it would be, not a text at all. As you descend, its meaning becomes the faces that line the airstrip, bright and eager as their skin is dark. They watch expectantly as you land. You open the door to a searing blast of heat and humanity. Welcome to Nomad Station.

Introduction
In Search of Surprise

LIKE MOST ANTHROPOLOGISTS, I was unprepared for what I would find. My wife, Eileen, and I had been married for just a few months when we flew in 1980 from Michigan across the Pacific. The two of us were going to live for two years in a remote area of the rainforest north of Australia, in the small nation of Papua New Guinea. I was twenty-six years old and had never been west of Oregon. I had no idea what changes lay in store either for me or for the people we were going to live with.

Well into the twentieth century, the large and rugged tropical island of New Guinea harbored people who had had little contact with outsiders. In the area where we were going, initial contact with Westerners had not occurred until the 1960s. The 450 people whom we encountered had a name and a language that were not yet known to anthropologists. As individuals, the Gebusi (geh-BOO-see) were amazing—at turns regal, funny, infuriating, entrancing, romantic, violent, and immersed in a world of towering trees, heat and rain, and mosquitoes and illness. Their lives were as different from ours as they could be. Practices and beliefs that were practically lore in anthropology were alive and well: ritual dancers in eye-popping costumes, entranced spirit mediums, all-night songfests and divinations, rigid separation between men and women, and striking sexual practices. A mere shadow to us at first, the dark side of Gebusi lives also became real: death inquests, sorcery accusations, village fights, and wife beating. In the past, cannibalism had been common, and we later discovered that a woman from our village had been eaten a year and a half prior to our arrival. As I gradually realized, the killing of sorcery suspects had produced one of the highest rates of homicide in the cross-cultural record.

The challenge of living and working with the Gebusi turned our own lives into something of an extreme sport. But in the crucible of personal experience, the Gebusi became not only human to us but also, despite their tragic violence, wonderful people. With wit and passion, they lived rich and festive lives. Vibrant and friendly, they turned life's cruelest ironies into their best jokes, and its biggest tensions into their most elaborate fantasies. Humor, spirituality, deep togetherness, and

3

raw pragmatism made Gebusi, for the most part, great fun to be with. I have never felt more included in a social world. And what personalities! To lump them together as simply "Gebusi" is as bland as it would be to describe Lady Gaga, Brad Pitt, and Bart Simpson as simply "American." The Gebusi were not simply "a society" or "a culture"; they were an amazing mix of unique individuals.

Anthropology is little if not the discovery of the human unexpected. I initially went to the Gebusi's part of the rainforest to study political decision making. Armed with tape recorder and typewriter, I wanted to document how communications with spirits during all-night séances produced concrete results—the decision to mount a hunting expedition, conduct a ritual, fight an enemy, or accuse a sorcerer. But spirit séances were more like off-color YouTube clips than a political council. The spirit medium sang of spirit women who flew about seductively and teased men in the audience. The male listeners joked back while bantering loudly with one another. In the bargain, their own social relations were intensified, patched up, and cemented. That community results could actually emerge during the night-long séance seemed almost beside the point. And yet, the results were sometimes really important, including one spiritual pronouncement that ended up forcing some villagers to leave and form a new settlement. Sorcerers could be scapegoated and threatened with death; people could be accused or found innocent of infractions. Politics, friendship, and sidesplitting humor combined with sexual teasing, spirituality, and conflict in ways that made my head spin.

You might imagine the first time I tried to translate a Gebusi spirit séance from one of my tape recordings. I sat with male informants in all seriousness as the machine played. At first, they were astonished to hear their own voices. But they quickly shifted from amazement to howling laughter. Then they attempted, image by laborious image, line by laborious line, to explain to me the humor that I had committed to tape. With no reliable interpreters, I was learning the Gebusi language "monolingually." As it turned out, the spiritual poetry of their séance songs bore as little relation to their normal speech as hip hop does to the sentences of an anthropology textbook. The Gebusi responded to my confusion by gleefully repeating the jokes that I had recorded. Although I was unable to turn nighttime humor into daytime clarity, I certainly gave the men a good laugh—and fueled my own uncertainty. Seeing our strange interaction, the women said that many of the songs I was trying to write down were "no good" or "rotten."

For the most part, Gebusi were not only jovial but considerate, quick to apologize, and adept at making the best of difficulties. I ended up liking most of them a lot. As I came to understand their rituals, beliefs, and customs, I strongly appreciated their culture. But I remained keenly aware of my own ethical and moral values, derived from elsewhere. What was I supposed to do with my sense of morality when it collided with theirs?

As in my own dilemma, cultural anthropology has been driven by competing desires. Anthropologists want to appreciatively understand the cultures they study. But they also confront the difficulties and injustices they observe. In Western scholarship, the goal of appreciating other cultures on their own terms was highlighted during the eighteenth and nineteenth centuries by European theorists such as Giambatista Vico and Johannes Herder. Broadly speaking, they argued that cultures should be viewed in the context of their own time and place. Later, the same principle was emphasized by the "founding father" of American anthropology, Franz Boas. Similarly, in recent decades, cultural anthropologists have been passionate to understand foreign peoples through the lens of their customs and beliefs. Why should Western ways of life be considered superior?

On the other hand, anthropologists are also mindful of problems and inequities in the societies they study. Some of these injustices have been fueled by the intrusion of outsiders. During centuries of colonialism, for instance, Western powers have exploited or enslaved people from many regions, including North and South America, Oceania, most of Africa, and large parts of Asia. Such incursions have often subordinated or stigmatized large portions of indigenous groups on grounds of cultural or social difference, race, ethnicity, religion, gender, or age.

But such injustices are not always linked to external forces. Among Gebusi, the domination of women and the scapegoating of sorcerers grate roughly against the splendor of Gebusi ritual performance, spirit belief, and communal festivity. These paradoxes cannot be explained away by the impact of colonialism or Western intrusion.

Such counterposing trends underscore the challenge that anthropologists face as they investigate problems and suffering that are caused or abetted by local customs. Cultural anthropologists often have trouble reconciling the wonder of cultural diversity with the difficulties caused by subjugation or violence in the heart of the societies they study. Accordingly, ethnographers during fieldwork frequently see social life through the crosshairs of ethnocentrism, sexism, racism, ageism, religious intolerance, or other forms of scapegoating. In the process, anthropologists often become more self-aware of the ethical standards that they themselves hold. They also risk projecting these standards onto the people they study. This was the dilemma I myself faced when I began working among the Gebusi.

Ultimately, the Gebusi surprised us beyond the delightful "good company" of their social life and the violence of their sorcery beliefs and gender practices. It was only later, after returning from the field, that I realized how rare it was even in New Guinea for long-standing customs to flourish with so little inhibition. But my bigger surprises came when I returned to live and work with the Gebusi again and again. I suspected each time that new influences had swept through during the intervening years. And each time, I braced myself to take whatever I would find at its new face value. But how could I know what lay in store?

By 1998, my old community had, by its own choice, picked up and moved from deep in the rainforest to the outskirts of the government airstrip and administrative offices at Nomad Station. Previously isolated in their forest settlements, the Gebusi were now part of a multiethnic community in and around the station at Nomad, which includes more than a thousand persons speaking five different languages. They also had a new sense of themselves as members of the nation of Papua New Guinea, including at their new big celebrations on National Independence Day and, on a daily basis, in the lessons that children received at the Nomad government school. Most of my Gebusi friends were now stalwart Christians who worshipped at one of three local churches. Men and boys had organized rugby and soccer teams, the "Gasumi Youths," that played refereed matches against rival ethnic groups each weekend on the government ball field. On Tuesdays and Fridays, Gebusi women lugged heavy net bags of food from gardens and the forest to Nomad market in hopes of earning a few coins. New crops such as manioc, peanuts, and pineapples sprouted in the gardens, and sweet potatoes were now a starch staple and grown for sale at the market.

Gebusi entertainment had also changed. Spirit séances had been replaced by modern music sung to the accompaniment of guitars and ukuleles. On Friday and Saturday nights, young people tried to find a "party," "video night," or "disco," dancing to cassette tapes of rock music. When children drew pictures of what they wanted to be in the future, their pages filled with colorful portraits of pilots, policemen, soldiers, heavy-machine operators, nurses, teachers, rock singers, and Christians in heaven. Traditional dances had become a kind of history or folklore and were rarely staged in villages. Because shamanism or spirit mediumship had now become defunct, Gebusi had no reliable way to communicate with their traditional spirits. As such, sorcery inquests following death had been replaced by Christian funerals—and violence against sorcery suspects was practically nil. Gebusi themselves said that they had exchanged their old spirits for new ones associated with a more developed way of life. In the process, however, they had become subordinate to outsiders who were in charge of activities and institutions associated with the Nomad Station.

By 2008, Gebusi had changed strikingly once again. Due to logistical problems and lack of funds, the Nomad airstrip had been closed. Government officials had left. As a result, the Nomad school, health clinic, and sports leagues were shut down, and the market was desultory. With access to the larger world mostly cut off, Gebusi, remarkably, had rejuvenated many of their long-standing customs—while also taking a stronger role in their local Catholic church. In character and emotional tone, they seemed to be much more in charge of their own lives and society. If Gebusi seemed uncommonly "traditional" during my first work with them, they had become surprisingly "modern" sixteen years later. Then they resuscitated long-standing beliefs and practices—and combined them with modern trends more on their own terms. This trend has continued to the present, as government presence continues to be minimal or spotty at Nomad going into 2012.

My fortune has been to forge a deep and lasting connection with a remote people who maintained amazingly rich traditions, sought out and developed a locally modern way of life, and who more recently have found solace and meaning by drawing on earlier customs in new ways. The experiences of Gebusi can't, and don't, reflect those of other peoples around the world. But they do illustrate how people develop and change their lives over time. Like the Gebusi, societies across the world become more modern while also retaining and extending their own unique identity. As an anthropologist, it is encouraging to see that cultural change in the contemporary world is as diverse as colors refracting through a prism. By examining these refractions, we can understand how people in various world areas share experiences that are increasingly modern and global, but in ways that remain distinctive or unique to them. Some peoples resist outside influences. Others blend old customs with new ones. Some agitate for their own autonomy, while others accept national or international authority. Though these may be alternatives, they are more commonly mixed within societies.

Exemplars of this process, Gebusi provide me a convenient framework for introducing topics that are often covered in anthropology courses. These include distinctive features of livelihood or subsistence; how kinship organizes people into groups; patterns of social and economic exchange; dimensions of leadership, politics, and dispute; religious beliefs and spiritual practices; matters of sexuality and gender; the construction of ethnicity and race; the impact of colonialism and nationalism; the role of the anthropologist; and, through it all, the dynamics of sociocultural change. Rather than describing the Gebusi in general terms, I present them as individuals whose lives have unfolded along with my own over the course of three decades. My goal is to let the Gebusi come alive for you, to convey their past and their present, and to connect the dramatic changes they have undergone with those in contemporary anthropology.

➥➥➥

BROADER CONNECTIONS: *Cultural Anthropology*

- Through their experiences of **field work** and their writing of **ethnography, cultural anthropologists** such as Bruce become highly engaged with and attuned to **cultural diversity.**

- Exposure to cultural diversity leads anthropologists to appreciate **cultural relativity**, including the value of each culture on its own terms.

- Anthropologists are also attuned to **social inequality**, including how differences of sex, gender, age, ethnic identity, religion, or other factors lead some people to dominate or subordinate others.

- Some aspects of social inequality derive from external constraint or coercion, including **colonialism, imperialism,** or **nationalist domination.**

- Other aspects of social inequality may derive from **internal social discrimination or stigma,** as influenced by long-standing beliefs and practices.

- In current practice, many cultural anthropologists are *both* **appreciative of cultural relativity** and concerned about and **critical of social inequity**.

- Collectively, changes among Gebusi over time illustrate **traditionalism, globalization** and how people become "**modern.**"

- Because Gebusi develop and draw upon larger influences in their distinctive fashion, they become **"locally modern"** or **"alternatively modern"** in their own way.
- Because **cultures and their changes over time are not easily predictable,** their development is especially **interesting, surprising, and exciting** for anthropologists—as well as instrumental in providing **new knowledge and understanding** about our human world.

PART ONE
1980–82

CHAPTER 1

The author snaps fingers in a welcoming line of adult Gebusi men. (PHOTO: Eileen Marie Knauft)

Friends in the Forest

THE BANANAS WERE ALL piled up, hot and grimy. Steam floated up from the pile—as if the air around us could have gotten any hotter. Some were stout as well as long, but most were slender, and a few were quite tiny. But their variety in dozens was a mystery to us then. All of them had been carefully scraped, but long strands of soot and globs of charcoal remained from their time in the fire.

What to do with this mound of starchy bananas, presented to us so formally in that first village? Kukudobi villagers had probably not seen a white person since five years before our arrival. At that time, the Australian patrol officers who had tramped to major settlements once a year and counted the local inhabitants suddenly left for good, along with the other Australians. Like a tempest in the forest, our arrival had certainly caused a hubbub. Children fled and men gasped with curious excitement. Emerging from under the trees, the four local men who were carrying our supplies took the lead, and we followed them ("When in Rome…") to the central longhouse. We sat down cross-legged, and a flood of villagers did likewise around us.

They must have done the cooking quickly or known about our arrival in advance, because it wasn't long before the smoldering stack of starch was brought in on a palm leaf platter and laid down with gusto in front of us. I was suddenly the focus of intense public scrutiny. Short men with bamboo tubes through their noses looked on from all around. I was too embarrassed to check with our carriers or even with Eileen about what I should do next. Everything was heat and stickiness. I took one of the sooty plantains and began to munch on it, trying to show appreciation. The bananas were dry, but we forced ourselves to chew through one and pick up another. The people around us started to grin as we swallowed their food. Our progress was slow, however, and judging from the size of the platter, our task was hopeless. Using my hands, I signaled that the pile of food was large, my stomach was small, and many people could certainly be fed. What a relief when they broke into pleasant conversation and stretched out their arms, sharing the bananas throughout the longhouse. We had apparently passed our first test.

11

Anthropologists often talk about "the gift," especially in Melanesia. How people put hard work and sweat, good intentions and hopes into tangible things that they give to one another speaks volumes about human connection. Gifts are at once a social economy and a materialized emotion. As Marcel Mauss suggested, gifts reflect and reinforce social bonds between givers and recipients. In American society, gifts at Christmastime are loaded with meanings that are reflected in whom we give presents to, how much thought and investment we put into the gift, and what reactions or returns we get by way of reciprocity.

As in many parts of New Guinea, Gebusi believed that gifts should be given to visitors who were peaceful. Their most basic gift was the fruit of their most regular work as well as their primary source of nutrition: starchy cooked bananas. Well beyond the giving of basic food, however, material exchange was linked to human connection. Gebusi relationships were defined by the things that you gave or didn't give to others. Later on, I established an "exchange name" with each man in our village—based on something that one of us had given to or shared with the other. Gusiayn was my "bird-egg," and Iwayb was my "Tahitian chestnut." Based on gifts that I gave myself, Yuway became my "fishing line," and Halowa my "salt." Whenever we saw each other, we called each other by these names, and our relationship was referred to similarly by others: "Here comes your 'bird egg;' there goes your 'salt'." To have a social identity and to have given and shared something that was memorable were one and the same.

In that first village of Kukudobi, we were fortunate to have accepted those starchy bananas and to have eaten a few and shared the rest. It was a simple act, but symbolic in ways we could barely appreciate. The patrol officers before us had also come to forest villages—once a year, to count heads for the colonial census. But they had brought along their servants, or "houseboys," to cook the tins of meat and bags of rice they had hauled in. In our case, word had already spread that we were look- ing for a rainforest village to live in, and that we ate local food. So we received a hopeful reception of cooked bananas. The other features of Gebusi welcoming eti- quette were not yet known to us—the calling out of gift and kin names, the hearty snapping of fingers with each host, the dramatic sharing of smoke-filled tobacco pipes among men, the drinking of water from twelve-foot-long bamboo tubes, and the palaver that lasted until the hosts arrived with great whoops to present more food. But even in that first village, the lead card of social life, the giving of food, had been extended, and we had accepted. It was a good start.

As we soon found out, all the villages we visited wanted us to live with them. Though bossy, the Australians had provided a trickle of outside goods, and when they left, the trickle had dried up. Local people craved the trade items they now associated with us as white-skinned outsiders: cloth, salt, beads, fishing hooks, soap, and, especially, metal tools. In contrast to a blunt stone adze, a steel ax goes through a rainforest tree like a knife through butter. Metal axes made it easy for people to clear bigger garden plots, grow more food, and build stronger houses. Metal knives and machetes found many additional uses, from skinning animals to clearing weeds.

Besides stoking a passion for trade goods, the Australians left a political legacy that the Gebusi roundly appreciated: they pacified the Bedamini. More numerous and aggressive than the Gebusi or their other neighbors, the Bedamini people had traditionally sent war parties deep into Gebusi territory. Their tactics were brutally efficient: surround an enemy longhouse at dawn, set it ablaze, and slaughter the inhabitants as they fled. Gebusi had been victimized repeatedly by these raids; in some cases, whole villages had been wiped out. Not infrequently, the Bedamini would cut up the bodies of those they had slain and carry them home for feasting. It is important to distinguish rumors of cannibalism from the actual practice. But its occurrence has been well documented and admitted among Bedamini—and by Gebusi themselves following the killing of sorcery suspects.

Being but 450 people against the Bedamini's 3,000, and with fewer residents in most of their settlements, Gebusi were no match for Bedamini war parties. If Australian patrol officers had not stepped in and stopped Bedamini raids, the Gebusi might have been only a remnant people by the time we arrived. As it was, thirteen years of colonial influence had gradually curtailed Bedamini expansion. By 1980, Gebusi were still visibly scared of the Bedamini, but they were seldom killed and no longer massacred by them. Despite, or perhaps because of, colonial intervention against their enemies, Gebusi themselves had rarely felt the boot of colonial domination. Australian patrol officers had been rough, but the benefits of their military intervention far outweighed the costs of their brief annual visits. Among Gebusi, the officers' main objectives were to update the local census and to lecture the villagers, via interpreters, about keeping the village clean and not fighting with one another. The Australians viewed the Gebusi as victims of the Bedamini rather than aggressors. Gebusi were portrayed as "quiet tractable people," and the Australians seldom intervened in their affairs. Hence the irony that, even as the Bedamini were being pacified by armed colonial patrols, the Gebusi were left alone to continue their own sorcery inquests, executions, and even cannibalism within their communities. Living deep and scattered in the rainforest, they concealed their actions from Australian interference.

Though the Gebusi appeared at first to be a pristine people, in fact they were not. What we took to be "traditional" had flourished in the wake of the Australian pacification of the Bedamini and in the larger clearings, gardens, and villages that the Gebusi had produced with steel tools. Because Gebusi associated physical growth and social development with spiritual support and fertility, the benefits of Bedamini pacification and of steel implements affirmed their religious values as well as their social life. Like streams that converge in the forest, material production and spiritual reproduction came increasingly together in major Gebusi rituals, especially during the initiation of young people into adulthood. Increasingly during the period of Australian patrols, Gebusi lives swelled with the combined power of religious, sexual, and social force. Ironically, then, colonial intrusion gave the Gebusi the freedom to develop many of their own customs and beliefs. In some ways, Gebusi became even more "Gebusi-like" than they had been before. Although they seemed unacculturated to us at the time, Gebusi and their traditions underscored the importance of changes all around them. A tribal powerhouse had been laid low while the neighboring Gebusi had been left to cultivate their own customs. By the 1980s, Gebusi resented Bedamini not so much for their former raids as for being recipients of government development projects that the Gebusi wanted for themselves.

That Gebusi combined an exuberant tradition with a desire for contact with outsiders made them a perfect fit for us. Little wonder that we were enamored of them or that they wanted us for themselves. At first, however, we weren't interested.

***

Our journey had begun with a blank spot on a map. That was where my graduate advisor and I had thought, back at the University of Michigan, that I would find the most fascinating people. The largest scale maps then available were produced by the U.S. Army—in case even the remotest parts of the globe needed military intervention. The map of Papua New Guinea's Western Province showed an unknown space that stretched across a swampy rainforest north of the Tomu River. The two of us thought that the culture of the people who lived there could be roughly triangulated on the basis of what was known about groups that lived twenty-five to forty miles away in different directions. There was no name for the peoples of the Tomu River, but I talked by phone to a missionary who had completed some aerial survey work in the area. He thought that the closest people were probably the "Kramo." Armed with this information, I obtained funding from the U.S. National Science Foundation and the U.S. National Institutes of Health to study political consensus formation led by spirit mediums among people called the Kramo in the remote rainforest of Papua New Guinea's Western Province.

But there was a good reason for the blank spot on the map: no one lived there! We finally accepted this fact after leaving Kukudobi and trudging for what seemed like forever to the distant village of Honabi, at the edge of the settlements of the Honibo ethnic group. The inhabitants there told us consistently, and in as many ways as our inadequate language would allow, that there was nothing farther ahead of us but swamp and mosquitoes, both of which we had already endured to our limit. They also informed us that the few people, called the Kabasi, who had previously lived in this area had deserted it and gone to live near a crocodile skin trading post eastward at Kasigi. Even if we had wanted to continue our trek into their erstwhile territory, our carriers would not go with us. Our trail had ended. In professional terms, we had traveled to Papua New Guinea on doctoral research grants to study people whom we couldn't find or who didn't exist (see map).

Sensing our uncertainty and perhaps our fear, the Honibo people brightly insisted that we stay and live with them instead. Though they claimed that they had a tradition of entranced spirit singing, their assertions were hedged with ambivalence. When we probed deeper, they also admitted that they typically abandoned their village for several months during the dry season, split into tiny groups, and foraged for food even deeper in the rainforest. As the evening grew longer and the mosquitoes bit harder, the prospect of adapting to their lifestyle for two years seemed more dreadful than admitting failure. Not knowing what else to do, we opted to trudge back to the Nomad Station via the village that our carriers lived in, which was not altogether out of the way. The more we found out about this impending stop, the more interested we became. By this time, our carriers

The Gebusi and nearby groups

had become real people to us. Yuway was a wonderfully decent young man, as sensitive as he was tall, and strong for a Gebusi. He had a spontaneous sense of concern, interest, and patience even though we couldn't yet communicate verbally. He would wait to help us over slippery log bridges, and he often volunteered to shoulder the heaviest load. Gono never said much, but he was as sinewy and dependable as a stout tree, and he was always alert. Hawi was our nominal interpreter, and though his translations ultimately proved more troublesome than helpful, he was socially and physically agile. Finally there was Swamin, older than his unmarried companions by half a generation but more muscled than they. He would flash a captivating smile under his impish hooked nose and pepper his remarks with articulate bursts that, given the reactions he got from the other three, convinced us that he was both very funny and very smart. As Hawi informed us, Swamin was also a spirit medium who held communal séances on a regular basis.

When we finally reached their village of Yibihilu, the "place of the deep waters," we thought we had reached the local version of paradise. We had stumbled for days through a sea of leaves, mud, and vines under a closed rainforest canopy. We felt like the miniature children in *Honey, I Shrunk the Kids!* who navigated enormous obstacles in a galactic backyard of foliage. I yearned to look up and out, to see more than the next hidden root that could send me sprawling. The "place of the deep waters," by contrast, was perched on a forty-foot bluff overlooking a serpentine bend in the Kum River. The porch of the longhouse extended out over a canyon through which the river rushed before pooling in a serene basin some hundred yards wide and across which we could see a crocodile lazing in the sun. Farther downstream, the watercourse was calm enough to be traveled by canoe—which was far preferable to tromping through the muddy forest. At dusk, the sky above the river became a breathtaking sunset. The villagers would stop and stare. *Bubia maysum*—"The crimson is being laid down."

If the village seemed majestic, the people were yet better. Having learned more about us from our carriers in five minutes than the other villages had in five days, their kin and friends gave us the kind of warm welcome, especially in such a remote place, that made us feel on top of the world rather than at its end. As the traumas and troubles of our journey were discussed to the tiniest detail, the villagers laughed good-naturedly. That we were already trying to speak their language—however haltingly—was widely and enthusiastically noted. That we ate local food and that I had somehow carried my own backpack, which the men enjoyed trying on, were also taken as positive signs. There was also a bonus in that Eileen was present. White women had rarely been seen by the Gebusi, and probably never in Yibihilu. Eileen shared food and laughter with the women and played with the children. They were enthusiastic and responded in kind. If the men "had" me, the women took Eileen into their own world.

In remarkably short stead, our physical presence, our possessions, and our desire to speak the local tongue seemed to paint us as paragons of beneficence, a gold mine of goods, and a three-ringed circus of entertainment. Our hands were shaken, fingers snapped, and bellies gorged with countless gifts of food. Everyone seemed quite genuinely to want our friendship. If our reception was anything less than overwhelming, we were too euphoric to notice. As if we needed further encouragement, Swamin held an all-night spirit séance. Word of our presence had drawn villagers from surrounding hamlets. Given the convergence of so many people and the surge of good feelings, a songfest of celebration was almost inevitable. The stars shone as they do only when there is no competing light for hundreds of miles. The songs of the men swelled as the silhouette of the forest canopy loomed over us in the moonlight. Beneath the glow, their deep-throated harmony echoed through the village as if in a wild cathedral. The music was different from and more amazing than any I had ever heard. I knew that the Gebusi believed in a whole world of unseen forest spirits and places that come alive through the songs of the spirit medium. But as the sound washed over me, I knew almost nothing of its meaning. In the moment, however, this only added to the mystery and splendor of the Gebusi cosmos—a world of wonder I had come to explore.

There was so much that we didn't know about the Gebusi at first—including their name. Our ethnographic maps and the missionary who had told us about the "Kramo" had placed a group called the "Bibo" at our present location. But the people of Yibihilu found this terribly funny. They brought us a large starchy banana and indicated that this was the only "bibo" in their territory—one of their three-dozen varieties of plantains. There were no people called "Bibo." They said in no uncertain terms that their own identity, and also their language, was "Gebusi."

The discoveries of fieldwork had already brought us full circle. We had gone halfway around the world to study a Kramo people who didn't exist. We had projected their presence based on our incomplete maps and our imaginations. But the people we did find—and came to like so deeply—were, in name, an undiscovered group. As green and insecure as we were at the time, this was a comfort. In retrospect, though, our nominal "discovery" of the Gebusi exposed as much about ourselves as it did about our tribal friends: the Western drive to label other peoples and to project onto them our own sense of discovery. Like many anthropologists, we were starting to learn new things about our own way of life at the same time, and in many respects for the very reason, that we were trying to reach out and understand the lives of others.

Beyond the Gebusi's name, we also quickly encountered one of their central concepts—one that took much longer to understand. With predictable difficulty, we had been trying to explain exactly why we had come to the rainforest. Villagers were especially curious about this since we didn't fit the mold of whites they had previously encountered or heard about. Were we patrol officers who ordered people around and then disappeared for another year? No. Were we those white people they had heard about but never seen who held up a big book (the Bible) and exhorted villagers not to dance or be initiated but instead to sing to a new spirit? No, not that either. Then why had we come? We tried to communicate that we wanted to learn their language, to understand their songs, to watch their dances, to join them at their feasts—in short, to be with them as they lived and learn what they were like. In a flash, they seemed to grasp our meaning: we wanted to learn their *kogwayay*. They appeared so certain of this that we had no choice or desire but to agree with them. Of course, we had no idea what *kogwayay* meant. But in truth, they were entirely correct.

Kogwayay is—or at least was, during that early period—the single word that best describes the heart of Gebusi culture. In a way, the term represents their concept of culture itself—the beliefs, practices, and styles of living that are special and unique to Gebusi as a people. At one level, *kogwayay* refers to customs that make their culture different from others. As Gebusi themselves used the term, it refers especially to their distinctive traditions of dancing, singing, and body decoration. But what is the term's deeper meaning? The Gebusi were not much help here. For them, *kogwayay* was a catchall marker of cultural distinction rather than a tool for dissecting it.

When you think about it, it's not surprising that people have a hard time explaining concepts that are central to their culture. Such meanings are often "beyond words." Would it actually be that easy for your average American, Canadian, or Englishman to define and explain what "love" is to someone who had never heard of this term? In the case of *kogwayay*, we were fortunate that the word breaks down into three distinct units of meaning, what linguists call morphemes: *kog-*, *-wa-*, and *-yay*. *Kog* conveys "togetherness," "friendship," and "similarity." These meanings reflect the collective and communal nature of Gebusi life. Gebusi always prefer to do things with as many other people as possible, and they hate being alone; they are the opposite of loners. The *wa* component of the word is the Gebusi root of *wa-la*, "to talk." It refers to pleasant dialogues and conversations that are roundly shared. This is what the men did in the longhouse at night—they "*wa-la*'d" by sharing news and gossip, joking, fantasizing, and telling stories around the small glow of the resin lantern. This is the Gebusi equivalent of the late-night bull sessions that can echo through the halls of a college dorm. Hour after hour and evening after evening, I came to realize how rare it was for the Gebusi to get angry with one another in these gabfests. Disagreements were tempered by friendly smiles; embarrassments were covered by jokes and shifts of conversation.

Yay supplied the exuberant conclusion to *kog-wa-yay*, its exclamation point. Particularly for men, to *yay* or to *kay* is to cheer, yell, joke, and cry out as loudly and happily as possible—and preferably in unison with other men. These yells have bodily meaning as well. When a Gebusi calls out in concert with those around him, his "breath-heart" (*solof*) pushes out and mingles with that of others. To *yay* or *kay* is to send forth and unite human spiritual energy; it is a vital assertion of collective life.

Taken together, what do *kog-*, *-wa-*, and *-yay* mean? And why should we care? No single English word captures their essence—and this fact is important. As anthropologists, we are charged with learning and conveying concepts that are important to other people even and especially when these exceed our initial understanding. *Kogwayay* was clearly important to Gebusi. The word was frequently used and talked about, it evoked strong feelings, and it was highly elaborated in central rituals and ceremonies. In Gebusi culture, *kogwayay* was what anthropologist Sherry Ortner has more generally called a "key symbol." Collectively, the three meanings of the word—togetherness, talk, and cheering—conveyed core Gebusi values of happy social unity, of living in good company with one another. And *kogwayay* permeated Gebusi social life. This was evident on a daily basis and was epitomized at important events such as feasts, dances, spirit séances, and the initiation of teenagers into adulthood.

Although *kogwayay* was a powerful and deeply held concept, it did not stand alone. It highlighted the positive side of Gebusi culture, the bright side of their moon. Most peoples try to depict themselves in a good and favorable light, and the Gebusi were no exception. If you were asked to name central values in American and other Western societies, you might use words such as "freedom," "economic success," "love," "self-expression," "family values," or "tolerance." Of course, these are sometimes ideals more than realities. Many marriages end in divorce; people can be shackled by poverty; and discrimination based on race, ethnicity, sex, or age can be as deeply ingrained as it is illegal. A critic from another culture might argue that American society is cutthroat, egotistical, hedonistic, imperialistic, and much less equal or free than we like to believe. If culture is an assertion of ideals and values, these can sometimes hide problems or difficulties. In this sense, culture is a double-edged sword of beliefs and representations. On the one hand, it emphasizes values and ideals that are often, if not typically, good and healthy. On the other hand, trumpeting these values can downplay or deny less pleasant realities. Certainly it would be shortsighted to dismiss the importance of cultural values. Where would we be without them? So, too, it is good to appreciate the values of other peoples, including the Gebusi. But it is also important to recognize the underside of culture—realities that are neglected by cultural ideals. Both sides of this coin are important.

Where do we draw the line between an appreciative view of culture and a critical view of social inequalities? Do we emphasize the fight to free the slaves during the American Civil War? Or the history of slavery that made that war necessary? Do we emphasize the human benefit of toppling a dictator like Saddam Hussein? Or the tens of thousands of lives that have been lost as a result? Such questions have few simple answers. But asking them makes us more aware of both the positive power of culture and the problems it can hide.

Gebusi culture can be viewed in this same light. The good company of *kog-wayay* was a strong practice as well as a wonderful ideal. But *kogwayay* was also controlled and dominated by men. It was men rather than women who collectively cheered and publicly yelled. Men were the ones who gathered for public talk each evening on the large porch that overlooked the river. During this time, women were largely confined to whispered conversations in a cramped female sleeping room along one wall of the longhouse, away from the men and older boys. In terms of decision-making, it was typically men who determined which settlement their respective families would live in—who would have togetherness, and with whom. Men took charge of the events most strongly associated with *kogwayay*—ritual feasts, dances, spirit séances, and initiations. At feasts, men from the host village would proudly present visitors with piles of cooked sago starch— though this food was produced by women's hard labor. In the evenings, it was men who dressed up in stunning costumes to dance. At initiations, young men were the main focus and were decorated most elaborately. As if to deny the notion of motherhood, boys were nurtured to manhood not by females but, as described in Chapter 5, by the men themselves—through the transmission of male life force from one generation to the next.

Male control was especially pronounced at spirit séances. Late in the evening, men would gather in the dark longhouse and arrange themselves around the spirit medium while he sat, smoked tobacco, and went into a controlled trance. The medium's own spirit would then leave his body and be replaced by a soul from the spirit world. After a while, the new spirit's voice would start chanting through the spirit medium, first whispering and then singing in soft falsetto tones. As the words of the spirit became clearer, the men clustered around the medium and formed a chorus to echo him. Their singing encouraged the medium's spirit to sing louder and with greater confidence. Gradually, the spirit's chants became full songs, each line being repeated and chorused in full harmony and top voice by a robust male chorus.

Gebusi women, however, were excluded from the séance (though they could hear its content as they sat or dozed in their cramped quarters). Meanwhile, the men shouted, joked, and laughed in an all-night songfest of masculine bravado. Perhaps most strikingly, the primary spirits who sang through the male spirit medium were young women. And not just any women, but gorgeous young spirit women who longed to have sex and joke with Gebusi men. In effect, the men's séance singing voiced, projected, and received back their sexual fantasies of women—at the same time that real Gebusi women could be beaten by husbands or brothers for being flirtatious. By contrast, spirit women were literally embodied by the men themselves, first in the voice of the male spirit medium and then in the men's collective chorus. Spirit séances were, at least to some degree, a male fantasy that celebrated men's sexual desires at the same time that real Gebusi women were excluded, controlled, and sometimes disparaged.

Given this male bias, what were we to make of Gebusi "good company"? Was *kogwayay* merely a cultural value that disguised male dominance over women? This question brings us to the crux of anthropology's appreciation of cultural diversity, on the one hand, and its critique of inequity on the other. For the most part, Gebusi women accepted and appreciated the culture they lived in. At spirit séances, they sometimes took offense at male joking, but more often they indulged and genuinely enjoyed it. Women were excited and galvanized by ritual feasts and initiations, and they actively played their own roles at these events. On these and other occasions, they enjoyed interacting with women who visited from other settlements. It was true that Gebusi women often lived in the cultural shadow of Gebusi men. Sometimes they resisted their second-class status, but for the most part they accepted and embraced it. Women swelled with pride at their own and the men's accomplishments, even when men presented the fruits of women's work as their own. So, too, women tended to accept men's collective prerogative to take violent action against sorcery suspects and usually as well the right of a man to beat his wife.

In many if not most regions of the world, the activities and experiences of men and women differ. Among the peoples and cultures of New Guinea, the division between male and female realms is especially marked. Women had their own world, their own lore, and their own female-centered interactions. For my own part, I found the social life of Gebusi men to be largely a heck of a lot of fun. I enjoyed their banter and horseplay, smoked their tobacco through big bamboo tubes, joked with them, and participated in community feasts.

To both men and women, and for us as well, Gebusi children were a great source of pleasure and happiness. We ourselves took a particular liking to an impish little boy named Sayu. He was four or five years old and simply the most charismatic child either of us had ever known. His mother, Boyl, was an attractive woman with a broad smile and, we thought, the strongest intellect in the village. Her husband, Silap, was one of the more important men in the village, one of the principal founders of the main longhouse, and a feisty character with a quick smile.

In the beginning, we didn't know what would happen next. We knew that the people of Yibihilu were vibrant and welcoming and that their culture was alive with song and celebration. We had naiveté, energy, and trust in our purpose—and these were indispensable for fieldwork that was both deeply difficult and ultimately limitless. After several weeks of visiting, it was time for us and for the people of Yibihilu to decide if a house should be built for us at "the place of the deep waters." The villagers continued to be friendly, and some of them were becoming our personal friends. But they were also very different from us, and we felt the force of this difference.

One night, the conversation finally turned—uncertainly, via Hawi—to how long we would stay in Yibihilu. Dusk was turning into night, and the men and boys around me became silhouettes with bones in their noses and feathers in their hair. Trophy skulls of pigs and cassowaries swayed from the rafters. A chunk of resin sizzled on the stone lamp. I looked up and saw people and personalities I was beginning to know. But they also appeared alien. Some were covered head to foot with the scaly skin of ringworm. Others had streaks of soot or caked ulcers on their skin or large cracks in the thick callouses that lined their feet. Their toes splayed, as if they had been born to stride along mossy log bridges that we inched across timidly. Even when sitting down, I towered over them. My gawky six-foot-plus white frame stood out against their dark bodies, which averaged five feet four inches at full height. Their skill and prowess in the forest dwarfed my own. How quickly and silently they could climb a tree, club a lizard, shoot a fish, or ford a stream. I knew that until recently they had eaten the flesh of persons killed as sorcerers. Their polished arrows were propped in the corner. Many layers of their culture remained obscure to me. The joy of our beginning made me question whether my giddiness would change to disillusionment when the novelty of our warm welcome wore off. But the dice, it seemed, had already been rolled. After undergoing years of scholarly training, journeying halfway around the world, and enduring mosquitoes and leeches, and with my personal and professional identity on the line, how could I turn back? They asked, "How long do you think you will stay?" I heard myself say, "Two years." My head swam as I heard the hubbub around me. But in the best Gebusi tradition of "everything is going to be fine," the discussion quickly turned to where our thatched house was to be built. On this side of the village, or on that one? The following morning, strings were laid on the ground to mark where the walls would be. And our house was built above them.

BROADER CONNECTIONS: *Fieldwork and Culture*

- **Cultural anthropologists** such as Bruce conduct **long-term ethnographic fieldwork** and study culture through **participant-observation.**

- **Gift exchange** and **reciprocity** are important ways that human social interactions are established and reinforced—including with anthropologists in the field. Gebusi employ exchange and reciprocity in **food-giving** and in **gift-exchange names** between friends.

- **Cultural anthropologists** are often distinguished from government administrators, missionaries, or aid workers in that they **typically try to participate in local means of reciprocity** and exchange. Professionally, cultural anthropologists attempt to **observe and learn about diverse** peoples rather than actively trying to change their customs, behavior, or beliefs.

- Many peoples of the world have been influenced by external threat and pressure either from outside their country or nation (**external colonialism** or **imperialism**) or from inside it (**nationalist domination** or **internal colonialism**).

- The impact of external influence or colonialism is diverse; **Gebusi** largely appreciated **Australian colonial presence**, but the neighboring **Bedamini** people, who killed many Gebusi in raids, resisted and resented it.

- Among Gebusi and other peoples, **culture is a shared public system of meanings, beliefs, and values.**

- **Cultural change** not only alters practices and beliefs but can reinvent them in new ways over time **(the reinvention of culture** or the **reinvention of tradition).** Gebusi culture intensified in part because Australians pacified their tribal enemies while introducing them to modern goods such as steel knives and axes.

- Most peoples assert **cultural values** that they emphasize and share as a **positive belief system** (or as a **cultural ideology**). Among Gebusi, deep cultural values are reflected in *kog-wa-yay*—the "good company" of togetherness, friendly talking, and exuberant or playful cheering or yelling.

- *Kogwayay* among Gebusi can be seen as a **key symbol** in Gebusi culture— a cultural concept or emphasis that is widely shared, prominent, emotionally powerful, and frequently demonstrated.

- In many societies, positive cultural values are complemented by troubling or challenging features of social domination, conflict, or disorder that are downplayed or papered over. Among Gebusi these include **gender domination** of men by women and the **scapegoating** of people through **sorcery accusations.**

- Cultural anthropologists often undertake **long-term ethnographic fieldwork** that is at turns both enjoyable and challenging or difficult. This is true both in remote areas, such as the Papua New Guinea rainforest, and in highly developed areas, including anthropological fieldwork in modern cities in Western or non-Western countries.

CHAPTER 2

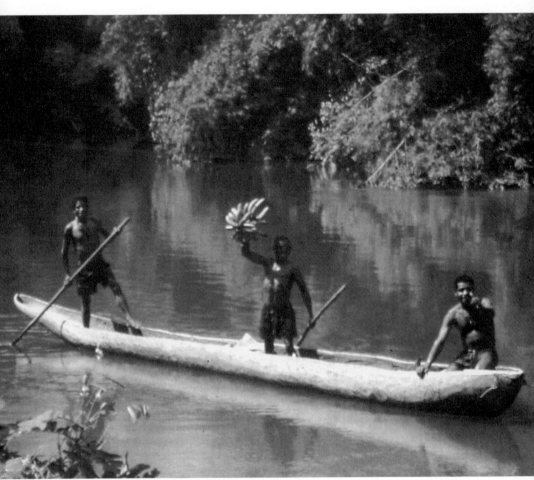

Men bring back bananas from gardens along the Kum River. (PHOTO: Bruce Knauft)

Rhythms of Survival

BOYL SLUNG HER LOAD of leaves to the ground as the other women staggered into the village and followed suit. The foliage had been stripped from sago palms, folded, and then loaded onto their backs in net bags that were supported by tumplines across their foreheads. These leaves would form the bulk of our house, as they do all Gebusi dwellings. We hardly guessed that a house made mostly of leaves could provide shelter against up to fourteen feet of rainfall each year and in temperatures that can often top 100 degrees. But they do. The leaves are carefully pinned to wooden strips about five feet long, from which they extend by almost a yard. Hundreds of these leaf strips are lashed like shingles to the roof beams of the house, with just an inch or so overlap between each strip and the one above it. For the village longhouse, which measured 74 by 34 feet, the tens of thousands of leaves needed for the structure easily weighed several tons. The bulk of the dwelling was the massive roof, which peaked almost twenty-five feet high in the air and sloped over the house's windowless walls until it almost touched the ground.

We were intrigued to see our own house take shape. Yuway and the other men scampered over the frame like skilled acrobats, hoisting log supports and the heavy ridgepole. Without measuring tape, plumb line, or any materials other than wood, leaves, and vines, they built the roof and then the rest of our house with all the confidence of a first-rate construction crew. The Gebusi overcame a lack of formal training with practical ingenuity and intimate knowledge of forest materials. Their indigenous numbers are just three: "one" (*hele*), "two" (*bena*), and "two plus one" (*bene bwar hele bwar*). Anything greater than that is simply "many" (*bihina*). Counting was as irrelevant to the Gebusi as their physical skills were finely honed. As ad hoc engineers, they were astounding. This is not to say that arithmetic has been undeveloped in the history of other non-Western cultures. Western counting systems are themselves based on Arabic numerals that are mid-Eastern in origin. In New Guinea itself, some societies have developed elaborate numerologies. Like the ancient Babylonians, the Kapauku people of West New Guinea developed a base-sixty number system, which they used to count items into the thousands just for fun. But one group's chosen passion is another's apathy. Although the Gebusi shortchanged their numerals, they had a rich vocabulary for a seemingly endless variety of plants, vines, and trees, each of which had special properties and uses.

If culture humanizes the environment, the Gebusi longhouse was their biggest accomplishment of material culture. Being the main gathering place for the fifty-two residents of Yibihilu, the "house long" (*masam sak*) was their tangible sign of village cooperation, physical prowess, and collective labor. Materially minded anthropologists describe culture as "adaptive" because its creativity and symbolic diversity has allowed humans to survive in so many different physical environments—from the Arctic to the tropics and the deep deserts, and practically everywhere in between. Whereas nonhuman animals are more limited by genetically determined or "instinctual" paths of behavior, we humans add an enormous capacity for learning and for organizing our efforts through full grammatical language. As Leslie White put it, culture gives us an "extra-somatic" way to adapt to the world around us—beyond the constraints of our bodily physiology.

Given the prominence of the Gebusi longhouse, it surprised us at first that it was often almost empty. The longhouse was the permanent residence of just two extended families, with the others living in smaller houses in the community clearing. But the longhouse had been built by the community at large and it functioned as the general evening gathering place and site of community celebrations and collective rituals. Although humming with energy when the village was full of people, the central dwelling gave way to the surrounding forest as a focus of dispersed activity during the bulk of most days. Hawi goes off with a group of young men to spear fish. Boyl and her husband depart to collect bananas from a distant garden and to see if tubers are ready to harvest. Two young girls leave with their adult sisters to forage for fresh bamboo shoots, to rummage in the nest of a wild bush hen for eggs, or to scoop for freshwater prawns under rocks in the stream. Along the way, they keep a keen eye open for a stray bush rat or snake that could be clubbed with a stick or sliced with a knife. Men carry bows and arrows and look for signs of a wild pig, a sleeping lizard, a possum on a low-lying branch, or a cassowary—a large, flightless bird—scavenging in the brush. Even a good-sized tarantula can be seized for the cooking fire. The Gebusi eat practically anything that moves.

By late afternoon, those within a reasonable distance return to the village for an evening meal and general conversation. The atmosphere is languid and friendly as families congregate. Men sit together and share large bamboo tube pipes filled with powerful home-grown tobacco. Women chat as they stoke the hearth and cook the bananas. Back in the forest, some families are too far away to return for the night; they make a temporary camp and sleep in a makeshift shelter or lean-to. Imba and his wife, Walab, walk for a day to distant clan land, accompanied by their siblings and children. The men in the group chop down and split open a stately sago palm; then the women pound the soft interior of the tree into pith. Deep in the forest, it can take women two weeks or more to process the pith and leach its pulpy fiber into heavy bundles of caked sago flour. In the meantime, the whole group lives in the forest. Imba and his male kin hunt and forage; the children play together or set off with a group of adults to gather breadfruit or Tahitian chestnuts from stands of trees. The minicommunity sleeps in a temporary shelter of poles and sticks covered with sago leaf thatch to keep out the rain. When the sago palm is completely processed, the fruits of the women's labor are bundled in bark, wrapped in leaves, slung on their backs in big net bags, and hauled to the river, where the sago can be brought back to the settlement by canoe. For weeks on end, the heavy parcels will supply starchy flour that can be easily stored and then wrapped in fresh leaves and cooked directly on the fire.

Beyond its food, the rainforest is ripe with meaning. Hogayo lingers by an old settlement where his father was born; Walab stops to drink from a stream that belongs to her mother's family line. Memories are associated with each stand of trees, creek, small hillock, or patch of old garden land that has since been overgrown. For the Gebusi, to walk through the forest is to relive past experiences and to remember what the forest has provided their kin, their ancestors, and themselves. They rediscover how the trees have grown, when their fruits will be ripe, what animals have left traces nearby, and when the area can be revisited to reap one or another natural harvest. The forest is not simply "land," it is a living cornucopia with meaning and nuance in each nook and wrinkle. Gebusi describe their lands with fondness and nostalgia. They name individual places and luxuri- ate in their tranquil distinctions. When the Gebusi sing at dances and séances, many of their most haunting songs recall places in the forest.

Between daily trips and more extended ones, the residents of Yibihilu spent almost half their nights—45 percent, to be precise—in the forest or at another settlement. In earlier days, they could easily scatter to the bush if they knew or thought that enemies or foreigners were on the prowl. It is no surprise, then, that the early Australian patrol officers struggled to locate groups of Gebusi in the forest. Partly out of frustration, they labeled the local population as "nomads." Indeed, they designated the whole region as the Nomad Subdistrict and named the regional government station the Nomad Patrol Post. In fact, though, they were mistaken. Anthropologists define nomads as people who have no permanent residence—people who shift their settlement every few weeks to forage and hunt—or to tend their livestock. Sedentary peoples, by contrast, build durable houses and live in long-lasting settlements. Certainly, the Gebusi longhouse qual- ifies as a durable residence, and even in precolonial times, Gebusi villages lasted for several years. Though the Gebusi travel extensively across their lands, they are "sedentary" insofar as they identify themselves as members of a specific set- tlement and spend over half of their nights in their principal residence.

If the Gebusi lifestyle sometimes flirts with being seminomadic, it is tempered by the benefits of growing food in gardens that can be reached by an hour or two of walking from the main settlement. Notwithstanding festive attractions of communal village living, Gebusi survival depends on growing crops, especially bananas, in cleared gardens. In their part of the lowland rainforest, large game animals aren't plentiful. These are mostly wild pigs or cassowaries, which look like strange, small ostriches. Though the Gebusi eat and enjoy the more numer- ous smaller creatures of the forest, these don't supply many calories on a daily basis. It is doubtful whether the Gebusi could survive on the basis of hunting, fishing, and gathering alone, that is, without the plantains and other foods of their gardens.

The biggest task, at least for the men, is the felling of trees. Though most families maintain individual gardens, large ones also may be cleared as a communal project. After several weeks at Yibihilu, we went with some villagers to see how this was done. We left in high spirits, the men whooping and the children frolicking. It was going to be a big garden. As we walked twenty minutes to the site, it felt more like a festive parade than a work brigade.

Along with the rest of the men, I took turns chopping trees and resting by the makeshift cooking fires while chatting, munching bananas, and smoking Gebusi tobacco. To my surprise, Yuway told me not to chop any of the trees all the way through; each time, I was stopped when I was only about halfway done. The other men were doing the same. Perplexed, I asked why. I became only more confused when Yuway and the others made dramatic pantomimes of noise and crashing. After two more hours of "half-work," hardly a single tree had been felled. My companions seemed content and even expectant while I remained baffled. Our work pace dwindled until only a handful of men were left at one end of the large plot. There, they attacked a particularly large and majestic piece of timber—while the rest of us were waved off to the far margins of the area. Everyone took great pains to tell me that I should not, under any circumstances, wander back into the garden area. Knowing that the Gebusi had deep spiritual ties to their land—and that many of their spirits lived in large trees—I thought that the land might now be under a spiritual taboo. Perhaps special rites or spells would be performed by the senior men to supplicate the spirits of the largest tree before felling it, so the spirits wouldn't be angry about the destruction of their "home." Maybe after that, I thought, we would finish chopping the biggest tree's smaller cousins. But I was wrong.

A few minutes later, the enormous tree began to creak and groan from the continuing blows of the senior men's axes. Though towering above the lesser trees, a thick skein of vines and foliage knitted it to its neighbors. Finally, it tottered and thundered down with a torrential crash. In falling, its force exploded to those it was linked to in domino fashion, and they, in turn, to trees across the entire acre of half-cut timber. In a flash, hefty trunks were toppled and flung in all directions, like telephone poles ripped up by a falling master pylon. It was frightful, wonderful, and awe-ful—an arboreal tornado. Then, as quickly as it started, it was over. All that remained were the whoops of the men, the blizzard of leaves that filled the sky and fluttered to the ground, and a sea of fallen trunks and limbs. Stunned, I had to sit down.

As I regained my bearings, my confusion persisted. The trees had been felled with remarkably little effort, to be sure. But now their fallen mass smothered the garden land beneath. How could the plot be planted, much less cultivated? Yuway and the others were unconcerned. They pointed out that banana suckers and root crop seedlings had already been stuck in the ground days before. When I had arrived at the site and the trees had still been standing, I had not even noticed them. Although a few of these plantings were now crushed by the fallen limbs, the vast majority of them were merely now sheltered from the blaze of the sun and the pelting of rains by the fallen branches now hovering just above them. Without this covering, the new seedlings would wilt in the tropical sun or be washed away by torrential storms. As the foliage of the felled trees decomposed, the crops beneath would sprout through these fertilizing remains and would then be strong enough to grow unshielded. Though the garden now looked like a chaos of fallen limbs, it was, in fact, a finely honed and ingenious system of cultivation. Anthropologist Edward Schieffelin gave the practice a fitting name: "felling the trees on top of the crop."

As already mentioned, the main food planted in Gebusi gardens is plantains—starchy bananas. These require almost no weeding, grow quickly, and don't bear fruit until the plants have hoisted their caloric pods beyond the reach of wild pigs who would eat them. As a result, Gebusi dispense with having to build fences to keep animals such as pigs away from their crops. Theoretically, the bananas could be eaten by birds and fruit bats when they ripen, but most of the plantains are starchy rather than the sweet variety that attract flying freeloaders. In any event, villagers usually harvest the fruit before it is ripe enough for birds and bats to eat. The hard plantains can be eaten after simply throwing them on the fire; as the thick banana skin gets charred, the fruit inside just softens and cooks. Retrieved with wooden cooking tongs, the bananas are then scraped of their charcoal and eaten straightaway.

As their plantains suggest, Gebusi grow crops without much labor. Since they let the land lie fallow to regenerate for many years before recutting and replanting it, their food-raising qualifies as "horticulture." By contrast, anthropologists typically define "agriculture" as cultivation that requires great effort—practices such as irrigating, fertilizing, plowing, fencing, and/or terracing, which Gebusi avoid. These techniques increase the quantity of crops that can be raised on a given piece of land—and the number of people that can live on it—but they exact a heavy price in either physical labor or mechanized intervention. Gebusi stay happily at the other end of this continuum. Because they have plenty of land, they have little need to labor mightily in any one plot. Even their best garden plots are abandoned after one or two plantings. As the rainforest reclaims its terrain, weeds, shrubs, and then trees reemerge. A new layer of nutrients enrich the poor clay soil. Ideally, the grandson of the man who planted the initial garden comes back to reclaim and recultivate it. In so doing, he draws upon the ancestral substance of the regenerated land as he fortifies his own essence and that of his family. As such, the Gebusi's cycle of reproduction is spiritual and cultural as well as caloric and demographic—the rejuvenation of land, food, people, and spiritual connection. Because land is plentiful, it is easily lent to friends as well as kin, thus extending and intensifying their social and spiritual network. As such, land and its spiritual energy are a widely shared resource.

Across generations, Gebusi have maintained an ample supply of food, though their part of the rainforest is not particularly bountiful. In the process, moreover, they don't seem to have strained themselves unduly. Certainly, they endure stints of intense labor. Women carry more than their share of heavy loads through the rainforest, and they transport firewood, food, and even their babies in net bags slung on their backs. Although men can also bear these burdens, it is women who give the Gebusi their ultimate "carrying capacity." Even for women, however, many hours on most days drift by in relaxation—conversing, eating, and playing with children. And men have even more time for social pursuits. Their palavers extend for long hours into the evening. Every week and a half or so, they also gather for an all-night spirit séance. After this extended songfest, men and boys typically sleep for a good part of the following day. Added to these festivities are all-night ritual feasts and dances that energize the entire settlement and that occurred about once a month during my first fieldwork.

Marshall Sahlins has called simple human cultures "original affluent societies." Though their technology and material culture may be rudimentary, people in such societies are typically able to spend hours each day socializing or lazing around. Although obtaining food and shelter requires work, this effort ebbs and flows not so much as a struggle against nature but in relaxed harmony with the environment. From the icy Arctic to the parched deserts of central Australia, simple human societies have survived with plenty of time to spare. Against this standard, the growing complexity and advanced technology of modern societies reduces rather than increases our leisure time. On most nights, the Gebusi get a good nine hours or more of sleep. Here in the United States, I am lucky to get seven. Each of our so-called labor-saving devices brings new demands for productive work.

If Gebusi lives throw the frenzied pace of modern society into relief, they also possess their own afflictions. Their deeper struggle has not been so much to acquire food as to fight off illness and, as discussed in the next chapter, to endure human violence fueled by sickness and natural death. The Gebusi's biggest enemies have ultimately been very small. Mosquitoes bring the scourge of malaria. Parasitic worms cause chronic and draining illnesses. Communicable diseases such as tuberculosis and introduced influenza wreak havoc. In the hot, humid climate, cuts and scrapes easily fester and form putrid skin ulcers. All these ailments sap energy and could be combatted by better nutrition. But Gebusi are at pains to improve their diet. Though their staples of plantains and sago brim with starch, they give little protein. Forest animals can be hunted, but they are hard to catch on a regular basis or in large numbers. Hunting more frequently deep in the forest would also expose Gebusi to yet more mosquitoes and malaria and would put them at greater risk of accident and injury. Malnutrition is hence a problem. Young children often have the tiny limbs and distended "sago belly" of a diet that is high in starch but low in protein. Ultimately, the "affluence" of Gebusi leisure is itself an adaptation to their environment: it is more efficient to conserve energy and relax than to work harder while only minimally improving nutrition.

The same is true of the Gebusi approach to raising pigs. Gebusi love to eat pork but don't like the work of raising the animals. They would have to feed them every day and also fence gardens nearby to keep the pigs from rooting them up. So they take the easy way out. When the opportunity arises, Gebusi capture wild piglets in the forest. They feed them leftover food, carry them around in little net bags, and, to an extent, tame them. But as the pigs start to grow, Gebusi turn them loose. The critters live in the forest on their own but still come back to their Gebusi owners for occasional handouts of food. As a novel result, the pigs are neither wild nor domestic but somewhere in between. When a major feast comes up, Gebusi use a special twist on a tactic found in the Hänsel and Gretel fairy tale. To entice their pigs back, Gebusi lure them with pieces of banana or sago, which they leave by the pig's tracks in the forest. They then extend a trail of food for the pig to follow right back to the village. Like Hänsel and Gretel in reverse, the pigs find their way unwittingly home, where they can be slaughtered fresh on the spot. Keeping their pigs semidomesticated doesn't allow Gebusi to raise very many of them—barely one for each extended family. But it does provide a reliable source of meat for their most special occasions while avoiding the heavy work of having to feed, tend, and restrain pigs or even carry them back to the village when slaughtered.

This leads to a larger point. Anthropologists use concepts and categories to class societies according to their type of livelihood or subsistence, their mode of residence, and their form of political organization. But these categories are not rigid in practice, and people like the Gebusi easily defy them. Gebusi subsist through gardening as well as foraging and hunting actively in the forest—they are "horticulturalists" but their practices also reflect "hunting and gathering." In residence, their lifestyle is mobile and almost "seminomadic," yet they build durable houses and are "sedentary." They efficiently raise pigs, but the animals are only "semidomesticated." And in terms of leadership, Gebusi have neither the aggression and status-competition of so-called big-men (which are often associated with the political organization of "tribes") nor the more fully egalitarian and decentralized leadership that has often been attributed to "band" societies of foragers or hunter-gathers. Personally, I like the fact that the Gebusi are "in-betweeners." Like many peoples when considered closely, Gebusi hybridize and cross-cut many of our concepts and terms of classification—including those commonly employed in introductory textbooks. This doesn't mean that basic terms of classification are "wrong"; they can be useful for suggesting broad similarities and differences across societies in different world areas. But such generalizing terms don't fully grasp the details of a particular society or culture. In this sense, general concepts and individual cases are complements: ethnography can convey human richness and fascinating detail while comparative anthropology or "ethnology" provides categories for comparative or global understanding.

As revealed both by general concepts and case study descriptions, the diverse ways that people pursue their livelihood and organize their society is a testament to human creativity and to the power of culture as a means of adaptation. I am continually fascinated by how people not just survive but find meaning and purpose across different environments in different parts of the globe. This capacity will need not just to continue but intensify in the 21st century as humanity confronts the increasing challenges of climate change and our potential to pollute and degrade our planetary environment. As ecological threats grow ominous, humans need greater resilience and creativity to pursue long-term adaptations.

For their part, and amid their own many challenges and difficulties, Gebusi have basked in their environment. A storm blows in suddenly and doesn't let up for hours.

Rain pelts and pockmarks the village; it carves gullies and then little canyons in the central clearing. The streams swell and the rivers roil and flood. Bluffs of clay become slides of mud, and traveling anywhere becomes slippery and sloppy. Plans are canceled. But rather than curse the weather, Gebusi simply take the day off. Toasty in their houses, men light up their pipes and chat while women play with children, put some plantains on the fire, or thread more inches on the large net bags they are making. Someone tells a story or a myth. Plans unfold for a coming feast. Those returning in the downpour make fun of how wet and muddy they got. Sometimes, as if to defy the rain, they whoop loudly and march through it proudly.

When a dry spell descends and the rivers shrink, men make plans for spearing or poisoning fish. The low, clear water exposes their prey and makes them easier to catch. Hawi was one of the best fishermen. His favorite stalking place was above the rapids in a quiet pool of the Kum River. He would swim underwater and jab at his targets with a pronged spike. One day, he speared the biggest fish of all—it must have weighed twenty pounds or more. To the people of Yibihilu, landing this giant prize was akin to winning the Super Bowl. Cries of joy and amazement filled the air. As word spread, a feast became inevitable. More than good fortune or skill, the taking of the huge fish affirmed the goodness of the village, the beneficence of the river, and the harmony of the villagers with their forest spirits. Portions of the fish were shared among each and every inhabitant of Yibihilu, the "place of the deep waters." Hawi has always been my "fish," my *dio*, based on the piece of fish that he shared with me that afternoon. In the evening, Swamin held one of his biggest and most dramatic séances. In song after song, his spirits described how the big fish had given itself up to Hawi's skill and the strength of his village. The lives of the fish people, their comings and goings in the river, came alive in vivid detail. The other fish were ripe for the taking, the spirits said. The men in the audience went wild.

Although the Gebusi seemed for the most part to luxuriate in their environment, we as Westerners were hard-pressed to follow their lead. Daily physical maintenance was a major challenge. During the course of two years, ailments and illnesses became inevitable: the headaches and chills of malaria; digestive disorders; intestinal worms; skin lesions, boils, and rashes; and jungle rot that thrives in your body's most private parts. Our lives were made bearable by a small arsenal of medications, both for ourselves and for Gebusi. Not being doctors, it was often hard to know how we could or should try to help our friends with medicines. But the people of Yibihilu were good role models for us: they accepted infirmity when it came and made the best of life while it lasted. Tabway was afflicted with a putrefying ulcer on her thigh. Her leg would shudder in torment, but her face would stay calm or even show a soft smile. Sefomay's foot was permanently and painfully swollen to twice its normal size. She would joke that her "leg was rotten"—but her spirit was not.

Sickness and death visited Gebusi at every season of life. Malaria, pneumonia, filariasis or "elephantiasis," tuberculosis, influenza, and diarrhea were at once causal and contributing factors. Gebusi were distressed by microbes, parasites, clogged lungs, contaminated blood, and swollen spleens. By the time they reached what we would call middle age, most of them were physically wizened. Almost all adults had had at least one bout of a near-death illness. Sickness dovetailed with poor nutrition, since weaker bodies have a tougher time fighting infection. Of girls who lived to be five, only one in three survived to age forty. For boys of similar age, only about one in six lived to their fifth decade.

If Gebusi could not cheat death, they savored life while it lasted. They enjoyed simple pleasures, smiled often, laughed easily, and celebrated when they could. Notwithstanding their crusades against sorcery, there was little they could do to reduce their physical risk—either from disease or from one another. The deaths that we witnessed were met with quietude and acceptance. The warm hands of friends gave way to piercing wails only at the end.

Gebusi ailments put our own in perspective. On a daily basis, our two biggest challenges were heat and insects. Such "little" things are almost embarrassing to admit, but chronic discomforts loom as large in fieldwork as they are typically neglected in scholarly accounts. If heat and humidity turned our papers limp and our shoes green with mold, we easily felt the same way. The following extract is from my field notes:

> You can't be cool when the humidity and temperature both exceed 98.6. I sit in the shade of my house and calm myself inside and out. Mental strain fuels sweat and throbs my head. I stay absolutely still, motionless, relaxing, eyes closed. The sweat beads, then dribbles from my brow, chest, and thighs. I splash with water from my basin, but more sweat replaces it. I go to my sleeping room, a bit darker, and take off all my clothes, every stitch. I kneel on the floor beside my sleeping net. Fractions of confinement make a difference. The mesh of my sleeping net holds extra heat that radiates from my body, so I do not go inside it.
>
> The three-point stance is my naked attempt to relax in the heat. I can't lie down, since this creates hot contact between my side and whatever I am laying on; a puddle of sweat quickly appears. My best posture keeps an illusion of repose for ten minutes or so with the smallest possible part of my body touching the floor and as much as possible languid in air. The three points of contact are the tip of my big toes, kneecaps, and elbows. This reduces my surface area of contact to a few scant inches. If I get it right, I can hang my head without having to support it with my fingers (since sweat erupts wherever skin touches skin). So my head hangs limp an inch or two off the floor. My mind calms, so does my skin. The sweat still collects across my cheeks and drips from my nose. It splats onto the floor, but softly, slowly.
>
> After ten minutes, I am as serene as I can be. Relaxation is key, since heat makes friends with anxiety and stress. Yesterday I misplaced my notebook and my frustration quickly steamed my glasses. My three-point stance won't cure the heat. But it makes it easier to live with.

For their part, the Gebusi hardly minded the temperature or the humidity. They often kept cooking fires smoldering in their houses, which have no chimneys. The added heat and smoke dispersed the mosquitoes and drove away insects that would otherwise infest the thatch and wood of the house. But it was different for us as fieldworkers. We were raised in northern areas of the United States. It was hard to tolerate the added heat and smoke of a continual fire in our house. So we opted for less fire—and got more bugs. Insects were a whole separate dimension of fieldwork. I couldn't ignore them:

> They are everywhere. Even sitting in a canoe in the middle of the Kum River, the creepies and crawlies land on you. Some of them are really strange looking, sporting weird colors and wild-flight torsos and ways of moving that come from another world. Magnified a thousand times, they would be perfect for the next alien thriller from Hollywood. But most of them are innocuous. You just pick or brush them off and move on.
>
> There are several exceptions. Oversize grasshoppers give a startle when they land on you suddenly. Five-inch spiders raise my adrenaline when I find them sharing the close confines of our outhouse. Cockroaches are everywhere. Hundreds of the big ones live in our cardboard cartons and eat the labels off our precious tins of food. But the mosquitoes I hardly even count as insects because they are so insidious. Not just because there are so many of them, nor because they fly into our thatched house without pause or restriction. It's the malaria and elephantiasis they bring. They wait like cowards until dusk before taunting you with their mock fragility. They lilt in squadrons on low power but somehow float just beyond your grasp, waiting like lunar modules to hit your pay dirt. Swatting hard only flits them away to a yet choicer landing place. "One small bite for one mosquito, one giant risk for mankind."
>
> There is a special insult to getting several bites. How many did you really receive in the dimness? Was it only two? Or four or six? Is that another new one now again, just beside the others? Did you *really* take your antimalarial pill (none of which are completely effective)? The best thing is to go inside the mosquito net—and that very quickly, because *nothing* is worse than having mosquitoes get *inside* your net. But we can't live under a mosquito net from six at night until six in the morning. We have to eat and wash, write our notes, and of course, talk with people. The evening should be one of the most enjoyable parts of the day. Wearing heavy clothes or lathering on high concentrations of DEET isn't feasible night after night. So we have no real solution, take our hits, and do the best we can. But going to the bathroom remains the worst. Mosquitoes love the bottom of the latrine pit, and they fly up in droves whenever something goes down the hole. They attack our most vulnerable parts when we are most exposed. Talk about a bite in the butt!

If heat and insects were our daily scourge, the Gebusi kept our irritations in perspective. Despite their own much graver ailments, their lives remained vibrant. This pulled us beyond the orbit of our own concerns. Call it cultural gravity—the ability of others' lives to sweep you up and draw you in to your own surprise and against all challenge. This is the deepest part of fieldwork, the part that makes you grow. We joked with the Gebusi, shared with them, took part in their activities, and became part of their world. Reciprocally, they seemed to enjoy us, accepted our idiosyncrasies, and included us in their activities as much as they could. In professional terms, this is what is often described as the primary field-work method in cultural anthropology: participant-observation.

Professionally, I think my biggest challenge was learning the Gebusi language. Given their remoteness, there was no way I could have done this ahead of time. We had received training in how to learn an unwritten language without the help of translators. In the field, bit by slow, painful bit, we learned to recognize and make sounds that do not exist in English. We compiled lists of Gebusi words and phrases—and puzzled over their meanings. In all of these tasks, Yuway was my most patient, insightful, and pleasant helper. Increasingly over the course of weeks and months, he and I became special friends. He even helped me tackle the complexi-ties of Gebusi tense and grammar, and these were the worst. The Gebusi like to pile meanings into verbs while leaving out nouns and other phrases. For instance, the question "Would he have killed me?" is spoken in Gebusi as a single verb, "kill" (*golo*), which is then modified by a string of suffixes to indicate a presumed subject, a presumed object, conditional tense, causative action, and interrogative aspect. The whole sentence is one word: *golo-hi-lay-ba*. Fortunately, we knew from the start that learning the language would be our most difficult task. After a few weeks, we could make simple communications in broken Gebusi. After a few months, we began to figure out what the Gebusi were saying to one another—not in the simple, slowed-down language that they used with us, but in the idioms, quick pacing, and assump-tions that they used with each other. My advisor wrote and told us not to get too discouraged. He suggested that if we focused on language learning for the first six months, we would be okay. He also said that our language abilities would continue to improve and that two-thirds of our understanding would likely emerge during the last third of our fieldwork. So we would have to be patient. He was right.

Along the way, we developed our own rhythms of daily adaptation. Fieldwork is at heart its own brand of optimal foraging. As the Gebusi shifted their activities to gain the most from their surroundings, we tried to do the same. For me, however, our desire to participate, to observe, and to record our experiences became a dance between "living with" and "writing up." Days during fieldwork blended language learning, observation, note-taking, interviews, writing, and reflection—amid the con-stant intensity of public social living. I was continually surprised at how long it took me to type up my notes and organize them into larger topical files. Even when not much was going on in the village, I seemed to be behind in my work. It became painfully obvious that fieldwork was not a process of quickly discovering "the truth." My learning about Gebusi emerged gradually through a blur of confusing experiences and competing interpretations. I repeatedly found that my language skills were defi-cient, my interpretations misleading, and my assumptions simply wrong. I remember during our first weeks pointing to various objects with my index finger and asking in simple Gebusi, "What is it?" (*ke ka-ba*). But no matter what I pointed to, the answer I got was always the same, "*dob.*" I was completely perplexed. The mystery was explained when I learned the meaning of *dob. Dob* was the finger I was pointing with! Understanding was always a process of learning from our mistakes. We began at the lowest rung, asking nonsensical questions like "Is your son a girl?" But just as quickly, we learned to laugh at our foibles. It helped a lot that Gebusi laughed so good-naturedly along with us, just as they did at their own mistakes and problems.

As time went on and comprehension improved, I came to see cultural anthropology as a kind of dialogue—a conversation between Gebusi meanings and our own understandings. The trick was to have each side of this cultural equation make sense in terms of the other. This process was rooted in participation and observation, but it continued afterward in writing and reflection. Writing ethnography is almost invariably a process of trying to explain clearly events and actions that were, in fact, confusing or opaque when observed and experienced to begin with.

During fieldwork, this process linked us directly back to our relationship with the Gebusi. In our lives and our work, a balance between give-and-take was key: the ability to admit error and try yet again, to receive as well as give, to be acted upon as well as act. In this, Gebusi were wonderful teachers. Reciprocity was at the heart of their social life: they maintained a vigilant balance between giving and getting, between acting and being acted upon. As we increasingly came to realize, balanced reciprocity pervaded many if not most aspects of Gebusi culture, including their relation with their physical environment, their distribution of food, their ritual celebrations, their marriage patterns, their connections with the spirit world, and even their patterns of death and killing. The ideal of balanced reciprocity was one of the most personally and professionally important things that I learned from the Gebusi. Apart from their gendered divisions, they were egalitarian to a fault. They reinforced this norm by constantly striving to maintain a balance between receiving and giving.

> The big feast was yesterday. Today, our friends are happily eating food that the visitors brought and gave them in exchange for the lavish meal our settlement hosted. Since my household contributed fish and rice to the communal effort, people now want to repay me.
>
> This morning, a member of each major family in the village came and presented me with a bird egg. I was deeply touched. Most memorable was five-year-old Kawe, who has become my "biscuit" exchange-name friend. I saw him coming from across the village. With the confident stride and smile of a grown-up, he looked at me from twenty yards away and walked over directly, never shifting his gaze. Stopping in front of me, he flashed his cutest tooth-missing grin and extended his little hand that held his egg. He placed the egg in my palm, turned around, and walked back proudly, never uttering a word or looking back. I will never forget it.

BROADER CONNECTIONS: *Subsistence, Health, and Language*

- Gebusi are **sedentary horticulturalists**—who also **forage and hunt.**
- Gebusi's ingenious means of rainforest survival illustrate how culture is **adaptive.**
- Culture provides humans an **"extra-somatic" means of adaptation,** per Leslie White.

- Gebusi grow food, but nonintensively, through **horticulture**, as contrasted to **agriculture.**

- Gebusi also **forage** widely in the forest, including **gathering** wild plants and **hunting** animals.

- Gebusi live in **durable houses** on most days and thus have **sedentary residence.**

- Gebusi also move so widely and frequently in the forest that they are almost **seminomadic.**

- Simple human societies like the Gebusi have **leisure** to the extent that Marshall Sahlins has called them **"Original Affluent Societies."**

- Like many remote or poor peoples, Gebusi endure severe **health challenges,** including **malaria, childhood malnutrition, elephantiasis (filariasis), tuberculosis, worm (helminthic) diseases, and influenza.**

- Gebusi have **low life expectancy**, and death strikes them at any age.

- Like many anthropologists, Bruce's biggest **cultural challenge in fieldwork** was **learning the Gebusi language.**

- Gebusi language included culturally recognized sounds or **phonemes** such as nasalized vowels that are not distinguished or "heard" as different sounds in English.

- **Morphemes** are the smallest units of **meaning** in language. In the Gebusi language, morphemes included the many prefixes, suffixes, and "infixes" of Gebusi verbs—and the three components of *kog-wa-yay.*

- Bruce took many **fieldnotes** as events were happening. Writing these up and configuring them provides a foundation for producing coherent **ethnographic descriptions** or **ethnography.**

- As is also the case in many or most societies, establishing social **reciprocity** was personally and professionally indispensable to **fieldwork** among Gebusi.

CHAPTER 3

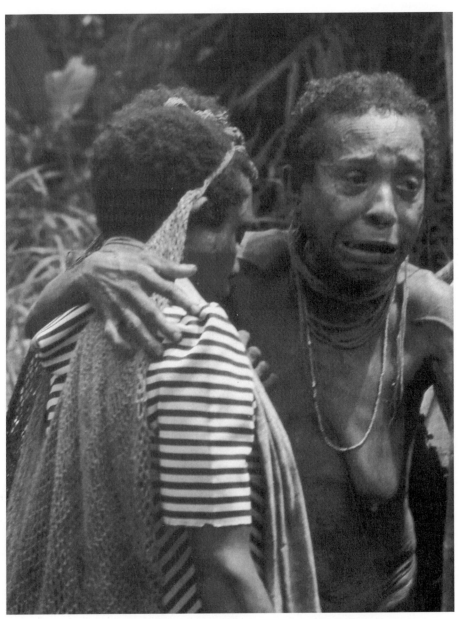

A woman mourns the death of her husband. (Photo: Eileen Marie Knauft)

Lives of Death

IT IS HARD TO WATCH A BABY DIE. Its scrawny body cries until its wails lose force and leave a ghostly little corpse. It was also hard on us that Gebusi men didn't seem to mind. During our first five weeks in the field, we saw first one baby die and then another. As the mother wailed with grief, her women-kin gathered in support. But the men continued to joke and smoke in the longhouse, and the boys played gaily in the village clearing. Only the baby's father stayed close by, and even this was with an air of detached waiting—until the small body could be quickly buried. Managing babies and managing death were both women's work; if women bore the day-to-day challenge and joy of caring for new life, they also bore the sting of its death. Along with Eileen, I visited the mother in each case to lend support. But both times I felt, as a man, that the most courteous thing I could do was to leave. As the second infant was dying, I talked with Owaya, its father. He said that the baby was dying "just because." But then he wondered whether a woman from Wasobi might have sent sorcery to kill it. As I later found out, the Gebusi attributed all natural deaths to sorcery. But they really only investigated the deaths of adults and older children.

The Gebusi don't think of infants as fully human until they are about seven months old, when their first teeth emerge. Until then, a human spirit is not thought to be completely rooted in their bodies, and they aren't even given a name. Many infants only flirt with life; a third of them die during their first year. The community in general and men in particular seem to protect themselves from identifying too closely with so many young lives that end so quickly. But this distance is not shared by the mother, red-eyed and weeping, nor by her closest female kin. The father, for his part, seems awkwardly in the middle, experiencing neither the women's emotion nor the other men's distance. But the other men treated me jovially, as if nothing had happened. At heart, I was confused. It was my first real lesson in the contours and constraints of Gebusi emotion.

Just three weeks after the second infant died, a third death hit the village: Dugawe killed himself. Unlike the infant deaths, which were taken as "normal," this one shocked the community. No one could remember a man having killed himself. Although we didn't foresee it at the time, Dugawe's death drew us into a whirling cultural vortex. Confusing events and experiences flew by; we struggled to piece them together. People we knew and liked suddenly did things we could not believe. In retracing this path—its twists and turns, and my own confusions—I came to know much about Gebusi life and death, the importance of kinship in their society, and how, during fieldwork, one begins to make sense of a foreign culture.

At first, I didn't believe Yuway and Silap when they came to tell me the news; they seemed so matter of fact. But within minutes, we rushed off to the forest so they could retrieve Dugawe's corpse. When we arrived, the dead man's wife and two other women were weeping by the body. Silap brushed them aside and wailed loudly. Dugawe had been Silap's extended "brother-in-law" (*gol*) and "initiation-mate" (*sam*). Gebusi settlements coalesce by bringing together men—and women—from different family lines. This differs from societies in which the settlement and its social life cohere around the core relatives of a single "clan" or "lineage." For Gebusi, by contrast, people co-reside in a village based on diverse and tangled networks of kinship and friendship. Silap and Dugawe had not been members of the same male line, but they had long lived in the same village, had become friends, had been initiated together, and were distantly related through marriage.

After Silap finished wailing, the women came back to resume their crying. They called to Dugawe, telling him how sorry they were about his death and how much they wanted him back. Their raw emotion was said to soothe Dugawe's lingering soul and ease its gradual passage to the land of the dead. Meanwhile, Silap smoked tobacco with Yuway and waited for other men from Yibihilu to arrive. None of them seemed upset, much less distraught, as they discussed how to take Dugawe's body back to the village. Wondering why he had killed himself, I went with others to inspect the body. Dugawe had been a strong, handsome man, but now his face was pale and slack, already beginning to swell in the tropical heat. I looked for signs of foul play. Perhaps his death was a murder disguised as a suicide. But the only sign of struggle was a mark on the front of his faded T-shirt; something had poked and scratched down its fabric for a couple of inches. The shirt was not punctured, however, and nothing had pierced Dugawe's skin. To the men, though, the tiny scratch exposed a larger canvas of anger and shame. As I later found out, Dugawe had fought that day with his wife, Sialim, before committing suicide. During the scuffle, she had held an arrow, thrust it toward him, and scratched his shirt. Their fight had been about a sexual affair that was generally acknowledged between Sialim and a young man, Sagawa. Publicly cuckolded, Dugawe had been furious. He had wanted to hunt and kill his wayward wife, and perhaps her lover as well. But Silap and others had discouraged him from doing this. Incensed but lacking other recourse, Dugawe had fought with his wife. He was further shamed by her scratching his shirt, his prized possession. When she went off to fetch water, the men said, he took tubes of poison that he had previously made for killing fish in the stream and, in a fit of rage, had drunk them all. Empty tubes with the smell of the potent toxin were found nearby. Dugawe had died a writhing death after poisoning himself in anger against his wife. But he was so much bigger and stronger than she. Why was his anger so self-directed?

It all seemed confusing. For the moment, all I could do was try to keep up with events as the men lashed Dugawe's body to a stretcher and marched it briskly back to Yibihilu. By chance, two women came through the forest from another direction and converged on us. They were fictive "mothers" of Dugawe from an adjacent community who had come to view his body. Upon seeing his corpse, and his wayward wife trailing behind us, they virtually exploded. Screaming, they tore straight into Sialim. She turned to avoid them, but the lead woman walloped her on the back with a steel ax she was wielding, blunt side forward. This was followed by another heavy blow. The woman then turned and threw herself on Dugawe's corpse, pawing it and crying in great screaming sobs, as if her emotion would wake it up. Simultaneously, the second woman resumed the first one's attack, screeching at full pitch and poking and shoving Sialim with a pointed stick as if she were going to drive it right through her. Silap and Yuway rushed in to hold her back while another man wrestled Dugawe's closest "mother" away from the corpse. The rest of the men quickly picked up the body and raced with it down the trail and out of sight. Yuway, Silap, and I followed closely, with the women coming more slowly behind.

When we finally arrived at Yibihilu, Dugawe's body was laid in state in his family house, a scant twenty-five yards from our own home. A crowd of women screeched and wailed while others arrived in short order. Many of them pummeled and berated Sialim, who hunched and whimpered but could not run away without neglecting her duty to mourn her dead husband. Our neighbor, Owaya, came up and waved a firebrand in her face. Unleashing a withering diatribe, he punctuated his anger with shouts of "Si-nay!" which, as I came to learn later, means, roughly, "Burn! Cook! We'll eat you!" This was what Gebusi traditionally did to persons executed as sorcerers. Owaya whacked Sialim with his burning stick and then shoved it into the net bag on her back. She gasped, whimpered, and shuffled several feet farther away.

Inside the house, we gathered with the women who had come to weep over the corpse. Like Dugawe's "mother," some of them flailed hysterically when they first arrived. After a few minutes, the atmosphere gradually calmed. But then a man with blackened face and body lunged suddenly through the doorway. Crying loudly, he cocked and drew an arrow in his bow with full strength and released the bowstring with a sharp snap. In my shock, I didn't realize that he still held the arrow with the other fingers of his shooting hand—he had snapped the bowstring without releasing the arrow. Yelling, he then repeated his diatribe—while plucking his bow individually at each of us who was in the house. Silap then rushed up and interposed himself. With calming words, outstretched hands, and a wan smile, he gingerly and gradually began to placate the intruder. As Silap and the attacker moved outside, I went with them and saw more than twenty warriors from other settlements, who were now massing. Almost as quickly, however, the men of Yibihilu were also gathering, not as antagonists, but to placate them. Armed with large stoked tobacco pipes, they snapped fingers and extended repeated hits of powerful tobacco to each visitor in turn. Their actions seemed to melt the tension like a cool rain in the heat of the day. In short order, the visitors retired to the longhouse and were provided resting mats. They began to relax. We did, too. Those of us from Yibihilu scurried to find and cook bananas and give them in hospitality.

An hour or so later, a government constable arrived from the Nomad Station. Silap and some other men had taken the rare step of sending word to the Papua New Guinea police about Dugawe's death—and inviting one of them to come to Yibihilu to investigate. Why? Apparently they were worried that the authorities might receive a different tale of Dugawe's death from some other source. After a long conversation through several interpreters, the constable finally wrote a brief entry in his police book: "Reason of death: Suicide caused by his wife fooling around." Though the constable's inquiry was completed, discussion about Sialim continued. Given the anger against her, it was decided that she should go with the officer back to Nomad straightaway and stay there temporarily for her own protection. The main events of the day were then over. The piercing wails of women haunted the night.

By the following morning, Dugawe's body had bloated grotesquely. His swollen limbs oozed corpse fluid, and his peeling skin exposed putrid red and yellow-green flesh. His belly and even his genitals had swelled with the gases of decomposition. I will never forget the stench, which burned up my nose, down my throat, and into my brain. Equally powerful were the actions of Dugawe's female relatives. With unearthly sobs, they draped themselves physically over the corpse, lovingly massaged its slime, and drew back its skin. Then they rubbed their own arms and legs with the ooze of the body. Corpse fluid on one's skin is a tangible sign of grief, of physical as well as emotional connection with the person who has died—making one's body akin to the deceased. Seeing this, it was said, Dugawe's departing soul would know how much they cared for him. Just a little, this would ease his pain and anger at having died.

The men of Yibihilu dug Dugawe's grave by his family house. Then the women rolled Dugawe's corpse onto Silap's back. As he strained and stood up under the weight, the body's arms flung out dramatically to both sides. The women shrieked. Men rushed to steady the corpse and help Silap place it in the grave. Dugawe's possessions—his bamboo pipe, bow and arrows, and so on—were quickly arranged in the grave by his female kin. Bark was placed over the corpse, and then the hole was filled in. Just as directly, the men retired to the longhouse to rest. The closest female relatives threw themselves on the mounded grave and wailed.

Prior to fieldwork, the only dead body I had seen was the sedate face of a friend of my parents during an open-casket funeral. Now I was shocked and repulsed by the events surrounding Dugawe's death. It seemed hideous that his corpse was allowed to decay and that our women friends wallowed in its stench before it was buried. But I also began to see that this raw transformation—of a human being into a decomposed natural object—was an emotionally and physically honest view of death. Dugawe's disfigurement showed me the fact of his death like nothing else could do. His demise was not hidden, not made pretty, not covered up in attempts to "spare grief." Were Gebusi customs improper? Or, was my own culture's tendency to gloss over and downplay the reality of death off-kilter?

I ultimately found that the dramatic actions of Gebusi women with corpses puzzled me less than the more reserved conduct of Gebusi men. As they went to the longhouse to smoke, joke, and drink bowls of root intoxicant, they acted as if nothing was wrong. When I heard that a visiting spirit medium would hold a public séance, I thought he would commune with Dugawe's spirit and inquire about his death. Instead, the séance was a songfest of ribald entertainment. Why was this? The men said that Dugawe's spirit was too angry to talk, and that in the meantime, since they were all together, they thought it best to relax and have a good time.

It was all rather bewildering. Which of the details surrounding Dugawe's death were relevant, and which were superficial? How did Gebusi funeral practices and sorcery beliefs influence their social relationships and their emotional lives? I tried to connect the dots by writing descriptions and reflections. But even as the picture stayed fuzzy, additional questions arose. What did Dugawe's sexual and marital problems with Sialim reveal about Gebusi gender relations? And to what extent were the circumstances of Dugawe's death exceptional or anomalous in Gebusi society? As I struggled for answers, further events both sharpened my questions and posed new ones. Gradually, the events following Dugawe's death unfolded into a sorcery investigation—an inquiry into who had "killed" him. Its twists and turns helped me answer the questions I had, but not in the ways I expected. In retrospect, I realized that this trail of discovery revealed much about the practice of ethnography as well as about the customs and beliefs of the Gebusi. In short, I was engaging the complications and confusions—and the dawning greater awareness—of studying culture through ethnographic fieldwork.

Though the big funeral feast for Dugawe took place just two days after his burial, it ended up being a sideshow to events that occurred weeks later. And by the time this sorcery investigation resumed, my opinion of Sialim had changed. At first, I thought she had acted irresponsibly. She had carried on a sexual affair with a young man named Sagawa, and she had apparently shamed her husband into killing himself. But additional facts painted a different picture. As Eileen found out from the women, Dugawe had years earlier killed not only his first wife but also his own small son. These murders had been so awful that villagers had informed the police, and Dugawe had served a five-year term at the Western Province prison in Daru. To our knowledge, no other Gebusi had ever been incarcerated there—or has been since.

When his prison term was over, Dugawe had returned to the Gebusi and married Sialim, who had recently been widowed by the death of Dugawe's "brother." Gebusi widows often end up marrying a male family relative of their dead husband. This custom is common in various societies around the world; anthropologists call it "marriage by levirate." When a woman marries a real or extended brother of her dead husband, it often keeps her residence, her labor— and her children—within the family line of the man who first married her. This can help keep intact the structure and patterning of marriages in the society—and

sometimes women desire it of their own accord. Knowing Dugawe's history, however, Sialim did not want to marry him. As newlyweds, they fought, and he frequently beat her. On one occasion, she finally sought recourse from the patrol
officers at the Nomad Station. Given her bruises and Dugawe's violent past, the
police had arrested him again and held him at the local jail. It was while he was
in jail that Sialim took up with Sagawa, her young lover. Perhaps she hoped that
her relationship with Sagawa would become a de facto marriage before Dugawe
was released from jail. But Dugawe was discharged earlier than expected. Enraged,
he wanted to kill Sialim and her partner. But Silap and the other men of Yibihilu
persuaded him that he would then receive an even longer prison term than the
one he had already endured. Amid this tension, Dugawe took up again with
Sialim. But after their fight in the forest, he committed suicide.

From a Western feminist perspective, it could be argued that Sialim could
hardly be blamed. She had been saddled with an abusive marriage and a murder-
ous spouse. She had tried to find refuge, sought solace with another partner, and
then stood up for herself when Dugawe beat her. What villagers took as a sign
of travesty—her fighting with her husband and scratching his shirt with an
arrow—could have been a desperate attempt at self-defense. However, Sialim was
rebuked not only by the men of Yibihilu but especially by Dugawe's female kin.
She had gone outside the community, gotten her husband jailed, and cheated on
him. To make matters worse, her romantic affair was with a young man who had
not yet been initiated into manhood.

What was I to think? I could criticize Gebusi as condoning violent sexism.
On the other hand, Sialim had violated standards of marital fidelity that were
deeply held by Gebusi. I felt stuck in the middle between these views. Most
importantly, though, we were concerned for Sialim's safety. It was fortunate that
she went off temporarily to Nomad.

As I slowly came to realize, Gebusi inquests into and retributions for lethal
sorcery usually did not take place until well after the victim had been buried. The
main exception was if the corpse itself, while lying in state, "signaled" who the
sorcerer was. As the corpse began to decompose, a sorcery suspect might be
enjoined by the community to vehemently shake the body while crying out his
or her own grief and sorrow. If at that unlucky moment the corpse gave a "sign"—
spilling cadaveric fluid, "moaning" due to gases in its lungs, or bulging its eyes
out or even bursting them, from the gas pressure of decomposition within the
braincase—the suspect could be axed to death on the spot. If the "verdict" of the
corpse was clear, there would be little protest over the execution of the alleged
sorcerer from even his or her closest kin. But this had not happened with Dugawe's
corpse. So the men of Yibihilu had soothed the anger of Dugawe's visiting relatives
by extending hospitality—snapping fingers, sharing tobacco, giving food, and
holding an entertaining séance.

My friends told me that further inquiry into Dugawe's death should not take
place in the heat of the moment but should be conducted more objectively over

a longer time—somewhat like a murder investigation in Western societies. For Gebusi, however, the purpose of the inquest was to ferret out the sorcerer who had killed Dugawe through spiritual means. In their belief, all human deaths were caused by people—either through sorcery or through violence. Even a man who had fallen out of a coconut tree and broken his back had been killed by a sorcerer: because the man had successfully climbed such trees many times in the past, a sorcerer must have made him lose his grip. Deaths from sickness were likewise attributed to sorcery—the sorcerer had caused the lethal illness. In the case of Dugawe's death, the Gebusi took it as self-evident that a sorcerer had either driven Dugawe crazy enough to kill himself or killed him and then used magic to make it look like suicide.

Five weeks after his funeral feast, the real investigation into Dugawe's death began. In a nod to neutrality, the inquest séances were conducted by a spirit medium who had had little personal connection with him in life. But when these séances were inconclusive, further investigation was led by our clever friend Swamin, the main spirit medium of Yibihilu. By this time, I had discovered that Gebusi sorcery had two main types. In one type, called *bogay*, the sorcerer was believed to secretly tie up the feces or other bodily leavings of the victim, causing a long, painful illness. The sorcerer then "killed" the victim by burning the fecal matter or other leavings. Anthropologists sometimes call this "imitative magic"—the magical use of supernatural powers based on the principle that "like produces like." The other main variety of Gebusi sorcery was called *ogowili*. In this, sorcerers took the form of magical warriors who attacked the victim in the forest, usually when he or she was alone. The sorcerer–warriors then killed the victim with arrows and clubs, ate out his or her insides, magically sewed up him or her, and then cast a spell that gave their victim amnesia. Although the person might amble uncertainly back to the village, he or she would die a sudden death shortly thereafter.

Bogay comes under the heading of what ethnographers call "parcel sorcery," that is, sickness sent by manipulating a parcel of the victim's leavings. By contrast, *ogowili* qualifies as "assault sorcery," a cannibal attack by magical warriors. For the Gebusi, *bogay* explained the torment of a long, lethal illness, while *ogowili* explained deaths that were relatively quick and sudden, as well as those caused by accident—and suicide. One way or the other, Gebusi believed that all deaths from sickness, accident, or suicide were caused by sorcery. In reality, we found no evidence that Gebusi actually practiced either type of sorcery—and we found much evidence to the contrary. But their own beliefs seemed unshakable.

In Dugawe's case, death was thought to have been caused by assault *ogowili*. Although such sorcerers are said to be men who take the form of a magical warrior, they may be manipulated to do this by a malicious woman. Given this, Sialim could be guilty of Dugawe's death if she had had sex with an *ogowili* and induced him to drive her husband crazy. For the Gebusi, this was plausible since Sialim was known to have had a sexual affair with Sagawa.

In his séances, however, Swamin's spirits suggested a different scenario. Rather than accuse Sialim, his spirits described how *ogowili* warriors had descended on Dugawe from a distant settlement while Sialim was away fetching water.

Though the assault sorcerers had disguised the evidence and covered their tracks, Swamin's spirits assured the assembled men that signs of their attack could still be found in the forest where Dugawe's death had occurred. Further, the *ogowili* might then be tracked back to their own settlement, where they could, at least in principle, be attacked in their human form to avenge the killing of Dugawe. However, to track assault sorcerers through the forest, the Gebusi needed spiritual help to guide them.

As Swamin's séance ended, at about five o'clock in the morning, the men of Yibihilu got ready to search for the assault sorcerers responsible for Dugawe's death. Uncertain what was going to happen next, I pulled on my boots and grabbed my flashlight in the predawn darkness. The men were carrying bows and arrows, and some had painted their faces black, like warriors. Eventually, we approached Abwiswimaym, the forest plot where Dugawe had drunk poison. The mood became tense as we searched for the ghostly form of an assault sorcerer ahead. Quietly and anxiously, men sought cover, pointed their arrows, and advanced warily on their spectral enemy. I pinched my arm to remind myself that we were not likely to find an actual person but rather the evidence of a magical attack by spiritual warriors lurking nearby. After a while, however, the area was declared safe; the assault sorcerers had apparently left.

Next, we searched upstream for the *buluf*—the magically transformed remains of the sorcerers' attack on Dugawe. With Swamin's spirits guiding us, we found an odd-looking stick that was said to be the "bush knife" that the sorcerers had used to cut Dugawe open. An indentation in the ground was the "footprint" of an *ogowili*. A discolored patch of dirt was Dugawe's "blood," which was said to have poured out during the attack. As incredulous as I was, the Gebusi around me seemed completely convinced. The very power of assault sorcerers rests in their ability to disguise their attacks and make the results look almost normal. We then tried to track the sorcerers back to their distant community. But Swamin's spirits lost their trail as we waded up a stream, and their path or direction could not be found again. As such, we could not determine the settlement of the sorcerers or their individual identity. The investigation did validate for the men the general information given by Swamin's spirits in his séance: Dugawe had been killed by an assault sorcerer from a distant village. But it was impossible to discover more, and no further action could be feasibly taken.

I thought this would be the end of Dugawe's story, but in Gebusi society as in our own, poignant events can cast a longer shadow. The verdict of Swamin's spirits provided something of a reprieve for Sialim, as she had not been directly implicated. During the next seven months, she spent more and more time with Swamin's own household. Eventually, she willingly consented to marry him—over the entreaties and objections of her young lover, Sagawa. Strong and robust for a middle-aged man, Swamin had been a widower. During our final year of fieldwork, he and Sialim seemed to be happily married.

Though this would have been a good Hollywood ending, it was not the one we ultimately came away with. It turned out that three years previously, before our arrival, Swamin had killed Sialim's own mother. The old woman, named Mokoyl, had been named as the parcel sorcerer responsible for the death of

Swamin's first wife. At the time, Mokoyl tried to prove her innocence by conducting a bird egg divination—cooking eggs placed inside a large damp mound of sago starch. Unfortunately, the eggs were badly undercooked. When Mokoyl had given Swamin one of the eggs to eat—which she was expected to do as part of the divination—he had vomited. This was taken as a sign that Swamin's dead wife was clutching his throat, refusing Mokoyl's food, and confirming Mokoyl's guilt. A few weeks later, about a year before we began our fieldwork, Swamin tracked Mokoyl alone in the forest—and split her skull with a bushknife. As the spiritual evidence confirmed Mokoyl's guilt, most in the community agreed that Mokoyl had been guilty and deserved to die, and her body was summarily buried in the forest. But villagers from another settlement, knowing she had been killed as a sorceress, dug it up and cooked and ate parts of it before it decomposed. In doing so, they indicated their own support for the killing. Government officers never found out about the incident.

If we add this last episode to the chain of events surrounding Dugawe's death, what conclusions can we draw? With the benefit of hindsight, reflection, and analysis, anthropologists are charged with making sense of diverse societies and culture. Experience becomes fieldwork, and fieldwork becomes ethnographic writing. But how does this transition occur? For me in the field, it was challenging. No Gebusi gave me a full narrative of Dugawe's death, its aftermath, or the events that preceded it. Rather, the story emerged from disparate and sometimes fragmentary events and observations over time.

As is the case for many anthropological fieldworkers, my methods of inquiry included participant-observation, formal interviews, casual conversations, text translations of tape recordings (in this case, of Gebusi spirit séances), and life histories of individual Gebusi that were backed up by genealogies and other systematic information that I gathered concerning residence, marriage, and mortality of those in the community and their ancestors. It was important to cross-check these sources of information, particularly concerning events that predated our arrival, to ensure that the resulting account was accurate. To these were added my daily entries and spontaneous reflections—sometimes insightful, but at other times misguided or off-base—concerning what was actually happening at the time. Within a few days—while the information was still fresh—I typed up my field notes and analyzed these in relation to other information I had gathered. Even concerning events that I myself saw, my awareness was often dim and partial at first—strong in emotional impact but weak in conceptual understanding. An initial event like Dugawe's death, dramatic as it was, became one end of a tangled skein. It sucked me into a thicket of crisscrossed meanings and histories. Figuring it out, writing it down, and getting a larger picture was quite a task—the "work" of fieldwork.

Magnifying this process, in which Dugawe's death is just one example, life among Gebusi was a continual stream of dramas big and small. These linked Gebusi together—and us to them—while gradually exposing what was a general pattern in

Gebusi society and what was individual or idiosyncratic. For instance, in the few weeks between Dugawe's burial and the inquest séances for his death, the villagers undertook spiritual investigations into seven other sicknesses, including my own, when I was stricken with my first serious bout of malaria. I found myself living in an intricate soap opera—truth more surprising than fiction. Lovers, killers, spouses, co-residents, friends, and relatives all had their parts in concocting a rich and sometimes toxic brew. No wonder that coming together in collective good company was so important to Gebusi—or that it was such an accomplishment!

What is participant-observation in such a world? And how can a fieldworker maintain a sense of ethics—and wits about him or her—in the process? In the present case, I observed and, to some extent, participated in the retrieval of Dugawe's body, his funeral and burial, and the spirit séances and sorcery investigations that followed. However, I did not want to participate in any attack on a suspected sorcerer. We tried to facilitate Sialim's departure to a safer place when sentiments against her were highest. This said, we worried that more severe violence might occur. Later in our fieldwork, when our understanding was better, an older woman in the village was accused of being a parcel sorcerer. In this case, we were able to act like kin supporters and side with the woman's family when she was forced to test her innocence by cooking a divination sago. Fortunately, no violent action was taken against her, but she nonetheless had to move out of the village with her closest kin. As this episode clearly indicates, cultural anthropologists often court risk and uncertainty as they decide what to observe and how and when to participate in the participant-observation of fieldwork. As also discussed in later chapters, the question of ethics in fieldwork is important not just to keep in mind but to continually pursue, including under conditions of modern cultural change. This is true in part for the very reason that, amid the surprises of fieldwork, it is not always self-evident how to handle situations that become difficult or delicate— or dangerous.

As an anthropologist, my human and ethical concerns have linked to my training and research as a social scientist. Between events we observed, those we were able to reliably reconstruct, and those we were able to participate in with good conscience, what larger patterns emerge concerning Dugawe's death, its precedents, and its legacy? What can we really "say" about Gebusi culture by drawing upon this story? We can proceed by way of review. This chapter began with a description of Dugawe's suicide, the attacks on Sialim, and the mourning and burial of Dugawe's body. Then came the surprisingly festive events of the funeral feast held to commemorate him. These were followed by a month of waiting. Then, after other aborted attempts, Swamin, the community's principal spirit medium, conducted a death inquest séance for Dugawe. Surprisingly, his spirits recast the death as an attack by male assault sorcerers from a distant settlement. A hunt in the forest for the sorcerers was inconclusive. Eventually, Dugawe's spirit was declared appeased and his widow, Sialim, was exonerated. Several months later, Sialim and Swamin were married. Rounding out this history were events that occurred prior to our fieldwork. These included Dugawe's killing of his first wife and son; Swamin's killing of Sialim's mother; the jailing of Dugawe for having beaten Sialim; and Sialim's sexual affair with Sagawa.

This web of incidents shows how major events among the Gebusi, such as Dugawe's death, are hardly isolated phenomena. Their causes and conditions link backward and forward through time. In viewing the larger picture, topics that may seem disparate—sickness and death, marriage, sex, sorcery, homicide, and suicide—come into interconnected focus. Further, a single event, such as Dugawe's death, can expose a host of broader issues: emotional dynamics among Gebusi, relations between men and women, the importance of spirits and spirit mediums, the impact of government incarceration, and even the role of subsistence practices such as fish poisoning. Far from being separate, these features resonate and twine together. As such, the anthropological concepts and categories we may use to illuminate this story—sorcery, divination, ritual antagonism, levirate, spirit mediumship or shamanism, spirit séance, accusation or execution, and so on—are like convenient hand-holds on a mountainside rather than the mountain itself.

What does Dugawe's story tell us about the Gebusi? Concerning Gebusi sorcery and gender relations, the events surrounding Dugawe's death illustrate that:

1. Gebusi women take primary responsibility for mourning and for emotionally identifying with the person who has died. Men investigate the death and take action against those deemed responsible as sorcerers.

2. Gebusi visitors' burials and funeral feasts express antagonism, but this aggression is undercut by the hosts' hospitality. Deeper anger is usually not expressed until proper inquests and divinations have been arranged.

3. The Gebusi believe that all adult deaths from sickness, accident, or suicide are caused by either male assault sorcerers (*ogowili*) or by male or female parcel sorcerers (*bogay*). Of the two, suspects for parcel sorcery (such as Sialim's mother) are more likely to be executed.

4. There is virtually no objective evidence that the Gebusi actually practice sorcery, but they firmly believe in its existence. Gebusi sorcery is a form of scapegoating. They "confirm" the identity of sorcerers through an elaborate variety of spiritual inquests and divinations.

5. Male spirit mediums play a key role in Gebusi sorcery accusations. The opinion of their spirits during all-night séances is highly influential, and they can direct the finding and interpretation of "evidence" that is used to validate an accusation.

6. Though spirit mediums should be neutral parties, the outcome of the sorcery inquest may end up benefiting the spirit medium who conducts them. In Dugawe's case, Swamin's spirits directed antagonism away from Sialim, whom he ended up marrying a few months later.

7. After sorcery inquests are completed, social relations are often reestablished between the families involved—even if an accused sorcerer has been attacked or killed. After Sialim's mother was executed, her relatives made peace with the killers. Sialim herself continued to live in the Yibihilu community after both her mother's killing and her husband's suicide. Indeed, she ended up marrying her mother's killer.

8. Sickness, death, sorcery, and marriage often link in a cycle of reciprocity or balance over time. Events that seem spontaneous, idiosyncratic, or even bizarre may end up illustrating deeper cultural continuities. In Dugawe's case, Sialim was attacked in reciprocity for his suicide. The earlier death of Swamin's wife was balanced by Swamin's killing of Mokoyl and then by the "replacing" of his deceased wife by his marriage to Mokoyl's daughter, Sialim.

The practices and beliefs described above were confirmed by the rest of my fieldwork with the Gebusi in 1980–82 concerning many aspects of their religion, politics, and social relations. In ethnographic writing—and in anthropology textbooks—one often finds remarks to the effect that "People X do or believe Y under condition Z." It should be noted, however, that in most, if not all, such cases, the summary statements collapse and compress a diverse tangle of ethnographic experience and information. As generalizations, such statements can be useful and are not "wrong." But in actual research and in human experience, they admit many exceptions and provide but a glimpse of the richness and diversity of human lifeways.

During our fieldwork, features of Gebusi life gradually became both more meaningful and more comparable or contrastive to our understanding of customs in other societies, including our own. This increased awareness sharpens our final lingering question above concerning Dugawe's death: How typical were the events surrounding it in Gebusi culture? This question looms large for ethnography. How do we know if we are observing events that are widespread or "normal" in a given society? Are we paying too much attention to some practices or beliefs at the expense of others? And what patterns of change have emerged to change the relationship between some practices and others over time?

In some ways, the events surrounding Dugawe's death were both normal *and* exceptional, both traditional *and* new for the Gebusi. On the one hand, the burial practices, antagonistic displays, sorcery inquests, and spiritual divinations that surrounded his death were "typical" for many Gebusi during the 1970s and 1980s. On the other hand, certain features of Dugawe's case were exceptional, even unique. His was the only male suicide in almost 400 adult Gebusi deaths that I was able to document and cross-check through genealogical investigation. He was also the only Gebusi who had killed his wife or his child. Not coincidentally, he was the only Gebusi we knew of from that period who had served a lengthy prison term. Quite possibly, Dugawe's experiences in prison and then at the Nomad jail increased his stress upon being released. Hence, his unique experiences may well have contributed to his ultimate suicide.

Sialim's actions were also unique; I know of no Gebusi woman before or since who managed to have her husband jailed for having beaten her. She was also exceptional in conducting an open sexual affair while her husband was still alive. These features—Dugawe's unusual violence and Sialim's forceful response—heightened or exaggerated features of male-female opposition in Gebusi culture. Their particular result relates as well to the legacy of Australian colonialism and the presence of Papua New Guinean constables at the Nomad Station. Without these influences, Dugawe would not have been imprisoned in the first place or jailed for beating Sialim.

And yet, these new developments blended as if seamlessly with general patterns of Gebusi culture. This included the subsequent marriage of Sialim to Swamin, which completed a cycle of balanced exchange both in death and in life: the death of Swamin's first wife was avenged by the killing of Sialim's mother and then structurally "replaced" by Swamin's marriage to Sialim herself. Sialim willingly accepted and in some ways pursued this resolution. Did she really care for Swamin? Was she grateful to his spirits for their help in saving her? Or was he simply a convenient protector? Did Sialim dispute the execution of her own mother, or did she accept this killing as legitimate—as some Gebusi do when their relatives are killed as sorcerers? It was hard for us to tell. Perhaps all of these were true for Sialim to some extent. Though it may seem odd or even shocking that a woman could marry her mother's killer, it is not uncommon in cultures around the world for people to live with those who have harmed them or their close relatives. In Western countries, including the United States, this pattern is common in cases of child abuse or spousal abuse; the victim may accept and even defend the person who has abused them.

Finally, the events surrounding Dugawe's death are distinctive if not unique in time. That they reflect general patterns in Gebusi culture does not mean they reflect Gebusi culture *now*. As we will see in later chapters (and as amazing as this would have been to me during my first fieldwork), Gebusi have to a large extent now given up their beliefs and practices concerning sorcery accusation. Though we want to draw conclusions from our work, including generalizations about a people and their beliefs and practices, we need to remember that these change over time, sometimes dramatically. Rather than downplaying or limiting this awareness, anthropologists are dedicated to understanding our changing humanity across cultures.

Events such as Dugawe's death and its aftermath challenged me to the hilt. They also yielded insights that were crucial to my understanding of death and dying, gender relations, scapegoating, and the power of human affiliation in the face of violence and suffering. Most ethnographers strive to find generalities while valuing the uniqueness of the people and events they study. They seek to appreciate cultures while exposing their ideologies and inequities. And they try to balance participant-observation with the importance of their own feelings and values. Like most ethnographers, I both succeeded and failed in all these respects. But the attempt was well worth the effort.

☙   ☙   ☙

BROADER CONNECTIONS: *Life Stories, Death from Sorcery, and "Doing Ethnography"*

- Like many cultural anthropologists, Bruce's **fieldwork methods** among Gebusi included **participant-observation, structured interviews, informal conversations, unstructured interviews, oral histories** (including life histories, event histories, residence histories, and dispute histories), genealogies, **census and residential surveys,** and **verbatim text transcriptions and translations from tape recordings** of Gebusi speeches, music, and spirit séances.

- **Anthropological ethics** and the **protection of human subjects** are important to cultural anthropologists. These include the principle of "**do no harm**" and, especially under conditions of danger or uncertainty, **reduce risk and increase benefit** to local people.

- Anthropologists need to be self-aware and **reflexive,** especially under conditions of danger or threat in the field, to make sure their own actions **minimize risk to others.**

- The **cultural construction** of the Gebusi **life cycle** includes pronounced beliefs about **infant identity and becoming human, maturation and adulthood** (see Chapter 6), the **cultural construction of disease and death** as caused by **sorcery,** and strong beliefs and dramatic practices concerning **death** and the **treatment of a person's corpse.**

- Gebusi **gender relations** include **male dominance** and sometimes **gender violence**—including by Dugawe and other members of the community against Sialim.

- Gebusi have believed in **sorcery** of two major types: *bogay,* or **parcel sorcery,** based on a belief in **imitative magic** and *ogowili,* or **assault sorcery,** based on **magical attack** by warriors against the victim.

- Gebusi **sorcery inquests** rely on spiritual guidance through **shamanism** (or **spirit mediumship**) and on various kinds of **divination.**

- Gebusi **sorcery accusations** illustrate the cultural projection of **stigma** and **social control** through **scapegoating.**

- The **anthropology of conflict and dispute** reveals important aspects of culture that may complement or **counterbalance emphasized cultural values,** as is certainly true of Gebusi sorcery inquests.

CHAPTER 4

Antagonists make peace by sharing a tobacco pipe over the grave of the deceased. (Photo: Eileen Marie Knauft)

Getting Along
with Kin and Killers

To FOLLOW THE PLAY, you have to know the characters. If the play is in sports, you need to know what sport they are playing, what team the players are on, and what the rules are. For me, lives in Yibihilu seemed halfway between a dramatic play and an intense sport. The sport analogy may be stretching things, because the "game" was to manage one's relationship to others in the community, not to defeat a rival team. Indeed, when men and boys in the village played soccer (which government officers had introduced), they preferred the game to end in a tie rather than having one team win and the other lose. In daily life, as on the field, Gebusi were organized into groups. And we had to know the groups and their rules of relationship to know what was going on. Suddenly, a dispute would break out. One group would start swinging clubs against another, which retaliated in like fashion— while a third group stood as peacekeepers in the middle, trying to break things up. It all happened spontaneously, and we couldn't tell why people grouped as they did. The same was true more generally—groups of people would casually depart to forage in the forest, give and receive gifts of food at feasts, or present costume decorations to initiates. Why did some people act together as a group as opposed to others? And why had some people been killed within the community while most others remained friends?

In societies like the Gebusi, cooperation and opposition are largely based in kinship and marriage. And if there is one topic that is specific to anthropology but largely unconsidered by the other social sciences, it is the organization of kin and relatives.

On the surface, kinship is simple. Each of us has a family and relatives. We know about parenthood and about our brothers and sisters; we know what marriage is, who our cousins are, and so on. But things are less obvious when we consider other cultures—or even when we consider our own more closely.

In Gebusi society and in many others, if you ask someone what group he or she belongs to, the person will tell you the name of his or her clan. A clan is a permanent social group whose members pass down membership through descent from one generation to the next.

Members of a clan generally believe that they should not marry one another and that they derive from a common ancestor. We say "believe" because all members of a clan may not, in fact, be able to trace links through a male or female line to an ancestor who they identify as having in common. Among the Gebusi, clan membership is passed down through the male line—a bit like the way last names in most Western societies have often been passed down. So we can call the Gebusi descent groups "patriclans." Within these, the subgroups that *can* demonstrate unbroken links of actual genealogical connection are called patrilineages. By contrast, most people in countries like the United States do not belong to clans or lineages—or to any descent group at all. They typically belong to "families" but not to larger, permanent named groups that are defined through descent and possess dedicated rights and duties. Among Gebusi, however, each member of a named patriclan calls all the other members of the clan "brother," "sister," "father," "father's sister," "grandparent," and so on, depending on their sex and generation—even though most of them are what Americans and other Westerners would call "cousins," "uncles," "aunts," and so on.

Ties of clan or lineage descent can be quite strong in forming alliances of collective cooperation—and of opposition to other kin groups. Take an example relating to marriage. When Saliam's first husband died, she was expected to marry the deceased man's patriclan "brother," Daguwa, who was a widower at the time. This "marriage by levirate" had the effect of keeping Saliam—and the daughter from her previous marriage—within a close branch of her dead husband's patriclan. This was true even through Daguwa was not the true brother but rather what we would call a cousin of Saliam's first husband. We can graphically show the family relationship that emerged between Saliam and her two husbands, in turn, by the standard symbols that anthropologists use to show kinship: a triangle for a man, a circle for a woman, an equal sign for marriage, a slash to indicate someone who has died, a vertical line for descent, a horizontal line for siblingship, and a slash across a horizontal line to indicate that descent or clanship cannot be demonstrated by actual kinship (see Figures 4.1 and 4.2).

If we want to be more complete, we can add Daguwa's first marriage and the children of the two marriages. Because this involves persons who died from homicide rather than a natural death, we can indicate these persons with an X rather than a slash. Likewise, we can indicate the order of each person's marriages with numerals in boxes (see Figure 4.3).

Though kinship diagrams take some getting used to, they are important ways for anthropologists to understand social relations among people in small-scale communities. Otherwise, keeping track of people's kin relationships can really be a mess! Kin diagrams can also alert us to things we might otherwise miss. For instance, Figure 4.3 reminds us that the marriage between Saliam and Daguwa was actually the second one for each of them. It also shows that Saliam had a surviving daughter from her first marriage, that Daguwa's first wife and son were killed, and that Saliam and Daguwa's own marriage did not produce any children. Finally, it shows that, despite Daguwa's violence, the clanship between Daguwa and Saliam's first husband helped him maintain his claim to her.

Figure 4.1
Key to kinship terms

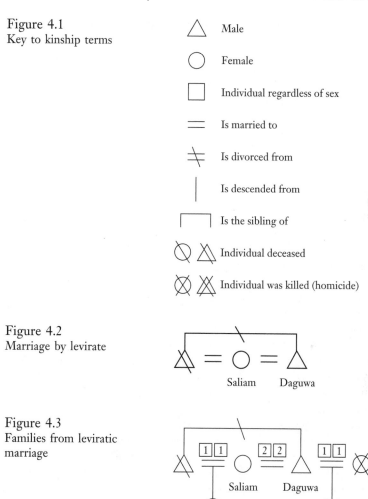

Figure 4.2
Marriage by levirate

Figure 4.3
Families from leviratic
marriage

What about the power of "sisterhood" between women as opposed to the bond of "brotherhood" between men? Because the Gebusi trace descent through the male line, connections of "brotherhood" and "sisterhood" pertain only as long as the links between generations go through fathers (see Figure 4.4). Put differently, generational ties don't turn Gebusi into members of the same clan if these are traced through mothers. For many of us born and raised in Western countries, the people we consider cousins can be related to us on either our mother's or our father's side. But for Gebusi, a cousin on the father's side is a "brother" or a "sister," whereas a cousin on the mother's side is typically not a member of one's clan at all.

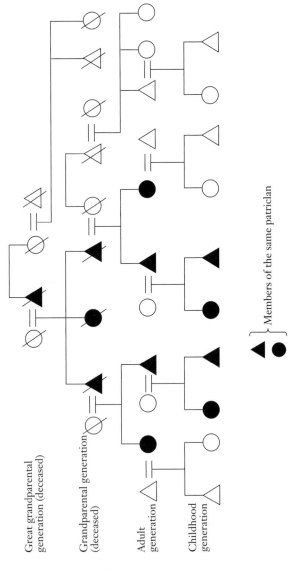

Great grandparental
generation (deceased)

Grandparental generation
(deceased)

Adult
generation

Childhood
generation

Members of the same patriclan

Figure 4.4
Gebusi clanship

꧁ ꧁ ꧁

Does this all seem complicated? It certainly was for me! Truth be told, kinship may be the driest and most boring part of cultural anthropology for students. In college, I thought kinship and calculus were similar: I knew they were important, but I couldn't really see the point—and I wasn't very good at them.

Across the globe, there are hundreds of ways that cultures group relatives together or apart, assign who is considered "really" related to whom, establish rules and patterns of intermarriage, structure alliances and oppositions between groups of kin, and so on. I started reading about this before going to graduate school—and I thought I would go crazy. But then I started doing fieldwork. Learning kinship in the abstract is, well, abstract. But then your friends are dating, marrying, fighting, giving gifts to one another, and all the rest, and you can't figure out who is doing what to whom and why *except* through kinship. Then kinship becomes not just important but a fascinating human puzzle.

As for marriage, Gebusi practice "preferential sister-exchange." When a woman marries a man of a given clan, a clan "sister" of the husband should also marry a clan "brother" of the bride; there should be a balance, so neither patriclan "loses" a woman without getting one back. This may sound like a strange way of getting married, as if women were pawns exchanged between groups of men. We may like to think that women and men should get married because they want to, not because they feel obligated. But among groups like the Gebusi, sister-exchange is more interesting and surprising than either of these alternatives.

First, the Gebusi ideal of marital balance is taken loosely and can be extended. Because Gebusi have complicated ways of extending "siblingship" beyond even the patriclan, they can sometimes find creative ways to define a woman as a kind of sister. Second, the bride-to-be has some veto power in marriage. If a Gebusi woman really objects to marrying a given man, her wishes often hold sway.

Alternatively, a teenage girl and a young man could become romantically attracted even though there was little chance that a "sister" of the young man would marry a "brother" of the young woman. These "unreciprocated" marriages provoked strong objections from the young woman's fathers and brothers. But the young couple could prevail if the woman was strong willed or ran away with her new husband. Though the parents or brothers of the woman would often beat her if they found her, many of these romantic unions endured and were ultimately accepted as marriages.

Marriage between certain kinds of Gebusi relatives was completely prohibited. All human cultures put a taboo on some kinds of marriages, such as that between a woman and her own true son. But other rules about who can or cannot marry vary widely from one society to another. In some cases, a large kin group is "exogamous"—you have to marry outside of it, and you have to find a partner for marriage within one-half, one-quarter, or even only one-eighth of the societies' descent groups. Western societies tend toward the other extreme: marriages are typically not prohibited except within the nuclear family and sometimes between very close cousins. In principle, this leaves the whole rest of society as an open field from which you can find a marriage partner. In practice, though, as in America, some kinds of marriages are preferred while others avoided. During a large span of American history, for instance, it was illegal for a white person to marry someone of African or African-American descent: race was "endogamous"— you were supposed to and were even required to marry within your racial group.

Gebusi are somewhat in between concerning in-marriage (endogamy) and out-marriage (exogamy). You generally have to marry someone outside your clan, with clans averaging eighteen persons in size. An additional clan or two may be considered "brother" clans based on vague ancestral ties, with marriage between them not favored but not completely prohibited either. There are a few other restrictions on marrying specific relatives. In all, for a village like Yibihilu, about two-thirds of the appropriately aged persons of the opposite sex are marriageable. Most Gebusi find their marriage partners within their village or in one or another community hamlet within an hour's walk of the main settlement. As such, we can say that Gebusi communities are largely, but not totally, endogamous.

On some occasions, a Gebusi woman actively wants to complete a sister-exchange. If a young woman likes her own brother and his new wife—not to mention the new wife's brother, her own potential spouse—then she looks forward to completing the matrimonial exchange. The two couples will typically live together as a joint family, and such family units tend to be strong and cooperative.

Ultimately, then, the notion that Gebusi sister-exchange is preferential means just that: sister-exchange is preferred if possible. But if not, that's life. In actuality, just over half of all first Gebusi marriages (52 percent) were sister-exchanges. Most of the remainder were what we liked to call "romantic unions" that did not follow the rules of sister-exchange. Despite pronouncements of Gebusi men that "we exchange women," women and men who wanted to marry without exchange often found a way to do so.

Features of Gebusi social organization helped them out. Within each Gebusi patriclan are smaller subgroups whose members *can* trace an actual linkage to one another via male descent: patrilineages. These are very tight and very small atoms of kinship defined through male descent. Overwhelmingly, their members live together in the same settlement. Given their small size, a Gebusi patrilineage might include only one young unmarried woman—or maybe none at all. Yet it is within the patrilineage rather than the larger clan that a young man's claim to use his "sister" for exchange in marriage remains strong.

If Gebusi patrilineages are small, and if members of the larger clan often do not live with one another, then who else do people live with? Typically, they live with other close kin related to them by marriage or via their mothers. For instance, more than 80 percent of men who have a living mother's brother live in the same settlement as this man. Seventy percent of men who have a true brother-in-law reside in the same village as he does. From a woman's point of view, this is good: it means that residing with her husband does not generally distance her from her own brother. And when she gets older, she is apt to live in the same village as both her son and her brother. In the mix, she usually resides with a range of close female kin on whom she can rely and with whom she can perform collective tasks.

Taken as a whole, Gebusi villages bubble with kinship relations traced variously through mothers, fathers, classificatory brother- and sisterhood, and intermarriage. The fifty-two residents of Yibihilu identified with thirteen different clans. The men of the village belonged to seven different clans and eleven different patrilineages. As many as one-third of them were totally unrelated to one another. As such, Gebusi villages are multiclan settlements rather than clustered around the men of a single patriclan. This helps explain why Gebusi place such a high value on collective good company across diverse lines of kinship and friendship; it helps keep their villages integrated and cooperative!

Having reviewed Gebusi social organization, we can now put the pieces together. In particular, we can ask what pattern emerges from Gebusi kinship and residence that combines very small lineages, preferential marriage by sister-exchange, and village residence based on diverse ties of kinship, intermarriage, and friendship. As we have seen, only about half of first Gebusi marriages are balanced through sister-exchange. And this creates a problem, because Gebusi lack any effective way to recompense an extended family or patrilineage that loses a sister or daughter in marriage. In some parts of Melanesia, Africa, and Asia, a woman's marriage can be "paid for" by valuable gifts given by the groom and his kin group to the close relatives of the bride. These payments are sometimes called "bride-price." Many anthropologists prefer the term "bride-wealth," though, because the transaction is not a human purchase but the opening round of wealth exchanges that may last for years between the kin of the groom and the bride.

Among the Gebusi, however, bride-wealth or bride-price was negligible. A groom might give small gifts to the mother or brothers of his bride, but these presents were not considered an exchange for the woman herself. Rather than material compensation, the Gebusi have practiced a direct or person-for-person form of reciprocity. The ideal, of course, is sister-exchange marriage. But when there is no return marriage, there is also no payment to mollify the bride's kin for her loss to their group. So what happens? Though this causes resentment, the Gebusi tend to sweep it under their cultural rug. Most in-laws claim they accept marital imbalance and get along well. Indeed, in-laws co-reside just as often when the marriage that links them is unreciprocated as when it is balanced through sister-exchange. Given their cultural emphasis on good company, it is not easy for Gebusi to admit or address tensions between in-laws.

Here is where issues of kinship, residence, and social etiquette link to Gebusi politics and disputes. And at least to me, this is where the discussion gets really interesting. It's one thing to know about kinship and residence, but it's more significant to use this knowledge to understand important trends that are otherwise hard to explain. For the Gebusi, these have included a very high rate of violence and killing associated with sorcery accusations. Why has the Gebusi rate of killing been so high, and who stands the greatest chance of being victimized?

One of the most important facts here is that Gebusi sorcery accusations are especially likely between kin groups linked by a marriage that has not been reciprocated. At this point, I should emphasize that the Gebusi themselves do not say this. As we have seen, Gebusi have a profound ability to emphasize good company and to suppress or dissociate from their anger. Even during a spirit séance when a community member is accused of being a sorcerer, the clan and lineage relatives of the accused usually say nothing. They may even continue joking so as not to lose public face. Gebusi believe that sorcery accusations should be proved by tangible evidence. As described in Chapter 3, these clues take a variety of forms, including a "sign" by the corpse, a packet of "skin and blood" identified by a spirit medium, leavings from the victim that have been "burned" by the sorcerer, or divination food that has been undercooked. To Gebusi, these represent tangible physical evidence—like fingerprints on a smoking gun. Why was the sorcerer accused or attacked? Because, Gebusi say, the objective evidence shows him or her to be guilty! This evidence is convincing to a wide range of people across different clans in the community.

Given this, how can I suggest that unacknowledged tensions related to marriage and sister-exchange inform Gebusi sorcery accusations? Here, we must shift gears. Gebusi's own explanations are crucial, but they do not tell the whole story. Beyond what people think and say, it's important to document what they actually do. Especially in small-scale societies, these actions often link to patterns of kinship and residence.

We all know that people may say one thing and do another. In American society, we may promise to marry someone "til death do us part." But almost 50 percent of marriages in the United States end in divorce. As an anthropologist, it is important—indeed, key—to consider the gap between ideals and actions. In doing this, however, we create greater distance between our perspective and those of the people we are studying. To say that many Americans who marry also get divorced captures neither the joy of a good marriage nor the pain of a bad one. It is a statistical assessment, not an emotional or humanistic one; it pulls us away from understanding human lives.

Anthropologists have often debated which is better—a close-up portrait that is rich with people's experiences, or a detached view that is more systematic and encompassing. Is a statistical depiction more scientific or more dehumanizing? My own opinion is that both views are needed—and that they need to be combined. Like using the zoom function on a camera, the anthropologist should sometimes focus on the details of individual lives and experiences, but she or he should also draw back—as in the present chapter—and look more dispassionately at the larger picture, statistics and all.

For the Gebusi, I tried to gain a societywide view by collecting census material, residence histories, and kinship information. By charting the genealogies of eighteen clans—as far back as Gebusi could remember—I documented the cause and circumstances of death for each deceased person. Then I double-checked each account with someone from a different clan, to ensure the information was accurate. This was a tedious task, as you might imagine. But the Gebusi were interested in the details, and I think they were proud to present them correctly. And when they didn't, they quickly realized that I could uncover their "embellishments" by obtaining a more accurate story from someone else!

We can now return to the question raised previously: How do we know that Gebusi who are related via unreciprocated marriage do, in fact, accuse one another of sorcery even though the Gebusi don't make this statement themselves—any more than Americans at weddings announce that the marriage may fail? Within Gebusi communities, statistics reveal that persons related by marriage are more than three times more likely to accuse one another of sorcery than would be expected by chance. In father-in-law/son-in-law relations, the rate of sorcery accusations is a whopping fifteen times greater than expected by chance. And in more than 70 percent of cases in which a relative via marriage is accused, the marriage that links the patrilineages of the accuser and the victim has not been reciprocated. Viewed broadly, this makes sense. Gebusi marriage is based on "person-for-person" exchange. So is Gebusi killing: the life of the sorcerer is taken "in exchange" for the death of the person who died of sickness. These aspects of positive and negative exchange link together. The lack of exchange for a woman in life increases the chances of violent revenge between the two patri-lineages when a person dies from an illness.

Killings of Gebusi were remarkably frequent. Of all adult deaths, almost one-third were homicides (129 of 394, or 32.7 percent). This rate of violence is even greater than that of the Yanomami, the so-called fierce people of the Amazon rainforest. Per person, this rate of killing exceeds the carnage of the bloodiest war in world history—World War II in Europe, including the Holocaust. Not all Gebusi killings were individual executions of sorcery suspects, but the majority were—61 percent. Another 21 percent were the result of Bedamini raids, in which large numbers of Gebusi could be killed simultaneously. Only 5.5 percent of violent Gebusi deaths resulted from battles or fights between massed groups of Gebusi warriors.

Gebusi adults of both sexes and almost all age categories could be killed as sorcerers. In relative terms, however, the persons most likely to be accused and executed were senior adults—which among Gebusi means anyone in their thirties or older. Although I don't have the numbers to prove it, I think there are several reasons for this. As they live longer, Gebusi accumulate more disputes and resent-ments, including via nonreciprocal marriages. When someone dies of sickness, there is a greater chance that one of these past disputes may consciously or unconsciously inform an inquest that finds a senior person guilty of sorcery. Also, older persons can get increasingly concerned with or angry about their own grow-ing list of friends and relatives who have died. Other people can then think that they may be angry enough to have become a sorcerer and take spiritual retribu-tion. By contrast, children are never accused of sorcery; in Gebusi belief, they are not old enough to know how to perform it.

Between the extremes of older persons and children, young men may also be accused of sorcery and executed. In the more distant past (the 1950s and 1960s), late adolescent males were commonly targeted as sorcerers. But one category of adults has been almost completely immune from Gebusi sorcery accusation: young women. In their mid-teens and into their twenties, Gebusi women were virtually never accused or attacked as sorcerers. From a society-wide standpoint, this is important. Young women are crucial to a society's reproductive and demographic survival. As unconscionable as it is in moral and ethical terms, the killing of older persons has less impact on reproduction. Few Gebusi women seem to give birth beyond their early thirties. Men are even more "dispensable" in demographic terms because a relatively small number of men may impregnate a larger number of women to repopulate society. Enormous numbers of European men were killed during World War I, but the population replenished itself quickly because so many young women were available for childbearing. In the case of the Gebusi, the relative immunity of young women from sorcery execution meant that the internal homicide rate, high as it was, did not preclude their collective survival. People lived in good company even as they killed those they suspected of breaking this rule, especially as they got older. A greater survival threat was posed by the Gebusi's neighbors, the Bedamini, who would indiscriminately kill Gebusi women and children as well as men during their fearsome raids.

What has happened to the Gebusi rate of violent death over time? As Australian colonial officers suppressed Bedamini raiding, from 1963 to 1975, the Gebusi who died of homicide declined from a whopping 39 percent of all adult deaths to 23.3 percent. This decline continued during the first seven years of national independence, during which 19 percent of adults died from homicide. Despite this general improvement, those killings that did occur were targeted increasingly against women. Why? First, Gebusi became increasingly reluctant to kill people whose murder might come to the attention of police at Nomad Station. Although officers seldom knew what went on in the villages, they might have learned about a killing from angry relatives of the slain person. In practice, the killing of a woman—particularly if she was an elderly widow—was not as likely to generate an outpouring of anger as when violence was directed against an adult male. Old widows were sometimes perceived as a drain on the community insofar as they had a declining ability to work, and their childbearing years are over. They were sometimes seen as irritable, uncooperative, and apt to use spiritual power to compensate for their physical decline. If an older widow did not have a grown son to support her, she could be a relatively easy target of a sorcery accusation. And if she was killed in the forest, away from the settlements, as was the case with Saliam's mother, chances were good that her death would not be reported to the authorities.

In some ways, Gebusi violence against sorcerers has gradually become more similar to that in Western history. From the late-fifteenth through the late-eighteenth centuries, some historians estimate that the Christian church killed approximately 300,000 women as witches. Fear of largely female witchcraft was found in significant parts of Europe and America during the 1600s and early 1700s, including in the famous witch trials at Salem in 1692. Among the Gebusi, however, sorcery was tied less to community hysteria than to resentment over high rates of death due to sickness and to marital imbalances that festered between in-laws. These tensions ultimately found expression in sorcery inquests, divinations, and accusations.

How have the Gebusi themselves viewed their killing? This question is important because violence was so frequently directed against those who were supposed to be friendly acquaintances within the community. To a surprising degree, Gebusi have rationalized these discrepancies away. For them, it is not murder to kill a sorcerer. Rather, it is a legitimate and proper way to dispense with someone who has him- or herself committed a terrible killing. In Gebusi belief, lethal sorcerers must be eliminated to keep the death toll due to sickness from climbing even higher. It may be hard for us to appreciate the degree to which the Gebusi have believed in their sorcery divinations and inquests. Outside the narrow context of sorcery inquests, most Gebusi *have been* good-natured and friendly, not angry or violent. In contrast to men in some other parts of Melanesia, Gebusi were self-effacing in public and more likely to minimize than to magnify their animosity. However, when the death of a close relative or spouse was followed by a community-verified sorcery accusation, even the most mild-mannered Gebusi man could become a killer.

In the aftermath of a sorcery execution, the killer and his supporters were rarely attacked; rather, the community tended to close ranks behind them. Just as the accusation needed to have "objective" confirmation from the spirits and support from different clans in the village, so, too, person/s who completed the execution could generally count on community support to uphold their actions. Faced with this reality, the surviving relatives of the executed person usually had little choice but to accept the result. Even when they wanted revenge, the men of the sorcerer's patrilineage were few in number—not numerous enough to prevail against the rest of the community.

Beyond our deep concern for the people who were attacked or killed—after all, to us they are innocent—what is the significance of Gebusi sorcery and violence? For one thing, their accusations reveal the role of culture in constructing or creating stigma. Cultural beliefs can powerfully validate discrimination, which makes the scapegoating of innocent people seem legitimate. Such justification can be abetted by structural tensions of social organization, kinship, and demography that lie outside the daily awareness of those involved. Given this, a scientific understanding of structural tensions within a society—beyond the ideas and beliefs of the people themselves—can be particularly important to complement and counterbalance the positive views and rich values held within the culture itself. In American society, tensions in family structure that result from class inequality, unemployment, racism, and gendered inequality clearly inform patterns of violence, drug use, alcoholism, and domestic abuse.

By understanding how inequality works among peoples such as the Gebusi, we may see more clearly how larger patterns of discrimination operate in other societies, including our own. Western cultural values of equality concerning race, gender, ethnicity, nationality, and religion are strongly assumed in discourses of human rights, freedom, and democracy. Amid this positive emphasis, which is important and which should not be minimized, we also need to document and analyze patterns of inequality and discrimination that persist in fact. As with the Gebusi, we may confuse how we would *like* society to function with how it actually operates. Just as we may believe in marriage despite a significant rate of divorce, we may believe in sexual, racial, and cultural equality and yet find that women are not paid as much as men for doing similar work, or that foreigners or racial or ethnic minorities are relegated to disproportionately low levels of income and status. In the mix, it is easy to neglect patterns of kinship and social organization that are important to ethnic or foreign-born minorities because their networks of affiliation are not well understood by most Americans and may remain outside legal recognition. In different ways, then, culturally constructed beliefs—and their discrepancy from actual behavior—can be as strong in our own society as we may discover them to be among the Gebusi. Cultural anthropology often looks to other cultures to rediscover our own beliefs and actions. Beyond their intrinsic value, features of social structure, kinship, community organization, and conflict or violence help us understand much about the human condition at home as well as abroad.

BROADER CONNECTIONS: *Kinship, Marriage and Social Organization*

- Gebusi social relations are hard to understand without making diagrams of **kinship relations in standard notation.**

- Gebusi **clans,** groups of persons "putatively" related by blood descent, average 20 persons and are traced through male descent (**patriclans**).

- Gebusi **lineages** of those with *demonstrated* male descent (**patrilineages**) contain only a few persons each.

- Gebusi clans are named, endure through time, have collective rights and obligations, and are thus **corporate descent groups.**

- Gebusi generally marry outside their clan, which means the clan is usually **exogamous.**

- Gebusi generally marry within their longhouse and associated hamlet community, which means the community is largely **endogamous.**

- Gebusi **marriage by levirate (leviratic marriage)** sometimes occurs between a woman and her dead husband's true or clan "brother"—as it did between Sialim and Dugawe.

- Kinship terms are often extended to a larger group of people through extension—**classificatory kinship.**

- The Gebusi desire to balance the marriage of a women between lineages or clans reflects a cultural emphasis on **sister-exchange marriage**.

- "Even Steven" or "Tit-for-Tat" exchange, which can be termed **direct reciprocity,** is evident in Gebusi **sister-exchange marriage** and also the

execution of alleged sorcery suspects in reciprocity for the death by sickness of the sorcerer's supposed victim.

- Unlike many ethnic groups in New Guinea, Gebusi place little emphasis on material transactions such as **bride-wealth** (or "bride-price") between the kin groups of the husband and the wife. In structural terms, the resulting resentment informs Gebusi sorcery accusations and violence.

- A comprehensive understanding of a society can combine **"experience near"** and **"experience far"** perspectives (per Clifford Geertz). These have also been described as **"emic"** versus **"etic"** views of culture, or **"insider"** versus **"outsider"** perspectives.

- Combining insider and outsider views of culture help balance our **appreciation of cultural values** with an **understanding of structural inequalities** between subgroups or classes of people.

CHAPTER 5

A Gebusi dancer embodies spirits at a ritual feast. (PHOTO: Bruce Knauft)

Spirits, Sex, and Celebration

GENDER, SEX, AND SPIRITUALITY among Gebusi differ greatly from Western practices; they stretch our envelope of understanding. Among these differences, Gebusi admit alternative expressions of sexuality, particularly for men. This is not to suggest that Gebusi practices are a model of sexual tolerance much less of gender equality. But neither is it to say that they have nothing to teach us. Notwithstanding its tensions and challenges, exposure to Gebusi sexual culture was a rich part of my fieldwork. Although I thought I was tolerant to begin with, I came away with a greater understanding of and respect for sexual diversity than I could have imagined. I also became more aware of gender discrimination than I had been previously. I am grateful that my Gebusi friends let me know about the sexual side of their culture. If sex is often a delicate topic, it is also an important one, and one that needs to be studied with special sensitivity.

My awareness of Gebusi sexual culture began with the male joking that laced events such as ritual feasts and dances, storytelling, and spirit séances. Here is an example of Gebusi male joking:

YABA [TO DOGON]: *Go over there and sleep with the women. Build your "fire" over there.* [Go over and have sex with them.]

SWAMIN [TO YABA]: *If he goes over there and lies down, where are* you [Yaba] *going to put your "forehead"* [phallus] *to sleep?! You'll just have to go over and lay your "forehead" on his* [Dogon's] *grass skirt!!*

YABA [TO DOGON]: *You're wearing a big grass skirt* [for me to lie on].

DOGON [TO YABA]: [You do and] *I'll pull off your loincloth!!*

YABA [TO DOGON]: *And you'll sleep there* [in my crotch]*!!*

[Whooping and laughter from the other men.]

DOGON [TO YABA]: *No! I'll give your loincloth to the women and take off their clothes for you* [so you can take the female role]*!!*

[More laughter from the men.]

69

SWAMIN: *The younger men must be getting tired from ladling out all their "kava"* [semen]! *I'll ladle out mine with a thrust!!* [Kicks out his foot.]

[General laughter.]

DOGON [TO YABA]: *Can you give some to me??*

YABA [TO DOGON]: *We'll have to lay down "forehead"* [phallus] *as a gift-exchange name!*

YABA AND DOGON [LEANING THEIR HEADS TOGETHER]: *YAY!!*

[Laughter and yelling.]

Simmering in everyday life, male joking found its greatest outlet on festive occasions and during celebrations. Jokesters didn't have to be related to each other; in fact, it was best if they were not. Dogon and Yaba were unrelated and didn't live in the same community; not being otherwise connected, they were all the more in "good company" for being able to joke together. These connections were made easier by men who were related to both jokesters. In the present case, this role was taken by Swamin, who was a community co-resident and distant in-law of Yaba's and a maternal relative of but not co-resident with Dogon. At the time, all three men were widowers in their early thirties. What about the content of their bawdy jibes? Were Yaba and Dogon really apt to have sexual relations or to use "phallus" as a gift-exchange name between them? No; their joking signaled nonsexual friendship. Much sexual joking, some of it quite physical, flirts with possibilities that aren't consummated. Thinking back, the same was true of the locker-room pranks played by members of my high school soccer team in Connecticut. In a similar way, much Gebusi horseplay is what could be called "homosocial" rather than "homosexual." Its humor derives from suggesting but not actually engaging in sex.

At first, I wasn't sure if Gebusi males engaged each other sexually at all. Groups to the east of the Gebusi were known to practice male-male sexuality, but peoples farther to their west did not. I thought that my Gebusi friends were more likely to be in the former camp than the latter, but how could I know? Their interactions were certainly full of suggestive jokes. A young man might shout in jest, "Friend, your phallus was stroked, and it came up!" But beneath the surface, how much was orgasmic fire and how much was playful smoke? I suspected that male trysts took place near the outhouse at night during séances and festive dances. To find out if this was true, I found myself sitting near the appropriate longhouse exit during these events so I could see who went out and if they "hooked up." I felt very uncomfortable as I did so—as if I was snooping around or being a voyeur. At the same time, I needed to find out. I didn't want to "project" sex between men onto the Gebusi if it wasn't documented—and other anthropologists would want to know one way or the other. Imagine how bad it would be to write about Gebusi "homosexuality" only to later discover that, in fact, the practice was rare or absent. Unfortunately, my Gebusi friends seemed unable to talk about the subject in a serious way. Any sober query was quickly turned into a joke. At several feasts, I ultimately did see pairs of males slip out toward the outhouse, cavort with each other in the night shadows, and return visibly relaxed a few minutes later. But these pairings were not between the principal joking partners. Rather, they tended to be between a teenage boy and a young initiated man.

Hawi later verified for me the substance of these sexual practices: the teenager manipulates the phallus of his elder counterpart and then orally consumes the semen. As was also the case with groups farther east, this insemination had an important cultural function: it supplied the uninitiated bachelor with male life force for his masculine development. Unlike girls, who were believed to reach maturity without intervention, boys were helped to grow and become stronger by receiving masculine life force in the form of semen. Hawi also verified that, as a rule, men who had been married for a significant time—like Swamin, Yaba, and Dogon—did not engage in trysts with other males even though they might joke about it quite realistically. In effect, they relived their earlier experiences through their sexual banter.

Armed with this knowledge, and being married at the time, I felt increasingly comfortable with my own place in the Gebusi sexual scheme of things. I learned to accept male joking, including with me, and to reciprocate in like fashion. On one occasion, I went with the men to a séance held by Swamin at a distant bush hamlet. Swamin's singing warmed up and even exceeded its normal heated pitch. In his songs, a voluptuous spirit woman boldly told the men that she was hovering on top of the house in which we were singing—and that she was longing to have sex with them. Pandemonium broke out as men yelled that they wanted to satisfy her desire. One of the upcoming initiates, Doliay, straddled a housepost and yanked it back and forth between his legs until the whole building rocked. Hawi bellowed that he couldn't wait any longer; he wanted to shoot his arrow up into the spirit woman. As the men doubled up with laughter, he grabbed his bow, drew back an arrow, and shot it right through the thatched roof. Egged on by the spirit woman, the younger men and teenage boys started pairing up and leaving for trysts in the darkness outside the longhouse to relieve their sexual frustration.

It was then that Mora stroked my arm, leaned his head close to me, and said, "Why don't you and I go off together?" He rubbed one of his fists up and down over the index finger of his other hand, and he motioned that I would be the one satisfied. I shouldn't have been surprised. Gebusi men had become open with me about their sexuality. After my initial shock, I thought I recovered rather well. I smiled back at Mora: "I'm really sorry, but, well, I'm already married. So I can't go off with you; it would be taboo for me." But I was as unprepared for his reply as I had been for his overture: "Don't worry. Didn't anyone tell you? We break those rules all the time. Let's go!"

I broke out in a sweat. I was not about to join Mora for a sexual tryst. But what would happen to the men's trust in me and their willingness to include me in their social and ceremonial life? Would Mora be angry and insulted? Would I compromise my status as a welcome observer? The men were already gearing up for the elaborate rituals and secret practices that would initiate the next cohort of teenage boys into adulthood. Would I be excluded from learning the keystone customs of Gebusi male culture? I already knew that insemination had cosmic and spiritual significance for Gebusi men as well as importance for the growth of teenage boys. The Gebusi word for initiation, *wa kawala*, meant literally, "boy become big." This "bigness" was promoted by ingesting male semen.

As I answered Mora, I tried to suppress my anxiety. I told him that going off with a young man for sex simply wasn't my custom, my personal *kogwayay*. I said that, back where I came from, some men did have sex with young men like him, but others did not—and I was in the latter group. So, I apologized, I could not go off with him.

Anthropologists are sometimes chided for generalizing about the people they study—for instance, that "the Gebusi practice sister-exchange marriage" or that "Gebusi men practice ritual homosexuality." Such generalizations can cover up much about personal variation. When Mora replied to me, he seemed to underscore this point. "That's okay," he said. "Some of us have sex a lot, but others don't do it so much." And with that, the séance went on as before. Relieved, I continued my role as observer and shadow participant—singing intermittently, asking questions, tape recording the proceedings, and joking, if anything even more good-naturedly than before.

As it turned out, Mora's reply was truer than I first realized. Though Gebusi teenagers do, in principle, complete their growth by receiving and retaining male semen, their own emerging sexuality is not so easily bottled up. Not uncommonly, the initiates-to-be found sexual release with each other. This was particularly true of Hawi and Doliay. We have encountered Hawi before—my initial helper and uncertain translator, accomplished fisherman, and energetic young bachelor. Among the cohort of soon-to-be-initiated young men, Doliay was his closest comrade. If Hawi was one of the oldest new initiates, Doliay was the youngest, perhaps sixteen years of age. He was also the shortest of the initiates, topping out at just four feet ten inches. But Doliay was a vacuum-packed firecracker. He was intense, funny, industrious, smart, and completely undaunted by the social and physical world around him. He was also remarkably strong for someone so small, as if his lost stature had been compacted into strength.

During the months leading up to the initiation, Hawi and Doliay became a hilarious pair. At séances, they would rush out together and then saunter back a few minutes later, happily spent. Reclaiming their energy, they would then stand together and jive. One of their favorite jokes was to reach suddenly with one hand as if to grab at the other's crotch—while holding the other hand back to guard against a similar riposte. Despite such jests, neither they nor the other men or boys made public displays of nudity or sexuality. This helped maintain the good-natured tone of collective joking, including the joking of the senior men, whose verbal antics far outweighed their sexual encounters. However, initiates-to-be like Hawi and Doliay made no secret of the fact that they consorted with each other sexually. Swelling with bravado, they boasted that they would never get married to women because they had each other as sexual partners.

According to academic views of "ritual homosexuality" or "boy insemination" that occurred in parts of Melanesia, boys who received semen were said to be discouraged or prohibited from having sexual release prior to initiation—lest they deplete the male essence of semen that they were accumulating. Rituals of manhood were supposed to be trials of severe self-discipline, in which boys were sexually or socially subservient to initiated men. But Gebusi defied these assumptions.

As if to confound my expectations yet further, Hawi and especially Doliay were interested in Gebusi women as well as in each other. Before the initiation, Doliay was caught alone with Nolop in the women's sleeping section of her family house. The escapade occurred in the middle of the night while a ritual feast and dance took place in the longhouse. Nolop had retired alone to her smaller house across the village while others enjoyed the festivities. During the night, Wosip, her husband, went back to their small house to get more tobacco. As he entered, he heard commotion and he saw a shadowy figure bolt from his wife's sleeping quarters, leap out a side door, and flee into the night. Sounding the alarm, he found his guilty wife alone in the chamber. And as everyone came running, Doliay was conspicuously unaccounted for.

The implications were scandalous. A teenager and not yet initiated, Doliay was some fifteen years younger than Nolop, whose oldest child was already twelve years old. Their encounter had probably been as brief and perhaps as opportunistic as it had been illicit. But clan genealogies were dotted with cases in which an unguarded widow or middle-aged woman had become pregnant from a younger man. Fortunately, Wosip was the most mild-mannered man in the settlement. He beat Nolop, though not as severely as most men would have done. Saddled with skin bruises and a scalp laceration, Nolop cried and whimpered, sat in public, and refused to wash off the blood that caked her skin. She recovered and reentered village life without further incident, apparently having paid the price for her indiscretion through the beating itself.

For his part, Doliay fled to another settlement until tempers cooled. Upon his return, he was not beaten—the Gebusi double standard remained in effect—but was chastised so severely that it appeared he might not be initiated. Denying initiation is a severe sanction for young men who flout the rule against having sex with women. Sagawa had already been precluded from initiation because of his affair with Saliam and her husband's subsequent suicide. Our silent friend Gono, who accompanied us on our initial journey through the rainforest, had also been excluded. Gono would have been the oldest of the initiates, but he had married a widow older than himself rather than waiting for ritual promotion to manhood. If it was possible for teenage boys to have sex with each other and sometimes, illicitly, with a woman, it was also possible for them to forgo initiation altogether and still become full adult men.

It was ultimately not surprising that men's fantasies of sex with women sometimes came to fruition: cultures often fuel desires that they also forbid. Among Gebusi, this tension was epitomized in folktales told by men prior to the initiation. These stories, called *gisagum*, portrayed escapades between a handsome unmarried bachelor and a gorgeous young maiden. The young couple was typically described as brought together by forces outside their control (such as the death of their parents) that forced them to live together and cooperate though they were not related and unmarried. The seductive behavior and subsequent restraint of the young couple provided the dramatic centerpiece of the story. Although the male audience was sometimes led to believe that the couple had sex, the continuing strength of the young man in the tales—as he overcame trials and defeated adversaries—showed that he had not weakened his resolve or lost his chastity. Most of the stories ended happily with the glorious initiation of the chaste young man and his subsequent marriage to the young woman. As icing on the cake, her relatives were so impressed with him that they typically made no requests for marital reciprocity.

At one level, these *gisagum* were morality tales. The hero maintained his virtue, attracted supporters, got initiated, and—most importantly—married the woman he desired. As support to this Hollywood ending, the tales also included villainous adversaries who were vanquished by the young hero's amazing feats of strength and fortitude. To the Gebusi male audience, however, the tales were anything but heroic or restraining. Instead, the erotic attraction between the young maiden and the hero served as a foil for the men to joke about their sexual arousal. Listeners would proclaim loudly that if *they* had been the young man in the story, they would have given up their chastity: "If it had been me, I would have had sex with her again and again!" Storytellers fueled rather than dampened such banter. Indeed, the tension between the hero's exemplary actions and the contrary declarations of the male audience was the centerpiece of the story's humor. Morality tales on the surface, the stories were a forum for men's bold desires to have sex despite cultural prohibition.

What about Gebusi women? Wives seemed to care little if their husbands had sex with teenage boys or with young initiated men. But they were furious if their husbands showed interest in other women. During spirit séances and story-tellings, women listened to the men's antics from their side of the sago leaf wall that separated them from the men's quarters. Sometimes, they responded with their own smiles and suppressed joking. Although women got angry if men fantasized about girls who were too young to have sex, they were not puritanical in general. As Eileen wrote, "Gebusi women regard sexuality as a positive force in the formation of marriage—as long as such relationships are based on reciprocal sexual longing."

Given the general Gebusi emphasis on sexual desire—both heterosexual and homosexual among men—did Gebusi women have their own lesbian relations? Though older and younger women are known to have had sexual relations among the Kamula, a group to the southeast of the Gebusi, there is little comparable evidence from any other society in New Guinea. Is sex between women rare in this part of the world? Or has it merely been underreported by male anthropologists, from whom it has been kept hidden? With tactful diplomacy and in private, Eileen asked women whom she knew and trusted if Gebusi women had sex with one another. Their responses were uniformly negative, and they ranged from incredulity to disgust: "No." "Certainly not." "How could that be possible?" "How would we even go about it?" "Is that really something that women do where you come from?"

In men's fantasies as well as women's realities, female sexuality among the Gebusi has been directed toward men. During men's séances, spirit women would get pouty and even angry if Gebusi men did not get aroused and joke with them. Fickle and capricious, a spirit woman could leave the body of the Gebusi spirit medium if she felt unappreciated by the male audience. This would force the medium's own spirit to come back to his body, thus ending the séance in the middle of the night. Such a premature conclusion would preclude the instrumental goal of the occasion—for instance, to ask the spirits about sickness or sorcery, or the location of lost pigs. In short, spirit women had to be kept happy and interested by Gebusi men in order for their séances to be successful. Contrary to what I initially thought, the "functional" and the "entertainment" sides of Gebusi spirit séances were directly linked rather than opposed.

For Gebusi men, spirit women were highly desirable but impossible to have sex with because they remained in the spirit world. The big exception here was the spirit medium. In his dreams and at séances, the medium's own spirit lived "for real" in the spirit world. He came to have a spirit world wife, children, and a whole set of spirit world relatives and friends. Among them, beautiful unmarried spirit women would sing through the medium's body and joke salaciously with the Gebusi men. The spirit wife herself would eventually bear the medium spirit children, including his all-important spirit sons. These helpful boys or young men would come to the medium and provide key information at critical points during the séance. The bulk of the medium's songs, however, were sassy tales sung by the spirit women. During the night, their blurred identities became an idealized fantasy of unbridled female sexuality for Gebusi men.

🌿   🌿   🌿

Having come full circle—from men's relations with each other back to their heterosexual desires—we can better understand Gebusi men's bisexuality. Gebusi dances are rife with erotic elements. The dominant features of the male dancer—including his red body paint, feathers, black eye-banding, and hopping dance steps—are strongly associated with the red bird of paradise, which is the preeminent form taken by young spirit *women*. Men in the audience refer to and joke about the male dancer as the red bird-of-paradise woman. In essence, the dancer impersonates a seductive spirit woman to whom the men in the audience say they are erotically drawn. In much the same way, in spirit séances, the spirit medium impersonates the female spirits. And this imagery is also accentuated by Gebusi women at dances. They sit offstage and sing haunting songs of loneliness and sexual desire while the men dance. As the men in the audience look at the dancer, hear the women's singing, and pine for the beautiful spirit woman, they joke about having sex with women—at the same time that they redirect their arousal as homoerotic horseplay onto one another. As such, male sexual desire for women is both genuinely heightened and redirected selectively among men and boys themselves.

The connection between same-sex and cross-sex desire, and between sexual frustration and redirected sexual aggression, is highlighted in the Gebusi notion of "longing," *fafadagim-da*. This is the men's most common refrain at dances and séances. To cry out, *"Ay fafadagim-da!"* is at one and the same time to declare, "I'm frustrated," "I'm lonely," "I have sexual desire," "I'm aggressive and I'm angry," and "I want sexual release one way or another!" That erotic arousal implies aggression and even anger may run counter to Western sensibilities. But it makes perfect sense to Gebusi. The spirit woman is alone in the forest; she wants a man but cannot be approached by most Gebusi men. So, too, the dancer at feasts and the young maiden in Gebusi narratives are beautiful but unreachable, alluring but frustrating. This makes men angry as well as playful and assertive in their joking. During the dance, the erotic and more humorous aspects of this aggressiveness are brought to center stage. But in spirit séances for sorcery, the rough edge of masculine frustration can galvanize a more sinister anger as well: the rage of loneliness and loss that is caused by death from sickness in the community. This is also described as *fafadagim-da*. Hence, it is no contradiction that Gebusi spirit séances arouse sexual desire at the same time that they can promote severe violence against suspected sorcerers especially in cases where men's sexual appropriation in marriage is not reciprocated, as this leaves their in-laws "frustrated." Connections between sex and violence that seemed completely strange to me when I was first with the Gebusi ultimately made cultural sense.

More generally, a cultural understanding of Gebusi sexuality in relation to "frustration," on the one hand, and more serious anger, on the other, helps move our understanding of Gebusi sexuality beyond basic categories of "homosexual," "heterosexual," or "bisexual" to key connections of understanding between Gebusi sexuality and their spiritual symbolism, social relations, and results such as sorcery accusation—as well as their ritual and religious expression.

What do the sexual practices of Gebusi tell us about human sexuality more generally? First, Gebusi customs underscore the degree to which sexuality and gender vary across cultures. Among Gebusi, men exhibited cross-sex fantasies, intentionally heightened heterosexual frustration, and bonding through same-sex relations. Women easily accepted men's sexual relations with each other but found the idea of sex between women quite unbelievable. Gebusi women valued their sexual relations with men, and infidelity in marriage was strongly discouraged, especially for women.

If we consider the distinctiveness of the Gebusi on a scale of global diversity, we can begin to appreciate how rich, variable, and often paradoxical human expressions of sexuality can be. In recent years, anthropologists such as Gilbert Herdt and others have documented the range of human sexuality diversity across the world, including same-sex, cross-sex, and bisexual practices and orientations. This variation is amazing. Even among the few million inhabitants of indigenous Melanesia, sexual customs have ranged from prolonged male chastity and beliefs in women's strength-sapping impact on men to fervent love magic and serial sexual intercourse—both heterosexual and homosexual among men—to collect or ingest sexual fluids for a variety of ritual and magical purposes. In many if not most of these same societies, monogamous marriage remained the norm for the majority of adults.

Even along the lines of its own codes of behavior, Gebusi sexual culture admits much variation for individuals. This was evident in the actions of initiates like Doliay and Hawi, and in Mora's overtures and subsequent responses to me. These underscore the degree to which sexual diversity includes both personal tendencies among individuals and collective differences between cultures. If cultural proclivities are variable in the realm of gender and sexuality, individual ones can also be diverse.

Cultures also vary in their types and degrees of sexual tolerance. Some societies are more accepting of a range of sexual behaviors; others are less so. Despite their emphasis on marriage and marital fidelity, Gebusi were relaxed concerning sexual relations between teenage boys and between them and young married men. In this respect, Gebusi practices blur the lines between what we might call homosexual, bisexual, and heterosexual behaviors. In many Western societies, these orientations are clearly distinguished—and bisexuality or homosexuality can be highly stigmatized. In one study in the United States, 29 percent of teenagers who identified themselves as gay or lesbian had attempted suicide.

Of course, Gebusi enacted their own constraints on sexual expression, including the beating of women suspected of infidelity or flirtatious misconduct. The way that cultures differently emphasize and tolerate sexual and gender diversity underscores the degree to which our own sexuality is influenced by both cultural and personal orientations. In this respect, the anthropology of gender and sexuality can have significant personal value as well as broadening our understanding of key features of human culture.

BROADER CONNECTIONS: *Sexuality and Gender*

- As Gebusi illustrate, **sexuality and gender are highly variable across cultures**.

- **Sexuality** is an **important but delicate topic of anthropological investigation** that needs to be **considered carefully and respectfully.**

- Gebusi men's practices of **bisexuality** and of **male transmission of life force** as semen from one generation to the next illustrate the **cultural construction of life cycle reproduction**.

- The tendency of Gebusi men to joke energetically about activities they might not actually practice highlights the importance of **distinguishing between verbal statement and actual behavior** in the study of social action, **including concerning gender and sexuality.**

- Bruce's response to Mora's sexual advances illustrate that, for their own personal reasons, cultural anthropologists may choose **to stay outside some cultural practices even as they attempt to understand and appreciate them.**

- Gebusi illustrate that **some cultures are more accepting of alternative forms of sexual expression than American society is**. Other societies are less accepting of sexual diversity than is the case in the United States.

- In societies such as the Gebusi and in Melanesia as a world region, **alternative practices of sexuality may coexist with normative monogamy (or polygamy) in heterosexual marriage.**

- **Sexuality is strongly and importantly linked to other features of culture**, including, among Gebusi, ritual and religious symbolism, sorcery accusation, and both camaraderie and violence within the community.

- **Gender and sexuality are variable by personal predilection or preference within cultures as well as between them.**

- **Understanding sexuality and gender in other cultures,** including the Gebusi, **may help us better understand the pattern and the diversity of gender and sexuality in our own society**.

CHAPTER 6

A male initiate (Yuway) in full costume. (Photo: Eileen Marie Knauft)

Ultimate Splendor

GEBUSI CELEBRATION OF LIFE, spirituality, and sexuality came together most fully and completely in the climactic events of the male initiation—the biggest and most elaborate spectacle in Gebusi society. Typically occurring just once in the lifetime of each major settlement, the initiation cycle began with the building of the village's central longhouse. The dwelling provided enough space to house relatives, friends, and visitors from the surrounding settlements during the initiation itself. At Yibihilu, the longhouse was built by six extended families from four different clans whose young men lived in the village and were initiated there. These six young men, one from each family group, ranged from about sixteen to twenty years of age. Their names were Hawi, Doliay, Yuway, Haymp, Momiay, and Hiali (the younger brother of Salip).

After the investigation of Dugawe's death was finally put to rest, our friends in Yibihilu began preparing in earnest for the initiation. During the next six months, much and then almost all activity in the village and its surrounding hamlets focused on the upcoming celebration. Beyond representing a passage to manhood, the initiation brought together the grandest features of Gebusi society and culture. For such a small and isolated group, the scale, effort, and energy that informed these events were amazing. In October and November, villagers spent several weeks amassing huge piles of firewood to be used to cook immense quantities of feast food. In December, January, and part of February, families went deep into the forest to cut and process sago palms. After the sago was pounded and processed into flour by the women, the heavy starch was put into large net bags and hefted in human caravans back to the village. In late February and early March, the men of Yibihilu dispersed into the forest to hunt and then smoke game, especially wild pigs and cassowaries. At the same time, women went off separately to process yet more sago.

Finally, it was time for everyone to reassemble in the village. The large pigs of the settlement—one for each of the six initiates—were tracked down, lured back to the village, penned in wooden cages, and fed to fatten them further. By March, the village was again a beehive of activity. Enormous piles of leaves and cooking stones were stacked next to the firewood. Food piles grew larger, including coconuts, greens, nuts, bamboo shoots, pit-pit, kava roots, and dried tobacco leaves. By the end of March, when everything was finally ready, the people of Yibihilu had worked and prepared for half a year. During this time, they had amassed enough food to feed virtually all of the more than 400 Gebusi–with plenty of extra for visitors to carry home.

If food represented the initiation's material foundation, the costumes of the initiates were its artistic centerpiece. As previously mentioned, the overall term for initiation is *wa kawala*, "boy/child become big." This refers simultaneously to the growth of the initiates and the process of getting dressed up in their elaborate costumes at the initiation itself. The costumes accrued from a far-flung network that spanned the entire tribe. People were mobilized from diverse settlements to obtain materials and construct the twenty different costume elements that made up each initiate's final outfit. The individuals who constructed these articles were linked to the initiates in a variety of ways—as a lineage or clan brother, a maternal relative, an in-law by virtue of previous marriage, or simply an unrelated friend. Leading up to the initiation, these many sponsors painstakingly made armbands, leg bands, waistbands, chest bands, feathered headdresses, shell necklaces, looped earrings, and other body decorations—all for the young man whom they had agreed to help initiate. Each initiate would also receive from their main sponsors carved hardwood bows accompanied by large sheaves of ceremonial arrows, each sporting a decorated bamboo shaft and an intricately carved and painted tip of bone or hardwood. Rounding out the gifts made for the initiates were newly made household items such as large woven net bags and big woven sago pouches. None of the items were displayed, much less given, until the final celebration.

During the weeks and months leading to the initiation, the effort of the community grew toward its final climax. But how? Gebusi have little in the way of leadership to orchestrate a large undertaking. Part of the answer lies in tradition. Based on past experience, families and household heads knew the sequence of preparations and the time needed for each. Just as importantly, they knew how other families and even those in other settlements would respond to the delays and complications that invariably cropped up during months of preparation. Collective discussion increased when people came back from the forest and met each other in Yibihilu. Though each extended family was ultimately autonomous, they were eager to trade information, strategize plans and contingencies, and keep track of each other's progress. The people of Yibihilu had already worked together to build their big longhouse. Now their task was to bring their human and spiritual vitality to fruition.

For purposes of organization as well as encouragement, the spirits of the Gebusi world were enthusiastically consulted. At each stage of planning, Swamin or another spirit medium held a lively séance. Hurdles of preparation were addressed, and positive resolutions charted. As Swamin described it, the spirits were planning to hold their own initiation at the same time that villagers would be holding theirs. Predictably, then, they were generous with advice and support.

Armed with otherworldly confidence, our friends at Yibihilu planned and worked with excitement, enthusiasm, and anticipation. During months of preparation, they overcame periods of poor hunting, cured persons who were sick, endured two additional deaths and associated sorcery inquests, found and retrieved semidomesticated pigs that had wandered deep into the forest, and arranged for a full complement of sponsors across different settlements for each of their six initiates. Their enthusiasm stoked a rising tide of good company. I had never experienced such a frenzy of friendship, laughter, and enjoyment along with plain old hard work. Everyone—women, children, men, and, of course, the initiates themselves—were swept up in the happy maelstrom. And just when we thought the level of camaraderie was about to level off, it would ratchet up to yet a higher level. The Gebusi continued to surprise us.

As we gradually came to realize, the festivities leading up to the initiation mirrored the basic structure of Gebusi feasting and ritual with which we had already become familiar. Elaborately decorated visitors would descend on the village in a show of force or aggression. They would then be appeased by gifts from the hosts—the smoking of tobacco, the drinking of water and kava, and the consumption of large quantities of food. Hosts and visitors alike would stay awake through the night while eating, talking, and generally having a good time. If the occasion was particularly festive, one or more of the visiting men would dance in costume as women sang and men joked lustily. Or an entertaining spirit séance would be held. At dawn, when everyone was tired and happy, outstanding issues of political contention or dispute would finally be addressed. With so many people from so many kin groups feeling so good, amicable resolutions were all but assured. The visitors would then return home, weary but happy, while the hosts retired for a daytime sleep. During the months prior to the initiation, this same basic pattern of hosting and feasting—and amicably discussing any issues of tension—was used to dedicate the longhouse, to commemorate the ear-piercing of younger boys, and to observe other celebratory milestones.

By mid-March, preparations had reached fever pitch. Oddly, the feast that formally inaugurated the initiation concerned a thin forest vine named *siay*. The name of the feast was *siay sagra*—literally, to "straighten the *siay*." Hundreds of strips of this sturdy fiber would later be wrapped around the wide bark waistbands that the initiates wore as part of their final costumes. In olden days, this strong waistband was like a piece of midriff armor that protected them from enemy arrows. The presentation of the *siay* to the initiates by their primary sponsors marked an official announcement of the initiation to come. It also established clearly which sponsors, including from other settlements, would be responsible for supplying various costume parts, bows and arrows, and other gifts to each of the initiates.

In planning for this feast to "straighten the *siay*," the men and boys of Yibihilu amassed dried meat from hunted animals. Meanwhile, the women and older girls processed yet more sago. To only a slightly lesser extent, the sponsors also had been occupied with these same tasks—the hunting of game and the processing of sago—to give to the initiate they were sponsoring. When all was ready, each initiate traveled to the settlement of his preeminent sponsor, his *tor*, and formally invited him to the *siay sagra* feast at Yibihilu the following evening. In response, the young man's *tor* presented him with a large roll of cooked sago, which the initiate carried back to Yibihilu. In economic and political terms, the *siay sagra* "sealed the deal in advance of the show." In social and emotional terms, it created a sense of good company among the wide range of settlements that would celebrate the forthcoming initiation.

Two weeks later came the ultimate festivities. These began with what anthropologists call a transitional, or "liminal," period for the initiates. As proposed by sociologist Arnold van Genep and later by anthropologist Victor Turner, major life cycle rituals are in many societies preceded by an "in-between" period that registers ambiguity between the person's previous position and the new one he or she will occupy. For instance, rituals of status elevation are often prefaced by rites of humility, submission, or teasing before the aspirant assumes his or her new role. For the prospective Gebusi initiates, their in-between status was signified by bold stripes of yellow ocher, painted on them from head to foot. The Gebusi word for yellow, *bebagum*, itself means "in the middle of" or "wedged in between." Along with the stripes of yellow paint, each of the initiates was festooned with a fringed headband, yellow forearm bands, yellow-painted waistband, nose plug, woven throat band, and a single long egret feather, which was stuck in his hair. Perhaps most striking, apart from the initiates' yellow body paint, was a broad white leaf attached to the inside front of their waistbands so that it hung down almost to their knees like a large penis. A topic of lewd joking and teasing by the men, the phallic leaf was a public and obvious symbol of the initiates' pent-up sexuality. Each of them was costumed identically, down to the smallest detail. As they lined up and stood with proper humility, it seemed as though their individual identities had merged into a beautiful and yet humble collective whole.

The initiates' biggest trial was to wear the new wigs that their sponsors now came to give them. The climactic festivities would shortly follow this ritual of "tying the bark wigs" (*uga togra*). But first, its painful prologue had to be endured. Wig wearing may not sound traumatic, but the adornment was made from large wads of sodden yellow bark. Tied in bulky bundles to narrow strands of each initiate's hair, the wig pulled down mightily on the initiate's scalp. In fact, the wet bark was so heavy—I estimated eighty pounds for each initiate—that after it was tied to the initiates' hair it had to be supported with a pole held by two helpers, who strained to raise it as each of the young victims, in turn, was ordered to stand up. All the while, the surrounding men crowded around the poor initiates, whooping and joking with abandon. The prime sponsor of each young man then trimmed off the wig's long trailing streamers, which reduced its weight to perhaps "only" twenty-five pounds.

Fighting back tears, the silent initiates were ordered to line up and listen to their elders. The senior sponsor of each initiate then came forward and lectured him on Gebusi values of generosity and virtue: "Always be generous with your kinsmen and in-laws, however long they live." "Don't be stingy with your food. Always give yourself the least." "When you come across your uncle's garden and see he has some nice food, never just take it." "If you ever steal, you will be rotten and no one will like you." "Whenever guests come, you must always snap their fingers firmly and warmly." "Never hide your tobacco away, always share your smoke with anyone who visits." Predictably, the greatest admonitions concerned sex: "You can never, ever chase after another man's wife." "Never flirt with your uncle's woman." "When you see a female 'bird' alone in the forest, you can't just go and 'shoot' it because you think you are 'hungry.'" "Don't you ever pry open the 'cooking tongs' [legs] of a village woman."

Although the sponsors started out seriously, their diatribes quickly lost steam; after a few minutes, their speeches labored to maintain an air of stern invective. As the sponsors finally got to their warnings about sex, the men and even the uninitiated boys could barely suppress their smiles and chuckles. Then, with loud cries of "SUI-SUI-SUI," the sponsors shooed the initiates outside to fetch water from the spring, a ten-minute walk away. Amid whoops and hollers, the men and even the boys accompanied the initiates, who carried water tubes and labored to walk while burdened with their wigs.

The initiates' trip to the watering hole turned out to be the prime occasion for revealing male secrets. In some New Guinea societies, elaborate restrictions surround the transmission of sacred male knowledge. In some cases, this information is doled out piecemeal over years. Measured against such standards, the Gebusi were amazingly carefree. As we approached the spring, the men spoke in only slightly lowered tones about the various foods that the new men, once initiated, would not be allowed to eat. Red pandanus could not be eaten because it formed a red paste, like menstrual blood. Slimy forest greens could not be eaten because, when they were cooked, they oozed like a woman's genitalia. River lobsters couldn't be eaten because they once pinched a woman in her upper thigh, which made them turn red. On and on went the list—until I tallied twenty-three food items that would now be taboo to the initiates. In each case, the "rationale" for the prohibition was the same: the food had some association, however circuitous, with women's primary sexual organs. As I later found out, initiated men were not supposed to eat these foods until their first or second child was born. But most of the taboos were observed only loosely in practice. I was told that a hungry man might easily break his food taboos when out in the forest, especially if experience had taught him that there was little harm in doing so. And though the list of dietary proscriptions seemed long, almost none of the items were frequent sources of protein.

As for additional male knowledge, there seemed to be none. At first I thought that Gebusi men must have deeper mysteries for me to discover. But I gradually came to recognize that the best-kept secret was the one I had overlooked: Gebusi men had few initiation secrets to reveal. Male sexual encounters with other men had not been hidden from women, and the initiates had taken no pains to hide their trysts. As for the telling of food taboos at the watering hole, the reactions of the younger boys were quite revealing. Although the men urged the boys to stay away and to cover their ears—lest premature knowledge stunt their growth— most of them edged closer. Some even cupped their hands behind their ears rather than over them, the better to hear the secrets. The men seemed unconcerned. In actuality, the telling of "secrets" was mostly an occasion of laughter and male bravado. Some of the men proclaimed that they would gladly die from breaking food taboos and by exposing themselves more fully to women's sexuality. Like their myths and séances, Gebusi male secrets were at least as much a source of ribaldry as they were sober declarations. Ultimately, the same was also true of the initiates' biggest trauma—the wearing of their bark wigs. Although the wigs were painful, the initiates quickly learned to manage them by hunching forward and shifting the weight onto their shoulders. By two o'clock in the afternoon, Hawi had cut off his wig entirely. When I asked him why, he claimed that it prevented him from preparing sago for the upcoming feast. By evening, only Yuway and Doliay still wore their wigs, and both of these were gone the following morning.

In some Melanesian societies, traditional rites of manhood were genuinely brutal. And they sometimes began when boys were only six or seven years of age. Ordeals sometimes included nose bleeding, penis bleeding, tongue bleeding, cane swallowing and vomiting, body scarification, and being beaten, berated, rubbed with stinging nettles, and forced to live in seclusion, in their own excrement, without food or water. In some societies, new initiates were threatened with violent punishment, including death, if they violated taboos or revealed male secrets to women. In contrast to these extremes, the Gebusi initiation was thankfully mild. Older men said that their rites of manhood had always been this way—more a celebration than a trial of pain or suffering. The same was true of some other groups in Papua New Guinea, including the Purari peoples of the south coast who, as it happened, were also vigilant headhunters. Once again, the diversity of cultures even within Melanesia was remarkable.

After wearing their bark wigs, our young friends enjoyed one last night of sleep—as much as they could get, amid their excitement—for several days to come. The following morning, after being repainted in yellow ocher (but without their bark wigs), they left to revisit their main sponsors in their respective villages. I decided to go with Hawi to Swamin's little hamlet at Sowabihilu. We found ourselves crammed into a mini-longhouse with fifty other people who had come there from settlements farther afield. A similar gathering was held simultaneously at the settlement of each initiate's primary sponsor. In the process, people coalesced at a variety of staging points the night before finally coming together at Yibihilu.

After a festive midnight hike back to the main village, lit by the moon, I awoke the next morning to find smoke from a score of blazing cook fires fingering up to greet the morning and shred the fog. The whoops of those stoking the fires and cooking the food soon mingled with the squeals of dying pigs, which stood in their cages as they were shot full of arrows by gleeful men. Singed and splayed to cook on top of the sago, the six large pigs—one for each initiate—would provide the most lavish meal since the last initiation, which had taken place in a neighboring community several years before. By mid-afternoon, the six initiates were finally ready to become truly "big"—to don their crowning costumes. We thronged around them and escorted them from the village a short way into the forest, where they could be dressed. The atmosphere was too festive to be exclusive, and in addition to the young boys who joined us, some of the women who had woven parts of the initiation costumes also came along.

Thoroughly cleansed of any lingering yellow paint, each initiate stood up to be painstakingly dressed as an electrifying red bird of paradise. The sponsors and helpers of each initiate took primary charge, painting with meticulous precision. Then they scrupulously dressed the initiates with the ever-so-carefully-made gifts of feathered headdresses, waistbands, shells, armbands, leg bands, woven chest bands, nose plugs, looped earrings, and more. The closest parallel, it seemed to me (although I had never actually witnessed it!) was the careful dressing of a traditional American bride prior to her wedding. The analogy wasn't completely far-fetched in that the initiation served, in its own way, as a kind of male wedding. Each young man would now be suddenly and imminently marriageable. All but one of the initiates would, in fact, be married within a few months. The additional gifts that the initiates received were a virtual trousseau to begin married life. In contrast to the initiation itself, the marriages that would follow—to women whose identity was not yet known—were strikingly unceremonial. As we later discovered, these unions were tense affairs characterized by worried courtship and adult irritation, and they were devoid of festive gift giving, costumed dancing, or public celebration. It was initiation, not marriage, that involved the cooking and distribution of the village pigs, and the publicly celebrated transition to virile adulthood.

If the initiation was like a marriage without women, the initiates themselves were almost like brides. The bright red paint that graced them from head to toe was the ultimate feminine color. Its association with crimson menstrual blood grew deeper as the various food taboos were retold to the initiates during their decoration. In the process, a large new phallic leaf was attached to hang down between their legs. Even more than the standard dance outfit (which also included images of other spirits), the initiation costume was a pure expression of the beauty, allure, and sexuality of the red bird of paradise—a spirit woman. But before they could be formally displayed and celebrated, the initiates had to be completely costumed and publicly paraded back to the village. Given the importance of this task, the initiates' sponsors refused to hurry despite the beginnings of an afternoon drizzle. Huddled under trees and with bystanders holding palm fronds and our umbrellas overhead to protect them, the initiates gradually emerged in final splendor. Each painted stripe, leg band, armband, and headdress feather was perfectly aligned and exactly identical on each of the initiates. I was deeply moved to see my young friends—Yuway, Hawi, Doliay, and the rest, whom I had come to know so well—so wonderfully transformed. Their grandeur was truly spectacular.

Against this aesthetic aura, the rain fell harder. The costuming was now complete, but a grand procession back to the village had become impossible. So we retired with the initiates to their family houses on the periphery of the village and waited for the storm to pass. Unfortunately, it did not. Instead, the rain grew stronger and stronger. We sat and sat as minutes became hours, from late afternoon into evening, and from evening into the night. It was an incredible, pelting rain, and it was completely unpredicted. Even as dawn broke, the water continued to thunder. The smooth village clearing had become a torrent of muddy gullies.

There were plenty of ironies. If the storm had held off for just another fifteen minutes (or if the sponsors had been a touch quicker with their decorations), the triumphal procession could have quickly taken place. Then we all would have been happily under the large sheltering roof of the longhouse. The visitors would have descended with great whoops to "confront" the initiates and have had their "anger" dispelled by the silent beauty of the initiates' immovable presence. The food would then have been served and eaten, and dances by the visiting men would have continued until morning. In short, everything would have gone according to plan. Now, however, the initiates, their sponsors, and the rest of us had stayed sitting up all night waiting for the rain to stop. Things were worst for the throngs of visitors. Festooned for their own grand entrances, they had retreated to the forest and huddled in makeshift lean-tos in a futile attempt to keep dry. Neither they nor we had had anything to eat. Everyone was very tired and very hungry.

Why couldn't the initiates simply be led under cover to the longhouse so the visitors could enter and the food be served? The answer was consistent: "Because the initiates' red paint would run down their bodies." Beyond the importance of having a triumphant procession, it was unthinkable to Gebusi that the beautiful red of the initiates, the congealed symbol of femininity that framed their masculinity, could be allowed to dissolve and drip down their skin. The specter of red liquid oozing down their carefully appointed bodies seemed tantamount to male menstruation—the destruction of masculinity rather than its crowning achievement. So we continued to wait for the rain to end.

To my amazement, almost no one got visibly upset. The principal exception was Silap, who cursed angrily and chastised whatever ghost was raining so literally on his parade. Almost everyone else eased into a kind of meditative doze, neither anxious nor despondent, but serene and trusting that all would work out. Despite the months of preparation and the sheer scale of the event—its social, spiritual, and material significance—the response to the storm was vintage Gebusi: quiet acceptance in the face of frustration. When the rain finally broke, in midmorning, my compatriots managed a few whoops of relief and anticipation. Cooking fires were now restoked and foods reheated. I went to check our rain gauge. It was filled to ninety-three millimeters—a bit shy of four inches of rain. This ended up being the fourth-biggest rainfall during our entire two-year stay—and the biggest within a month on either side of the initiation. Villagers shrugged it off as part of their unpredictable weather: "That's just the way it is."

The six initiates were finally lined up in front of the central longhouse. Shoulder to shoulder, they were individually brilliant but yet more spellbinding as a collective whole. Uniting the aesthetic and the material, they literally embodied the full power of Gebusi kinship and friendship, the breadth of their social connections across space, and the fullness of their sexuality and spiritual identifications. Together, the initiates crystallized the beauty, growth, gift giving, and forbearance of the Gebusi as a whole.

Into this electrifying vista, visiting men now rushed with abandon—a human stampede of celebratory aggression. Painted warriors bellowed, screamed, and sprinted through the mud as they plucked their bows and spiraled in a circle ever more tightly around the initiates in displays of happy mock antagonism—wave after wave, group after group. One man was carried in naked and covered head to foot in mud. His tongue hung out, and a huge fake phallus was tied to his waist. At least for the moment, he was a bloated corpse covered in cadaveric fluid—and indicting everyone around him as a sorcerer. As might have been guessed, even this gruesome display did not unsettle the initiates, who stood their ground with serenity even as children scattered from the "corpse" with ambivalent screams. Excited adults just smiled.

Eventually the attacks subsided and the feasting and celebration began in earnest. Festivities started with seemingly endless rounds of finger snapping, smoke sharing, kava drinking, and, especially, food giving. With thunderous whoops and hollers, the identity of an initiate's sponsor or other recipient was shouted. A representative from each of the six initiates' families then rushed to press a mound of food upon the pleased but besieged recipient. Special pleasure was taken in "force feeding" important visitors with great globs of dripping pig fat—pushing it to their faces until they had taken at least one or two gooey bites.

By midafternoon, it was time for the visitors to reciprocate and give gifts to the initiates—especially the prized hardwood bows and sheaves of elaborate arrows. Many of the male sponsors dramatically plucked the bow they had made before handing it to their initiate, showing him how strong it was. Previously allowed to use only unpainted arrows for hunting, the initiates could now use painted and people-killing arrows in ritual display and, as need be, in warfare. Exhausted as they were, however, the initiates could hardly do more than stand. Even that became difficult, and by evening, they resorted to propping themselves up while sitting lest they topple over in sleep and smear their costumes. As part of their proud ordeal, they had not talked, eaten, or slept for two days.

Seemingly oblivious to their plight, everyone else was now revved up for a full night of partying—eating additional food, smoking more tobacco, and drinking numerous bowls of kava root intoxicant. Jokes flew as thick and fast as the rain of the previous night. By now, the longhouse was packed wall to wall with people, with just a small space in the center for the dancers. The yellow light of resin lanterns and bamboo torches cast a golden glow across the faces and costumes. The outfits of the male visitors were as spectacular and creative as they were plentiful—including large headdresses of bird-of-paradise and cassowary feathers; red, black, and white face and body painting in innumerable patterns and combinations; bone and bamboo nose plugs and beads; leaf wreathes; and woven chest bands and armbands. Women were festooned as well: almost all of them had fresh grass skirts, bead or seed necklaces, and woven chest bands and armbands. Many also wore headdresses of fringed fiber strips and long egret feathers in their hair.

In addition to the usual male dancing, there was a special dance involving a few young women wearing their own red body paint, black eye banding, and red bird-of-paradise headdresses. During the plaintive songs of the women's chorus, the female dancers bounced up and down directly across from their male counterparts. Each of the young women held a long, thin rattle that she thrust up and down in front of her as she hopped opposite a male dancer—who pulsed up and down to the pounding beat of his drum. The sexual charge of these pairings was impossible to miss. The men in the audience went wild, and the women also joked and laughed from their sitting places beside the dancing area. To cap it off, a few women could be seen joking and flirting directly with men. It was as if, for a single night, the erotic mirth of the spirit woman had become acceptable for real Gebusi women as well as for men, at least in the realm of public joking. The night swept up everyone in joyful abandon. We will always remember its intensity.

※　　　　※　　　　※

The morning after was just that. As the visitors left, those from the host village crashed and slept, and so did we. While Gebusi had been busy partying, we had undergone our own initiation. Pumped by adrenalin and coffee, we had primed ourselves to observe and record what we had waited months to see—and what we knew we might not see again. Unlike the Gebusi, we didn't know what was going to happen next or when or how it would unfold. We worried that we would miss important events. I remembered the story of a well-known anthropologist who, working alone, fell asleep from fatigue at the height of a male initiation rite and missed a key sequence of color-coded costumes that he could never reconstruct. But in our case, we were cajoled good naturedly by the Gebusi not only to be present and observe but, insofar as we were comfortable doing so, participate as fellow residents of Yibihilu. This included our happily accepted offer to give food, especially rice and tinned fish, to help host visitors, and also to serve as secondary sponsors for the initiates. When men gave their *tor* initiates bows and arrows, I gave each of them several shotgun cartridges—"Western arrows," as they called them—for the hunting shotgun we had given the people of Yibihilu and which they cherished for providing them with extra meat. When initiates received their costume elements, we gave them each a pair of bright blue satin gym trunks that we had bought for them during a field break. These gifts were wildly popular and widely talked about, as it was (and remains) difficult for the Gebusi to obtain such items in the rainforest. In return, the families of the initiates gave us pork and sago. To each of the initiates, we became *tor*.

That morning, however, all we could think of was sleep. But just when we thought the initiation was over, an additional climax occurred. In early afternoon, we were awakened by loud noises and stumbled out of bed to see what was happening. The initiates were herded out of the village, their costumes retouched, and then paraded back in. This time, though, they were joined by two unmarried young women who stood alongside them in costumes that were, in body paint and feathers, virtually identical to their own. Together, the six young men and two young women linked fingers and stood in a single line. They bobbed up and down in unison as Tosi, the senior woman of the community, came forth to address them. Going down their line, she gently hit each of them with a sheaf of special leaves and chanted that they would henceforth be strong in heart, in breath, and in spirit. She said to each that he or she would have the inner energy of a buzzing hornet. Then she told them to be kind to and protective of others in the village. Finally, she declared for each the name of a young child to whom they were unrelated but whom they were charged to help and protect. With that, she turned and walked away. The initiation was over.

Thinking that we had seen everything the night before, we wrestled anew to make sense of this wonderful ending. Although women had been off-stage for many of the initiation's formal events, a senior woman had now become the center of its final ceremony. Young women had dressed up and danced as part of the previous night's festivities, but now two women dressed up like them and linked to them physically. The male bird of paradise—the woman who had ultimately been a man—had finally enveloped real Gebusi women as well. If this had been implicit in the previous night's dancing and joking, now it was formally proclaimed, with beautiful Gebusi women lining up directly with the men in costumes similar to theirs. What had seemed like—and in many ways was—a male initiation rite was also a large ritual celebration of male *and* female fertility, including the sexual coming-of-age of Gebusi women. The boundless sexual imagery of spirit women that was so dominantly appropriated by men in other contexts was finally accorded and publicly acclaimed for Gebusi women as well. It was almost as if, in its final moment of ritual celebration, Gebusi culture transcended its own deepest division between women and men.

This theme grew deeper that same night. Though the initiation was over, the young men and women were now adults—and free to dance on their own. Still dressed in their red initiation costumes, the male initiates added the feathered halo of the standard dance costume and danced for the first time with drums. Moreover, they danced in pairs with the young women who had stood alongside them at the initiation's benediction. Like their linkage earlier in the day, their ritual union encompassed the male-female beauty of the Gebusi as a whole.

Given these final events, how much did our understanding of the whole celebration need to be rethought? Was this a male initiation? Or not? As was often the case, the intricacies of Gebusi culture made a simple question deliciously difficult. On the one hand, young Gebusi women were painted similarly to the young men, lined up with them, danced with them, and were charged along with them during the final ceremony to protect a young child. Their maturity and sexuality were obviously on display alongside the young men. In social terms, their costume elements, though not as elaborate or copious as the young men's, linked the young women to those in the community who had given or loaned them these items.

On the other hand, in contrast to their male counterparts, the young women were not inseminated or otherwise sexually initiated. They were not subject to painful trials testing their stamina and did not receive bows and arrows or other major stocks of ritual or domestic items. They did not have pigs killed for them, did not have important gifts of food given in their name, and were not enjoined to observe special food taboos. They did not establish lifelong relations of initiation-mate and initiate-sponsor with others in the community. In contrast to the young men, the question of whether a given young woman would get dressed up in a red bird-of-paradise costume had been uncertain; it was answered only at the last minute by the young women themselves. Some of them had been shy and decided against it. As opposed to this, the planning and gift giving for the young men had been planned for months and were central to the ritual.

In a way, the inclusion of women as active but secondary actors paralleled other aspects of Gebusi ceremonial life. At the same time, the participation of young women in the final ceremony not just symbolized but embodied the central importance of Gebusi women's fertility along with the men's. If the initiation symbolized the height of the Gebusi male culture, it also extolled women and the Gebusi as a whole people. Spirituality, sexuality, materiality, kinship, friendship, and gender: they all came together in joy and happiness. Against all odds and impediments, against all sicknesses, deaths, and frustrations, the Gebusi somehow came together to celebrate their collective good company. It was a unity I had never seen or felt.

During our waning time of fieldwork with Gebusi after the festivities were over, I began to reflect more deeply on the strength of their culture. For all of the differences and extremes of Gebusi ways of life, I had learned from them positive human values and forms of happiness that were quite unprecedented and uplifting for me. As much as I wanted and needed to return to the United States, it was hard to contemplate leaving my Gebusi friends and their culture. I knew that adapting once again to the more scheduled and atomized features of life in America would be difficult. And that I would deeply miss the friends and the lifestyle I was leaving behind.

If the avenues of modern life tend to fragment into separate domains—the professional and public, the domestic and private, the leisure-based, the religious, and so on—here was a so-called simple society that managed to bring these aspects of life together in full celebration. To me, it was a testament to the human spirit that the Gebusi could create so much that was positive, beautiful, fun, and meaningful amid lives that were so difficult and tenuous. This is the way I like to remember them from that period: triumphantly asserting the richness and joy of their humanity.

BROADER CONNECTIONS: *Ritual Initiation and Life-Cycle Transitions*

- Gebusi initiation is a **rite of adulthood**, a **rite of status elevation**, or a **life-crisis ritual** by which young men, and to some extent women, become **full adult members of society**.

- Rich with **religious symbolism**, and as part of their **expressive culture**, Gebusi initiation also brings together and coheres **sexual, social, economic, and political dimensions** of their society and **asserts and affirms some of their culture's strongest values**, such as "good company" (*kog-wa-yay*). Major cultural celebrations frequently express and integrate cultural core values.

- Consistent with the transition stages of **rites of passage**, as suggested by Arnold van Genep and later by Victor Turner, Gebusi initiation involves (1) **preparatory rites and ceremonies; (2) a liminal or "in-between" period of category transition for initiates, and (3) climactic rites of social celebration and reintegration.**

- **Ritual initiation into adulthood** can be **severe or brutal** in some societies, but among Gebusi it is **mild-to-moderate**, including **the temporary wearing of heavy bark wigs** by male initiates.

- The **red bird of paradise** emerges as a **core symbol** or **key symbol** in Gebusi ceremonial life. As a **"polysemic" symbolic—a symbol with many meanings**—the red bird of paradise is literally embodied on the men, and, ultimately, on women.

- Gebusi initiation is consistent with the classic perspective of social scientist **Emile Durkheim**, who suggested that **religion reflects and projects the social features of a society into the spiritual realm.** Among Gebusi, the spirits are believed to have their own dances, and their own initiation, at the same time that the Gebusi do. The symbolism of the spirit world, and especially of the red bird of paradise spirit woman, is embodied on the initiates in their costuming.

- As well as being **observers**, Bruce and his wife were **participants** in the initiation through **gift giving** to visitors, and they also became a kind of **sponsor** *(tor)* **for the initiates.**

- The final rite of the initiation revealed that **Gebusi celebration of fertility and adulthood encompassed women as well as men.** Though women's gift giving and rites were not as elaborate as men's, the initiation **symbolized and socially enacted the unity and integrity of Gebusi as a whole.**

PART TWO
1998

Church poster: the "good heart of man," open to the "good news" and closed to pagan spirits. (PHOTO: Bruce Knauft)

Time for Change: Yuway's Sacred Decision

I feel like a neophyte all over again. Though at best not humiliating, fieldwork is always a humbling experience, and in a good sort of way. Arrows recently barbed at anthropology cast its knowledge as imperialist, gained at the expense rather than for the benefit of other people. But the gawky interloper is usually cut well down to size by the time he or she gets beyond the confines of the hotels, the taxis, and the urban elite to the place in question. Human leveling is ethnography's strength.

— FIELD NOTES, JUNE 1998

LEAVE IN 1982, COME BACK IN 1998—experience culture as a time machine to the future. Sixteen years is a long time for the Gebusi. So, too, for me, and also for cultural anthropology. While a whole generation of Gebusi were getting older and producing children, I went from young adulthood to middle age in Atlanta. My son, Eric, went from conception to high school. During the same time, the world also changed. Market economies, transnational influences, and national agendas spread to the farthest nooks of the globe. Cultural anthropology changed as well. If my fieldwork reflected anthropology's long-standing interest in remote societies, my restudy of Gebusi engaged its newer emphasis on change and transformation. In the interim, anthropologists' traditional interests in kinship, social organization, ritual, and exchange had broadened to include a full range of contemporary practices and institutions—markets, churches, schools, governments, nongovernmental organizations, and the mosaic of social and cultural influences that tie people to their region, to their nation, and to the world at large. Diversity of the contemporary world has become anthropology's concern.

Though my first fieldwork was limited in scope by its focus on a small and remote group of people, I hardly regret its results. Ethnography is as real and important as the lives it encounters, regardless of where or how numerous these are. Anthropology will be poorer if it gives up on the full range of human culture—from the most remote outpost to the most cosmopolitan city. But even at the time, external changes had already come to the Gebusi. In addition to steel tools and

97

pacification of the Bedamini had come cloth and occasional clothing, salt, soap, and matches, the yearly patrols of government officials, and the presence of the Nomad police when the Gebusi themselves called them. Subtler changes had also taken place. When I first encountered them, most Gebusi had already given up the traditional custom of tying their hair in dreadlocks in favor of cutting it short. A few men had even sported carefully shaved sideburns—recalling the hairstyle of the Australian patrol officers. And yet, at that time, many of the major changes that often impact peoples like the Gebusi, including missionization, wage-labor, cash-cropping, out-migration, mining, logging, and roads to other locations—had not affected them significantly.

State empires, commercial entities, and other wielders of power have criss-crossed the world for millennia. Commerce has girded the globe for more than five centuries. During the nineteenth and twentieth centuries, sections of the east half of the island of New Guinea were variously owned and colonized by the Germans, the British, and the Australians—until the country of Papua New Guinea gained independence in 1975. Though the flow and impact of many outside influences had been small among Gebusi during my first fieldwork, I anticipated that these had intensified during the 1980s and 1990s. And as anthropologists appreciate new worlds of experience, they also often find troubling new inequities. These include the unequal distribution of wealth brought by national and international influence, by the global market economy, and by powerful institutions that interact with local types of domination.

What had happened since my first fieldwork? Only snippets of information had reached me, and none of it was very revealing. Some colleagues suggested that modern developments—Christianization, education, migration, and economic development would have brought major changes to the Gebusi. Others emphasized that cultural values would keep many things the same. Even concerning violence, different outcomes were possible. By the end of my first fieldwork, I knew that violent death among Gebusi had declined to about half of its precolonial level. But Gebusi had continued to scapegoat and sometimes to kill one another as sorcerers without much government awareness or intervention. What had happened since then remained a mystery to me. Given the continuing absence of Australian officers—and the reluctance of national police to patrol in the rainforest—some colleagues thought that armed conflict among Gebusi would have increased. Violence had reemerged dramatically in many parts of Papua New Guinea, including in highland areas just seventy-five miles to the northeast of the Gebusi. The missionary who lived among the neighboring Bedamini people said that tribal violence had increased and would continue to do so. But the increasing association of Gebusi with activities in and around the Nomad Station, where the police were quartered, could offset this trend. So I was uncertain.

🌿   🌿   🌿

Added to my uncertainties about the Gebusi were ones about myself. During my first fieldwork, I was a fledgling twenty-six-year-old anthropologist—a researcher on a shoestring—with little to lose and everything to prove. I had youthful ignorance and unbridled faith in the understanding of cultures. These had galvanized the optimism that is essential not only to survive but also to keep one from considering too soberly the difficulty of the task ahead!

Sixteen years later, my hopes and expectations for renewing fieldwork with the Gebusi were peppered with anxiety. I was both more knowledgeable and more worried than before. Though I was going back to be with people I had known and liked, I also knew how tough it was to live in the rainforest. And the rainforest knows that a body at age forty-four is not what it was at twenty-six. In the United States, I had become a professor and the author of several books; I busied myself with the life of an academic. In contrast to my growing confidence as a scholar, I knew that fieldwork would again be a humbling experience. I wondered if my sense of being a successful anthropologist would fall like a house of cards. I was also concerned about the burden of my absence at home, and the problems that would arise if anything should happen to me. Finally, my uncertainty was intellectual. A middle-aged outlook often lacks the openness of a younger mind. How would I reconcile my expectation of change among the Gebusi with my appreciation of their cultural past? Anthropology crackles with debates between researchers who focus on global change and those who stress cultural continuity. Are societies more strongly informed by long-standing values or by recent transformations? Amid such questions, my desire to return grew stronger despite the difficulties it posed. And I really wanted to see my Gebusi friends. Their very remoteness became an additional reason to return—to study their changes.

So I committed myself to go back after sixteen years, and I was going solo. I told myself to treat whatever I found among Gebusi at its own face value—to wipe my slate clean of expectations, as much as I could. After months of finding funding, navigating bureaucracy, obtaining visas, buying supplies, reviewing old field notes, and shedding tears of good-bye, I left for Papua New Guinea. After two weeks in the capital of Port Moresby and several days in the district capital of Kiunga, I finally took the small plane to the Nomad Station. I landed for a half-year of fieldwork on June 25, 1998. That night, I wrote the following:

Tonight, this first evening back, I sit here with Sayu and Howe, who smile brightly as I type on this keyboard. We have just looked at the screen saver, which has amazed them totally. I am caught in a time warp between the pidgin English called *tok pisin*, Gebusi language, heat, fatigue, and my wonder and amazement.

First touchdown was a rush. Hawi was the airline agent who met me at the airstrip!! He had a gaunt face and a much receding hairline but was still strong and energetic. We hugged, shook hands, and snapped fingers about a dozen times. He told me he lives right at the Nomad Station—and that he has three sons and a baby daughter! Then he had to attend to the paperwork of the flight while my things were unloaded. I turned around and had the wonder of seeing age jump right before my eyes. One after another Gebusi whom I had known came up to greet me. The grown children were the most incredible. There was Sayu, our little friend about whom we joked that we would adopt and bring back to the States. He is strong, handsome, and smart! He has already become my closest companion and helper among the younger men. He combines his father's quickness and his mother's intelligence, perceptiveness, and friendship—or at least so it seems on my first impression.

Most striking among my adult friends are their hollow faces, withered bodies, and wrinkled skin that I remember as smooth. But my happiness in human connection transcends space and time. We embraced and snapped fingers mightily, including the women. Gazing into the eyes of those whom you know with fond memories from sixteen years ago, and who suddenly live again in the present, is totally thrilling and completely unforgettable. In Gebusi legends, reunions and welcomes are so warm and numerous that people's hands are worn bare by snapping fingers heartily and repeatedly. Today, I allowed myself the hubris of feeling the same way. My middle fingers are really sore from the finger snapping that I could not keep myself from continuing even if I had wanted to stop. It is like on my wedding day, when the joy of the event caused an actual soreness of smile muscles that were so irrepressibly stretched that they could not help but turn anything in the world to their overpowering good feeling.

Feelings notwithstanding, the day has been hot, and I have a mountain of decisions to make quickly. How many nights will I stay in this unpleasant little house at the Nomad Station? Where will I live after that? How can I build on today's rush of positive feeling? How should I reestablish reciprocity with my Gebusi friends? How will I cook? How many boxes should I unpack? Where are the specific parcels of utensils, sleeping equipment, cloths, toiletries, and so on that I need for this first night? (As expected, there are no real stores at Nomad, so I am glad that I have brought everything with me.) And yet, I simply must take time tonight to write the events of this astonishing day.

Amid the constant stream of visitors whom I did not want to stop, I somehow greeted everyone and found that virtually the entire generation of surviving Gebusi from Yibihilu now live in a "corner" of Nomad just across the Hamam River, about 20 or 25 minutes' walk from the Nomad Station. This is absolutely perfect, my ideal residential scenario! I should have easy access to the Nomad Station and its nationalizing influence while also being able to go with Gebusi back to the forest. Having stowed my things in the government house by about one o'clock, I couldn't resist the temptation to walk with my friends to their corner settlement and see for myself the lovely place where I will likely be living. It is all simply wonderful.

Within minutes, the Gebusi astounded me. Meeting me at the Nomad Station airstrip, the descendants of Yibihilu boasted a new flock of youngsters and of children-become-adults. Within a few days, however, I found that few men of my own age or older were still alive. Most of those whom I had known as adults had died, including Silap, Boyl, Swamin, Sialim, Sagawa, Tosi, Wosip, and Imba. Of the six young men we helped initiate, only three—Hawi, Doliay, and Yuway— were still living. I mourned the passing of friends even as I saw their personalities, amazingly, in their children, now pushing toward their own adulthood. In demographic terms, Gebusi were a new people and more numerous than before—up from 450 persons to about 615.

Change and turnover notwithstanding, and despite the heat and mosquitoes, it felt wonderful to be back. I was remembered fondly and welcomed joyously. Two children had been named after me during my absence. Once worn, the glove of friendship always seems to fit. Within one day of my arrival, Gwabi, who had been about twelve years old when I first knew him, insisted that I occupy the new thatched house that he had just happened to finish building beside his older dwelling in Gasumi Corners. With this as my base of operations, I quickly found myself immersed in Gebusi life, going both to Nomad and to the forest, and rediscovering the joys and trials of life in the field. I had worried about my ability to speak Gebusi after so many years, but this came back to me faster than I expected.

In short order, I discovered that the 122 descendants of Yibihilu and its surrounding hamlets had fashioned not just a new settlement but a new way of life. Now they were living on the outskirts of the Nomad Station, just a short walk from its airstrip, school, churches, market, ball field, and government offices. The settlement was no longer nestled in the full rainforest. Rather, it was sandwiched between the cleared areas that fanned out from the Nomad Station and the primary timberland that the Gebusi used to inhabit. From their vantage point at Gasumi Corners, my friends could still walk to their traditional lands in the deep forest, but their lives increasingly revolved around the institutions and activities of the Nomad Station. The result was what might be called a new structure of feeling in Gebusi culture. Within this new world, the social life of the primary forest, including our previous settlement of Yibihilu, was gone.

Internally, the new community still retained its kinship connections, including its links via marriage and maternal ties, as well as through clanship. But extended families and even nuclear families now lived separately in small individual houses that were scattered like islands in an archipelago across three hillocks and a stream. Strikingly, there was no longhouse—no central dwelling place as a focus of activity where people could gather. As a consequence, the traditional sense of good company—the togetherness, talk, and whooping/joking of Gebusi *kogwayay*—was greatly muted.

In terms of material goods, life was much as it had been before. Families had only a few more manufactured items than they did in 1980–82—perhaps an extra knife, a larger metal pot, or a shovel. The biggest visible change was the increased wearing of Western clothes. Unlike before, village women never walked around bare-breasted; they always covered themselves, if only with a ripped blouse. Even the men invariably wore a shirt with their shorts when they went to Nomad. Used clothes were intermittently flown in by the baleful and quickly sold at low prices for a profit by an itinerant trader or local official.

Along with their interest and new activities, Gebusi seemed to have developed a new sense of time. Before, in the relaxed world of the rainforest, rhythms of life had kept their own languid pace; people could simply not be hurried. There had been little attempt to mark specific times of day, and there were no words for the days of the week, the months, or even the seasons. We had easily lost track of days if we forgot to tick them off on our calendar. The Gebusi word for "tomorrow," *oil*, was the same as the word for "yesterday." The word for "the day after tomorrow" was the same as the one for "the day before yesterday" (*bihar*)—and the same was true of the word for "three days after today" and "three days before today" (*ehwar*). In terms of generations, Gebusi had used the same word for both their grandparents and their grandchildren (*owa*). And an adult man often referred to his own son as his "father" (*mam*). In the cycling of gardens and fallow land, a boy would ideally grow up to cultivate the lands of his father or grandfather and to eat of the sago palms and nuts trees they had planted for him there. Life had represented a spiritual and social circle. Even male life force had been physically recycled from one generation to the next. The ideal had been for things to repeat over time, not change.

Now, however, Gebusi days and even minutes were marked and measured. Everyone seemed to work under deadline to accomplish things different from, and hopefully better than, those of the past. The first Sunday after my arrival, I got a taste of what this meant. Sayu had said that the church service would begin when the sun was above the treetops. Gebusi sense of time had always been as vague as the morning mist, events invariably began late, and I figured I would be arriving before most of the others. But the houses along the way were curiously empty. When I got close enough to hear hymn singing, I realized I was late. Late! The idea had been foreign to Gebusi. But the clock-watching pastor had rung the metal chime first in warning and then five minutes before the service started. While I had missed the signals in the distance, everyone else was on time.

Beyond church services on Sunday morning, the new weekly schedule included schooling for local children from Monday through Friday. Classes at the Nomad Community School began promptly at 8:00 A.M. and lasted until 3:30 P.M. Mindful of time, the children of Gasumi Corners usually left for school before 7:00 A.M.—and got home after 4:00 in the afternoon. The school day was divided into sixteen timed periods, some as short as fifteen minutes. Their transition was frequently marked by the ringing of the school bell. For adults, and especially for women, Tuesdays and Fridays from 8:00–10:00 A.M. were market days. Weekend afternoons were slated for rugby and soccer on the government ball field, particularly for the men and boys, who arrived early so they wouldn't miss their starting time. Matches were timed and refereed by government timekeepers who sounded a large horn to mark the end of the half and the end of the game. Though most Gebusi could not tell time, all the men seemed to want wristwatches—so they could ask someone else the time or at least appear to be acting based on knowledge of the hour.

If time for the Gebusi was increasingly marked against a daily and hourly clock, its passage now reflected Gebusi hopes for—and failures of—progress and improvement. Tests on Fridays gauged the learning that students had accomplished each week. Unfortunately, few children from Gasumi Corners were on track to finish elementary school—and none were slated to go on to the high school in Kiunga. At the twice-weekly Nomad market, if food wasn't sold by the end of the session, it had to be taken home or given away. In sports, the Gebusi traditionally had played until the score was tied or until everyone had lost track. Now, they played on the government ball field, kept careful track of the score, and played to win by the final horn. In short, the strivings and shortcomings of the Gebusi's lifestyle were now measured against a timeline of hoped-for success.

Running out of time had not been a problem in 1980–82, but it certainly was now, with Gebusi struggling to meet new standards of progress and personal development. Perhaps nowhere was this more evident, surprisingly, than in the realm of spirituality and religion.

Yuway's eyes simply sparkled. "*Koya, koya!*"—"Friend, friend!" We must have gazed into each other's eyes, snapped fingers, and joked heartily at least a dozen times. I had come to his house, a mere five-minute walk from my own. Yuway had been my most helpful friend in 1980–82. He was an all-around good person and the tallest of the young men we had helped initiate. Shortly after the initiation, he had become a moon-eyed romantic with his fetching wife-to-be, Warbwi, and we had given him gifts to help with his marriage. That had been seventeen years ago. And here he was again, in the flesh! It was so good to see him. Every few sentences, we would smile and clasp each other again, as if to reassure ourselves that our reunion was real. We quickly brought each other up to date. He was touched to hear that I now had a son who was full grown and even taller than I. With subdued pride, Yuway told me that he and Warbwi now had four children: an adolescent boy and girl plus two younger sons. I joked with him that he must have been "busier" than I had been; we both broke into laughter.

As a few minutes passed, word spread that we two senior men were having a good jokefest together, and we ended up attracting a score of amused spectators from surrounding houses. Good-natured as he was, I realized that Yuway was slowly getting embarrassed by our traditional joking. Although I had taken our jests for granted, he started to suppress his grins. From the reactions of others around us, I could sense that old-time joking, though tolerated from me as a middle-aged man who knew their traditions, was funny in part because it was now a bit anachronistic, a touch out of place.

As if to punctuate my perception, Yuway finally told me with a smile that he was an SDA—a member of the Seventh Day Adventist Church. This was the most stringent Christian denomination in the Nomad area. I was naturally intrigued, and this led us to a thoughtful discussion of changes in Gebusi religion. Yuway said that he had come to Gasumi Corners from Yibihilu with the others some ten years earlier. Like most of them, he had also joined the Catholic

Church soon after. The Catholic pastor had been solicitous of the Gebusi and had even visited some of their settlements in the bush. Because the new church was between the new settlement near Nomad and the Nomad Station itself, the villagers thought that joining it would be a good way to help establish their new lives. As the people of Gasumi Corners got used to singing in church, Yuway said, they sang less with their own spirit mediums. The community's major shaman, Swamin, started going to church himself and then stopped singing to the traditional spirits entirely. So, too, with the other spirit mediums; they found themselves part of a community that was now singing to a new spirit, to a singular God. When the Gebusi go to church, they say literally, "We go to sing" (*gio dula*). Within a few years, the spirit séances that had galvanized Gebusi social life—and that had been such a large focus of my own work—had become history, a thing of the past.

Without spirit mediums, as Yuway explained, people in Gasumi Corners had no real way to communicate with their traditional spirits; their path of connection was "cut" (*gisaym-da*). No longer could they joke with the spirits, ask their advice about sickness or sorcery, or enlist their support for or opinions about fish poisoning and other activities. To my great surprise, the traditional world of Gebusi spirits had withered away. And with their departure, Gebusi social life had also changed. No longer were male sexual joking and camaraderie a focal source of excitement. The people of Gasumi Corners sang to their new God not in the dead of night but in the brightness of the morning, not with humor but with solemnity, not in a lively conversation with the spirits but, instead, with a subservient voice. Apparently the preacher and his God had simply been more powerful than the old ones. Together, they had the prestige and wonder of coming from afar, of being associated with wealth, success, and the accomplishments of a wider world. Although the lay pastor lived not far from Gasumi Corners, he was supported by the Catholic Church and flew regularly back to Kiunga and occasionally to his own home in one of the country's mountain districts. He was literate and well educated, wore nice clothes, had a house stocked with supplies, was able to call Kiunga on his own two-way radio, and was bent on presenting his way of life and his God as a model for Gebusi to follow. They willingly agreed.

Yuway told me that he himself had been one of the Gasumi leaders in the Nomad Catholic Church from 1992 to 1995. (I pinched myself to note how the Gebusi now kept track of years.) But after that, he felt more distant from the parish.

"Why did you join the Seventh Day Adventists?" I asked.

"Well, the Catholic Church is kind of 'soft'; I wanted a church that was 'hard.'"

"How's that?" By this point, I was remembering that the Gebusi word for "hard" (*gof*) also means "strong," "righteous," "angry," and "potentially violent"—as well as "difficult."

"If you are really going to worship God, it shouldn't be a small thing. It should be a big thing. You should really work hard to please God. And you have to be ready by Judgment Day. The Catholics make you work only a little hard. They let people keep lots of customs that God doesn't like—like dancing and smoking tobacco. The SDA Church knows that God doesn't like these and that they are wrong. They make their religion really hard by telling us we can't eat certain things that we like. They make us work a lot in the church yard, and they make us come for Bible learning as well as going to the long service on Saturday morning. They have pictures that show exactly what will happen to you if you have sin—you will burn in hell. With SDA, I know I am really a Christian and that I can go to heaven."

I paused to collect my thoughts. Yuway and my other friends had been so thoroughly "Gebusi" in spiritual outlook when I first knew them. Yet his answer revealed not just the onus but the attraction of a fundamentalist Christian faith. Yuway's comment also pointed up the key distinction that the Gebusi make among the three local churches. Catholicism was seen as the "easiest" faith because it had the fewest taboos. Catholics were told to attend church regularly, to worship God rather than other spirits, to avoid fighting, and to not drink kava—their lightly intoxicating drink made from roots. As long as these criteria were followed for a year or two—with some allowance made for backsliding—a Gebusi could be baptized as a Catholic by the priest or bishop on one of his sporadic visits to Catholic parishes in the province.

In many parts of the world, conversion to or fundamentalization of world religions—including Islam, Hinduism, and Judaism, as well as numerous forms of Christianity—has been on the rise. On the other hand, the particular way that a world religion is locally interpreted and expressed can be highly variable. In and around the Nomad Station, including at Gasumi Corners, the Christian churches were developed and run by fundamentalist Papua New Guineans who had come to proselytize the area from other parts of the country. This gave all the local forms of Christianity an aura of fundamentalism, though, as Yuway noted, some churches were perceived by the local population to be "harder" than others.

About 60 percent of those in Gasumi Corners had become members of the Catholic Church, while approximately one-fifth (22 percent) belonged to the Evangelical Church of Papua New Guinea. In addition to the Catholics' strictures, Evangelicals had a strong taboo against smoking tobacco and restrictions on participating in non-Christian rituals. The SDA rules were yet stricter. In fact, Yuway's family was the only one in Gasumi Corners to have joined their church. In addition to bans on smoking, drinking, dancing, and observing traditional rituals, the SDAs prohibited the eating of smooth-skinned fish and any kind of pork. This last was particularly significant, because eating pigs was still a prime feature of Gebusi festivities on special occasions. SDA adherents were told that each Saturday was a day for worshiping God in church; all other work or gardening, as well as forms of public entertainment—playing ball, attending feasts, or going to disco—were condemned as irreligious.

Because I knew Yuway to be a caring person, I wondered how his personal beliefs meshed with the SDA reputation for intolerance. He said with all earnestness that he had no anger against those who went to other churches or even those who went to none at all—which included a few in Gasumi Corners. I decided to push him a little: "If someone who is a good person goes to the Catholic Church or to the Evangelical Church instead of SDA, do you think that person can go to heaven when he or she dies? Or not?"

Yuway thought for a minute, but not too long: "I don't know. Only God knows these things. But for me, I think that someone who is good inside can go to heaven, and it shouldn't matter if they go to one church or another."

"What if they don't go to any church at all?"

"Well, if they are given the chance to believe in Father God but still don't do it, it might be hard for God to see them as a good person and let them into heaven. But it's not for me to say."

I was impressed with his answer. It was then that I remembered the arrows that Yuway had been fashioning when I had come up to greet him. Now they were lying next to him, elaborately carved and ready for painting with bright-red ochre.

"Those are really nice arrows. Aren't they the kind used to sponsor a young man at an initiation?"

"Yes, I'm sponsoring a young Wapsiayk (a young man from his clan) at Taylmi a month or two from now."

"Can you still do that and be an SDA?"

"Well, I won't get baptized into SDA myself until after the initiation. It will be the last time for me to eat pork in my life. And if I go just to see the initiation and not because I believe in its spirits, it's okay."

As I mulled over this last response, the sky opened up as if by divine intervention; rain suddenly came pelting down. Realizing that it was almost dark—and that the supper fire at my house had yet to be started—I smiled and snapped fingers quickly with Yuway before whooping loudly as I raced up the trail. I was thoroughly drenched by the time I reached home.

Reflecting that evening on the day's events, I was struck by Yuway's remarks in relation to what I was finding from Gebusi who were Catholics or Evangelicals. At Nomad, all three churches featured a fierce God of fire and brimstone—who threatened hell and demanded compliance. All of them held that Judgment Day could come at any time—and that repentance now was the key to salvation. All three churches were "hard," though some were "harder" than others. How was it that different Gebusi belonged to these three different churches—each of which drew members from diverse communities? While I had been visiting with Yuway that afternoon, his two married brothers, Keda and Halowa, had shown up. Keda was a lay leader in the Catholic Church; the previous Sunday, he had been asked to translate parts of the pastor's sermon for the congregation. Halowa, by contrast, was an Evangelical. Each of the three brothers, I realized, belonged to a different church. I found increasingly that Yuway had been right: Gebusi accepted each other's right to choose the religious denomination that suited him best. The "him" is significant here, because most wives attended the church that their husbands had chosen. If Christianity saved the soul of the individual rather than the group, so, too, each individual man, at least, could choose what church to belong to—and whether to believe in God at all. The Gebusi world of moral choices and consequences was no longer governed so strongly by kinship or clanship, but increasingly by a man's choice.

The second thing that struck me involved Yuway's plan to give initiation gifts to a young man while he himself was completing the arduous requirements for SDA baptism. How was this possible? Was Yuway being hypocritical? Or was this a classic case of "syncretism," in which two religions are blended together? Neither of these possibilities seemed likely to me; I suspected that something else was at issue. It turned out that Gebusi distinguish between witnessing a traditional ritual and actually hosting or performing in one. At a remote settlement like Taylmi—the last big Gebusi village that had not yet become Christian—one could attend an initiation the same way that Americans can watch an action movie or a historical epic without being considered a violent person or a creature of the past; they can view it as an entertaining drama or spectacle without adopting its values or lifestyle. Indeed, being exposed to "pagan ways" without succumbing to them can itself indicate commitment to Christianity.

It has often been noted that the process of Christian redemption is punctuated by trials and temptations. Preachers at Nomad repeatedly emphasized the danger of "backsliding" into sin and vice associated with tradition. Although the Gebusi willingly submitted themselves to the harangues of the pastor, it was their deviation from Christian thoughts or interests that spurred their sense of needing atonement—the pang of conscience that begs for moral cleansing. Exposure to and ambivalence about traditional customs was integral to the jawboning process of Gebusi conversion to Christianity. Hopes of salvation seemed directly linked to threats of sin.

Three weeks later, I experienced this dynamic by going with Yuway's family to an SDA service at a nearby hamlet. The pastor's message was bleak. And it became something of a marathon, exhorting the small congregation for a full two hours. Increasingly, they simply hung their heads. That evening, I wrote the following:

> The patience and passivity demanded in church—which I noted immediately among the Catholics—are brought to a firmer and sterner level among the Seventh Day Adventists. Today, the long sermon by the SDA preacher was a case in point. He placed great emphasis on the trials of Jesus: his forty days in the wilderness in the hot sun without food or water, his agonizing death on the cross, his suffering for us all. "Our own hardships are small; we should bear them easily and ask for nothing. We should think of Christ—be grateful that He suffered and died for us." The preacher's concluding harangue, which he repeated for a good forty minutes, was similarly somber. Saturday should be a day only for SDA worship. Food and market and other work activities should be finished Friday night. Saturday should be sober and worshipful, morning and night, with no entertainment or even cooking of food. This was the true way to worship God.

Where is the payoff in this scheme? The deadline is now—since Judgment Day can come at any time—but the reward is deferred. Against the austere trials of the present is the glorious image of life after death. Heaven was described as a place full of *bip*, or "cargo," a place where people are endlessly happy, without suffering or sickness. I was reminded of the dramatic cults that some Melanesians developed when they first encountered Western goods. These so-called cargo cults arose as local people attempted to obtain or "produce" European goods by means of magical rites or by mimicking Western behavior. In their conversion to Christianity, however, Gebusi bypassed such attempts, accepting that wealth and salvation would come in an afterlife and not right away. To attain this bliss, they could not ask for much during life on earth. But on the day of reckoning, the ultimate deadline, God would give an ultimate reward to those who had truly followed his path. My field entry concluded as follows:

> Now I can see, at least dimly, Yuway's attraction to this church. It is severe; it stresses the need to be hard and disciplined for God. This is the modern path of dignified compliance in and around the Nomad Station as well as a path for everlasting life. It measures the present not against a happy stand- ard of current success but against trials, and rewards, that were infinitely greater for Jesus. These give reward only later, in the future.

Yuway's choice foregrounds the path that the Gebusi were increasingly taking not only in church but also at school, in the market, and even on the ball field: to meet deadlines in the present, wait patiently, and hope for deferred success. All these contexts encouraged an ethic of disciplined action, of being on time and meeting deadlines, and of accepting the authority of outsiders.

❧   ❧   ❧

The most dramatic case of religious transformation involved Doliay, the youngest and smallest of the six young men whom we had helped initiate. Sev- eral years after my first fieldwork, Doliay married Boyl, Sayu's widowed mother. However, Boyl died shortly thereafter. Following her death inquest, he con- fronted the person accused of causing Boyl's death through sorcery—a man named Basowey. Doliay told me that his anger toward Basowey had pervaded his thoughts and actions. His plan for revenge took on a surgical and almost Zen-like focus. Although Basowey was almost a foot taller than he, Doliay sought him out and confronted him alone in the forest. He dodged Basowey's arrows and split his head with a bush knife. He then cut off Basowey's head and left it next to his body in the forest. Then he went to the Catholic compound, told the pastor what he had done, handed him his bush knife, and turned himself in to the Nomad police.

Doliay's killing of Basowey was a watershed. He was sentenced to six years at the national prison in the capital city of Port Moresby. No Gebusi had ever traveled so far. But Doliay hardly saw the city. While in prison, he became exceedingly self-disciplined. He learned to speak *tok pisin*, the national language, converted to Christianity, became a model prisoner, and even became head cook for the warden, who entrusted him with the key to the compound's entire store-house of food. In 1998, Doliay proudly kept the letter of reference and commendation that the warden gave him upon his release from prison. He recalled his jailers fondly and with great affection. He still wore the shirt that one of them gave him, and he named his first son Willy after a prison guard who had been his good friend.

Returning finally to Gasumi Corners, Doliay became something of an ideal Christian. Unlike those who hung around the pastor's compound in hopes of wheedling a favor or gaining a benefit, Doliay worked in the parish out of a sense of personal commitment. He told me that he waited to be baptized until coming back to Nomad because he wanted to be sure—really sure—that his bad ways were completely gone, that he felt no more hate in his heart. He felt grateful that God could forgive even as great a sin as his killing of Basowey. And he said that he would wait with a Christian heart until Judgment Day to see if God would accept him into heaven. I asked Doliay if he wouldn't be tempted to kill another person for sorcery, especially if one of his own children were to die of sickness. His answer was immediate: "No. No way."

"Why not?"

"It's not for me to take revenge. That's something for the 'Big Fellow' [God] to decide. Besides, the people of Gasumi Corners don't practice sorcery anymore. Even if they wanted to, they would be too scared of what I did to Basowey to send sorcery again. If my son died, it wouldn't be from sorcery!"

Against traditional beliefs, Doliay's view was revolutionary. Before, the Gebusi had universally attributed fatal illnesses to sorcery. And a man's demand for revenge was greatest when a member of his own immediate family died from sickness.

While Doliay had been in prison, his community had changed. Incited by the pastors, the villagers redoubled their rejection of violence against suspected sorcerers. The penalty Doliay had been forced to pay—six years in prison, away from his kin—intensified the reluctance of others to follow his footsteps. The killing of Basowey became renowned as the last execution of a sorcerer, the end of an era. In the wake of this act, conversion to Christianity swelled rather than diminished. Since then, as far as I have been able to determine, no Gebusi has been killed as a sorcerer—or for any other reason. This is fairly amazing: a society with one of the highest known rates of homicide has seen it drop to zero. I confirmed this lack of violence by detailing and then cross-checking the cause and circumstances of each of the deaths of the members and descendants of Yibihilu and its hamlets. To me, this underscores the degree to which human violence is not an ingrained or inevitable outcome, but one that is strongly shaped by attitudes and beliefs. And yet, the Gebusi belief in sorcery had been so strong, and their desire to seek vengeance had been so high, that I remained skeptical of this good-news story. I was a doubting Thomas—I needed to see in order to believe. Then Uwano died.

A certain depth emerges from the eyes of a man who knows his death throes are starting. Uwano was not old by our standards, probably in his late forties. Perceptive and a convivial joker, he had been my *arga*, my "breadfruit" gift-partner, since my first fieldwork. We had always greeted each other heartily. But by the fall of 1998, he was a shell of his former self, having only a tiny reserve of strength to fight his death. When I went to visit him at the Nomad Aid Post on his last night, the swelling that would soon consume his body had already taken his right arm and back. He gazed upward with a mixture of knowledge and confusion. Then he turned and seemed to recognize me, and a shadow of a smile flickered across his face.

I knew better than to tell him he would get better. I could only kneel down with a helpless smile, look softly into his eyes, and say *"Koya, koya,"* (friend, friend) as tenderly as I could. I took his hand in mine and stroked it. It was cold, already dead. He looked at me with that slight shake of head that is the Gebusi expression for, "There's no way; it's impossible." Then he was gone from me, eyes drifting into space. His little frame shook with a small spasm, which was all that his ravaged body could muster. He did not look back at me as I waited there. After a while, I crept out to the next room to talk with his relatives. The stark glow of the fluorescent bulb in that room with no furnishings cast them all in ghostly stillness.

We always project at death, I think—the Gebusi with their beliefs and me with my thoughts of final human connection. And hopefully Uwano, too, reaching out from his doorway on death's divide. He died a few hours later, on October 9, 1998.

I waited instinctively for the sorcery inquests to start. When I first knew Gebusi, it would have been unthinkable for a prominent man in the community to die without a full-blown inquest to find the sorcerer. But Uwano's body was carried back to Gasumi Corners for a simple Christian funeral. He was dressed in his best Sunday shirt, head wreathed with leaves, and buried with a graveside service led by a Catholic catechist reading from the Bible.

A few of Uwano's closest relatives grumbled that someone must have killed him. Men voiced vague fears that an assault sorcerer could be on the prowl. But there was no spirit séance, no accusation, no attempt to identify a suspect, and no attempt to take revenge. As if to satisfy themselves, the men walked off to one of Uwano's gardens. They pawed around aimlessly in case an obvious sign of a sorcery attack could be found. But their search was half-hearted, and they quickly lost interest. As one man said with a shrug, "If a spirit medium were around, we might have a chance of finding something. But there isn't." In effect, they were simply paying their respects to Uwano by visiting the place where they thought he might have become sick. Not wanting to waste their trip to the forest, the men gathered weathered logs near his garden and shouldered them back to the village for firewood.

In the wake of this experience, the Gebusi's descriptions of deaths that had occurred between my first and second periods of fieldwork finally made sense to me. In case after case, friends had earnestly recounted, "So-and-so simply died of sickness. We just don't know why. Only God can know. Maybe she was killed by sorcery. Or maybe by some other kind of spirit. Maybe Satan was trying to fool us into thinking that it was sorcery. Not knowing, we just buried the body and had the pastor read from the Bible." Although the dead person's closest relatives might suspect sorcery, there was little they could do. Without solid spiritual evidence, other people in the community would not support their claim. And if they did try to launch an accusation, it could backfire; the person accused of sorcery could turn the tables and charge the accuser with slander, even bringing the case to the police.

As I thought about all this, I had competing views about Gebusi Christianity. On the one hand, I felt that much of value in Gebusi culture had been lost. The vibrant wonder of their traditional beliefs had faded, and the poetry, symbolism, and musical awe of their spirit world were almost dead. In their place was a demanding new religion, trumpeted from elsewhere. In the history of colonialism and post-colonialism, including in the global spread of Christianity, the pressured or forced conversion of local people has worked hand in hand with powerful forms of social, economic, and political domination. Though the Gebusi had been thankfully spared coercive intimidation, they nonetheless had become passive recipients of outside spiritual as well as political supervision. On the other hand, Christianity and the way of life with which it was associated had reduced the Gebusi's extraordinary rate of violence. Indeed, their sorcery killings had stopped altogether. Social life was more peaceful than before. Men, women, and even children could walk to Nomad or in the nearby forest without fear of attack. Though the great camaraderie of earlier days was gone, so, too, was the threat of lethal violence. Life was tamer in many ways.

What about the experiences of Gebusi women? Previously, they had enjoyed the energy and splendor of the spirit world, but from the sidelines. Although spirit women were key figures in the traditional cosmos, Gebusi women themselves had been excluded from séances and had little influence in sorcery inquests; men controlled the spirit world and the use of violence. Now, however, women were Christian along with the men. The responsibility and the reward of being Christian—of repenting sins and gaining salvation—was individual for both sexes. In the church itself, pews were divided evenly, with women on the left side and men on the right. At the Catholic services, men and women attended in roughly equal numbers, but in SDA and Evangelical services, a decided majority were women. The church pastors and the primary lay leaders in the community were invariably men. And the authority of "Papa God," as he was called, was both stronger and more patriarchal than that of traditional Gebusi spirits. Sporadically but notably, men in Gasumi Corners would echo the tone of the preachers or government officials, adopting a lecturing and authoritative tone in their own community. Finally, the number of Gebusi marriages that were acrimonious as opposed to harmonious was about the same as before.

Adding to my conflicted feelings about Christianity was another uncertainty: To what extent were the Gebusi's previous beliefs really dead? If only vestigially, the Gebusi still worried about sorcery. In many parts of Melanesia—and in parts of Africa, Asia, Latin America, and even Western countries—belief in sorcery or magic has persisted or reasserted itself. Such beliefs have sometimes melded with Christianity or other world religions such as Islam, Buddhism, or Hinduism. In significant areas of Melanesia and Africa, sorcery beliefs play a major role in contemporary disputes and rivalries, including between political leaders. If these customs can continue in modern forms, couldn't Gebusi beliefs come back in new ways?

No matter what happens, however, and even if Christianity is later rejected or disavowed, its great influence will have a significant legacy. The hands of time cannot be turned back. And there is every indication that Christian influence among Gebusi has been growing stronger.

🌿 🌿 🌿

How can we explain changes in Gebusi religion and culture, comprehending the richness of their past, their present, and their indeterminate future? The complexities of the present can play havoc with the categories of the past. The Gebusi cosmos had been full of spirits from humans, birds, fish, lizards, and even trees. Contact with these spirits was made by spirit mediums or "shamans"— spiritual practitioners who had direct, if sporadic, access to the spirit world. Gebusi religion centered on animism and shamanism, suggested to be the oldest forms of human spiritual belief. However, Gebusi religion is now dominantly influenced by Christianity, a major world religion. Historically, world religions such as Islam, Buddhism, Judaism, Hinduism, and Confucianism, like Christianity, have been associated with state kingdoms or empires. Many of these religions boast a spirit world that is centralized or monotheistic, focusing ultimately on a single God or creative force. Such major world religions, often associated with the spread of external influence or domination, have become more influential in recent decades, including in remote areas such as the New Guinea rainforest. Although it once was thought that religions would decline as the world became more modern, the reverse is perhaps now just as likely. At Nomad as well as in many countries, including the United States, the growth of religion has been connected with politics and political interests. Government officials were among the strongest proponents of Christianity and among its strongest leaders. Christianity was even taught as a subject in the Nomad school—just as the teachers often read scripture or gave sermons on Sunday in church. More generally, connections are easily made between the local force of the State, a national or international church, and broader processes of being or becoming modern.

In the process, however, world religions are themselves shaped by the history and beliefs of different cultures. At Nomad, Catholicism, Protestantism, and Seventh Day Adventism are very different from how they are practiced in Western countries at the same time that they all remain strongly Christian. People often find ways to assert organic or homemade versions of spiritual and aesthetic expression even as—and even because—external structures and institutions impact them. These responses include personal experiences that are deeply meaningful and "effervescent," though they may not be religious in formal terms. One day, quite unexpectedly, I found this myself in the new community of Gasumi Corners. This is what I wrote in my field notes:

> Today by my house, I had little idea what hit me. The breeze sent a faint melody, beautiful and haunting, apparently from afar. I had never heard anything like it. I went magnetically toward the music, but I found no houses in its direction. "You want to hear the singing," Kilasui said, and he pointed me down the path. It led from the village to seemingly nowhere, but the music grew louder. Its sound was stunning and yet different from the séance songs of old. I wound through the brush to a small fire with breadfruit warming next to it. No one was there, but the music was now full all around me. I looked up. Smiling down like nymphs on high were seven radiant boys smothering each other in soft harmony.
>
> I drew irresistibly up into their tree, its white branches grown as if they knew where each step should be placed. It swayed with my weight, shaking with gentle laughs that echoed the boys themselves. They squealed in delight to have a gawky grown companion, white as their tree, take interest in their singing. Their antics and my own soon brought the attention of other children, some of whom also clambered into the tree and distributed themselves carefully, as if to steady a wobbly ship. Even without their hubbub, our actions could not have gone unnoticed. I now looked down to see a gathered crowd of women, yet more children, and even Sayu, who grinned up at me through the foliage. Their happiness, mine, and that of the boys made its own harmony, suspended in air with their song.

I had several indescribable minutes in that tree—the kind that convince you to the bone that you've done the right thing to go so far, that you have reached an enjoyment and a bonding that transcends culture and that words cannot express. The sky was bluest blue, a cool breeze laced the melody, and I looked out thinking I had captured the innocence and joy of forest peoples that others wrote about so nostalgically in decades past. I cannot fully share or reproduce that nostalgia; there are too many complexities, uncertainties, and problems for that. But those stolen moments of innocence, full and beautiful, when one finds oneself inexplicably a young boy again drawn up in a tree, caressed in a sea of angelic smiles, tender harmony, and rainforest awe, can be neither denied nor suppressed. These are moments that make life not just worth living, but a thousand times over. If music marks the sound of the soul and the wheels of time, the songs of the Gebusi present are as rich as their spiritual past.

BROADER CONNECTIONS: *Sociocultural and Religious Change*

- **Cultural change** is as **old as humanity** but it has **intensified with globalization** during the past 500 years and **especially during the latter part of the 20th century.**

- Like many people in remote areas, **Gebusi cultural change** included **pacification of** local peoples (such as the Bedamini) and introduction of metal tools and western clothing.

- In contrast to **colonized peoples in many areas,** there is little evidence that Gebusi had themselves been subject to **coercion or violence from Westerners, land alienation, taxation, forced labor, cash cropping, labor migration, or religious conversion by missionaries, religious zealots, or other colonial agents.**

- After the Gebusi from Yibihilu moved to near the **Nomad Subdistrict Station,** they experienced aspects of modern change shared by many peoples, including adoption of a world religion (Christianity), schooling, and a local market where items were bought with money.

- Cultural loss is a trend shared by many peoples. Among Gebusi this included the general decline of longhouse living, shamanism or spirit mediumship, sorcery accusations, initiations, and of general emphasis on *kog-wa-yay* or "good company."

- Becoming **"modern"** often entails **desire for quick material progress** over time. A new concern with temporal progress was also evident among Gebusi.

- Modern developments are often associated with **increasing intrusion or authority by external authority figures.** Among Gebusi, these included **external church leaders, government officials,** and **police,** and, in some ways, the **ultimate power of "Papa God."**

- **Modern development can include selected positive changes.** Among Gebusi, this included **a reduction of the rate of killing to zero since 1989.**

- After Uwano died, his body was **buried in a Christian funeral without a sorcery inquest.**

- Many peoples exhibit resilient or resistant forms of local expressive culture. Among Gebusi, these included **local singing by boys and young men.**

- When a cultural anthropologist **returns to the field,** as happened to Bruce, his or her **connections to local people often expand and enrich.**

CHAPTER 8

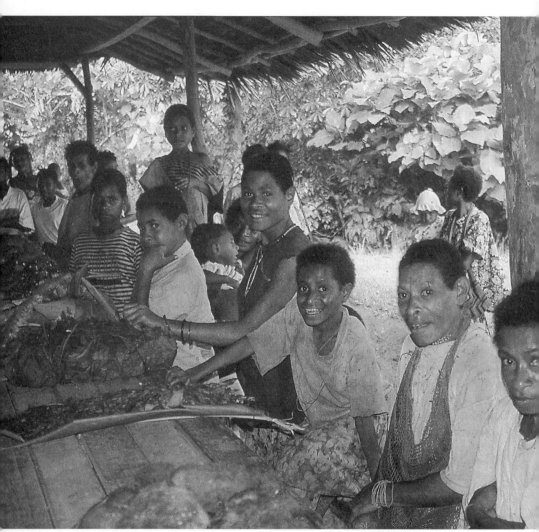

Women waiting to sell their produce at the Nomad market. (PHOTO: Bruce Knauft)

Pennies and Peanuts, Rugby and Radios

BOSAP WAS NOT HAPPY. The market was winding down, and her piles of bananas and sweet potatoes lay primped for sale like wallflowers that everyone saw but nobody wanted. The other women were similarly forlorn; their produce was still competing with Bosap's on the sellers' tables. Thinking to make light of the situation as well as to collect more information, I tried to view her glass as half full: "You sold at least a little, right? Maybe two or three sales at 10 cents each?" Bad questions, bad timing. Bosap's normally congenial features, already sober, flashed to a scowl. "Not interested," she said, and turned away. She had sold nothing.

So, too, in her life, Bosap had been passed over, though she usually took everything in stride. As she had laughingly said when I talked to her before, "No man wanted to marry me. But then, I didn't want to marry any of them, either!" Among the Gebusi, Bosap had the rare distinction of becoming an older woman, now in her mid-fifties, without ever having married. When she had been in her thirties, this hadn't stopped her from having a sexual affair with a young man in his late teens. It had created a scandal when Bosap became pregnant, but she had carried on with determination. She did not marry her young lover, who had not yet been initiated, nor any of his older clan-mates, who could have been willing to claim the infant boy and take Bosap as a second wife and domestic helper. Instead, Bosap raised Kuma by herself, with the help of her own kin. It was the pride of her life that Kuma had become a strong and decent young man who was now almost ready himself to be married. As long as I had known her, Bosap had maintained both her pleasant disposition and her ultimate determination to go her own way. Her good-spiritedness was attested by the fact that, even as an "old woman," she had never been suspected of sorcery in previous years, in contrast to many other older women in Gasumi Corners.

Because Bosap was usually friendly, I was caught off guard by her reply to my remark at the market. Bad sales were a touchy personal issue, and there were few buyers—mostly government officials and their wives from the Nomad Station. Nevertheless, women from Gasumi Corners and other communities continued to laboriously take their best produce to market in hopes of selling it. At dawn on Tuesdays and

117

Fridays, they packed their foodstuffs in cavernous net bags and hauled them across the Hamam River and down the muddy path to the Nomad market. Even on a "good day," many women came back loaded down with the same food they had brought. And prices were low. For the equivalent of 60 cents, a buyer could purchase a large bunch of ripe bananas, a pile of shelled Tahitian chestnuts, and a bundle of cooked bamboo shoots. Even at that, few people aside from government workers and pastors had money to spend on food, and their own wages were small, erratic, and undependably paid. But local women kept bringing food to sell, twice each week. The market was their way to have at least a small place in a cash economy.

Wanting some insight into this dynamic, I tried to find just how much food the women brought to market, how much they took back or gave away, how much they sold, and how much money they earned. As I realized from my encounter with Bosap, however, this was going to be tricky. Women were reluctant to disclose their many failures and even their few successes—for fear of jealousy. Only a very few of them could actually add up the value of the coins they received in any event, and they quickly shoved their proceeds into tightly wadded bundles. When transactions did occur, they were downplayed or shielded from public view. A purchaser would have the exact change ready and pay in a lump rather than publicly count coins. Sometimes, he or she would saunter behind the table, make the purchase privately, and furtively sweep the food into a net bag before walking away. Because prices for each pile of food were standardized, there was no need for bargaining or even, in many cases, talking at all.

In typical fieldwork fashion, I discovered this etiquette by unintentionally violating it. I had been pleased to see so many new foods for sale at the first market I attended. Wanting to stimulate the local economy and to obtain some items for my own dinner, I approached a woman who had bamboo shoots for sale. Lacking pocket change, I pawed through my various pockets and found that the smallest currency I had was a 2-kina bill. As I extended this to her across the table, I could see the color drain from her face. Though worth only one U.S. dollar, the bill was ten times the price of the shoots I was buying. The poor woman had neither the arithmetic nor the coins to make change. So she was forced to initiate a confusing chain of inquiries that rippled in domino effect through all the people around her. Ten-cent loans and other transfers of coins ricocheted through the crowd. After several long and awkward minutes, my requisite 90 cents in change was amassed and dutifully counted for me—as everyone looked on. By this time, I had half a mind to let the unfortunate women simply keep the change. Except for two things. First, I would be wildly undermining the standards of the market, which were predicated on fixed and standardized prices for each pile of food. Second, my transaction had attracted the attention of perhaps half of the 200 or so people at the market. Setting a precedent of overpayment could have jacked up the cost of my future purchases by as much as 900 percent! So I smiled gamely and apologized pleasantly, trying not to call yet more attention to my gaffe.

How much is a dime worth at Nomad? The episode reminded me of how cultural meanings, rules, and assumptions—whole worlds of understanding—may underlie the smallest of material exchanges. Back in the United States, I walk into a store and don't give a second thought to the impersonality of buying an item from a stranger, handing over money in public, receiving change, and of having other people witness it. However, this presumes a set of market assumptions that Gebusi and their neighbors were just beginning to confront. But—and this is the more important point—Gebusi were *more* rather than less motivated to engage in market transactions even though, and, indeed, in some ways for the very reason that, their skills and confidence seemed undeveloped. Notwithstanding the embarrassment of my conduct at the market, the woman I bought produce from had earned not just my 10 cents but the prestige of selling to an outsider who had money. Of all the sellers with bundles of bamboo shoots, I happened to have chosen hers. She and her kin now had the ownership, presumably collective, of not just some coins but a 2-kina bill that was received very publicly. Notwithstanding its awkwardness, the transaction also conveyed value, which I judged from the grinning palaver of the woman's kin as I walked away. If I had unwittingly trampled on local etiquette, I had also unwittingly reinforced larger assumptions of a market economy: that monetary exchange is at once public, impersonal, and prestigious.

Being either a good or a bad ethnographer (sometimes it is hard to know which is which!), I became increasingly interested in determining what market women at Nomad actually accomplished. Like the churches, the Nomad school, and the local sports league, the market is an interethnic affair—people come to it from various sides or "corners" of Nomad. These corners are inhabited by persons with different ethnic or tribal affiliations. As such, women from Gasumi Corners form only a small fraction of those at the market. But because they were from my own core community, I decided to keep them as my focus.

The first and easiest thing to discern was that most of the sellers were, in fact, women. By counting the sellers from Gasumi Corners on twenty-five different market days, I found that over 91 percent of them (285 of 313) were female. This paralleled my rough sense of the percentage of female sellers attending from other communities and ethnic groups. Although men and boys also came to the market, they seldom sold anything; they tended to converse with one another around the periphery of the selling area. Occasionally, they would saunter down the aisle of selling tables under the market's large thatched roof. And once in a while, they would buy a pile of peanuts for a dime. But the center of action—or lack thereof— was the women and their sales. All the women from Gasumi Corners participated; each would gather her best foodstuffs and bring them to market an average of once every ten days. In all, the market was the prime place for village women to conduct business—a place to be modern. Women also went to church, of course. And girls had become students along with boys at the Nomad Community School. Only at the market, however, were women not merely present but the dominant and central focus of attention. Though they tended to be quiet and retiring rather than talkative or aggressive, they did visit casually with their female kin and relatives, including women from other villages or communities.

How much money did women actually earn at the Nomad market? I couldn't easily ask them, but I found that I could count the piles of food they initially placed on the selling tables. As the market progressed, I could stroll casually up and down the aisles, chat with the women and note which piles of food had been reduced by sales and in what amounts. Because prices were standardized, it wasn't hard to determine how much the women had sold by the end of the market. Women who were lucky enough to have sold several items were willing to clarify, if I was unsure, how many units they had sold.

Over the course of twenty-five market days, I found that Gebusi women sold less than half the food that they brought to the market for sale. The rest was carried back home or given away. The women's average individual earnings per market day was 20 cents—for selling food weighing several pounds or more. More than 20 percent of the women who brought food to market on a given day sold nothing at all.

The inflated price of the things that could be bought at Nomad's tiny home-front stores underscored the challenge of the women's enterprise. The benchmark goods were 2-pound bags of rice and 12-ounce tins of low-grade fish. Each of these cost the equivalent of $1.50. This meant that the average woman's market sales from almost an entire month were wiped out by buying a single small bag of rice or a single tin of fish. Comparing the nutritional value of the rice or fish against the many hours and calories required to raise the food and haul it to market, it was obvious that the energy cost of women's marketing far outweighed the benefits gained from it. In this sense, Gebusi women's market activity seemed irrational. Why would they put more time and effort into an enterprise than they get out of it? This question grew poignant as I saw women from Gasumi Corners repeatedly hauling food to market and waiting aimlessly to sell it.

The onus seemed greatest for two young adolescent girls, Danksop and Waygo, who would sit wooden or sighing behind their piles of food for hour after hour. But the answer to my question was one that I should have realized all along. In a word: culture. As we ourselves know from the things we buy, there is much more to a purchase—and more to the work that pays for it—than the trade-off between the dollars we spend and the functional use of what we get. Why do we prefer a Ferrari to a Ford, Godiva chocolate to Hershey's, or a gold ring to one made of tin? Similarly, why do the Gebusi prefer a small bag of rice to a dozen pounds of potatoes? The answer is the same in both cases: items of value afford prestige and cultural status. If Gebusi marketing seems "irrational," it carries the value and prestige of earning money, of being modern. And it does this for those who are otherwise most shut out of the local cash economy: village women. If men obtain occasional paid work—cutting the grass on the airstrip, doing odd jobs for government officials, or acting as carriers for visitors on a trek—women earn coins at the market.

❧   ❧   ❧

I realized the cumulative significance of women's marketing when I found my "banker" in Gasumi Corners. Nolop was the cleverest old woman in the settlement. On the way back from the market one day, I joked that though I had money, it was difficult to buy things—I had bills but not enough coins. At the next turn in the path, Nolop quietly motioned me away from the others. "I've got coins," she said. "Come to my house." We then continued to our respective homes. After stowing my things, I walked back to her little dwelling. As I did so, I remembered her personal history. This was as colorful as it was fascinating—and helped explain her desire to exchange coins for my bills. I knew Nolop well from 1980–82; she had lived in the house that was second closest to our own at Yibihilu. At that time, she had been married to the easygoing Wosip and raising two boys. She had also been a bold character. Not only had Nolop been caught having a sexual affair with the uninitiated Doliay, but she was also the only Gebusi woman we ever knew about who had dabbled in the otherwise all-male art of shamanism.

Since we had left in 1982, Nolop had endured much. The cyst on her right wrist had grown larger, and it became hard for her to use her hand. About 1990, her oldest, cherished son had been gored to death by a wild pig. Almost immediately afterward, her gentle husband also died; villagers said that after his son's demise, he had lost all appetite and grieved himself to death. Nolop had been left with her remaining son plus a younger daughter, Kwelam. Shortly thereafter Kwelam became seriously ill from a bone deformity in her hip. But Nolop was as tough as she was smart—always ready with a witty smirk and an astute way to solve a problem. She had somehow finagled the medical officer at the Nomad Aid Post to have Kwelam flown out to the Kiunga Hospital for an operation—along with Nolop herself. While in Kiunga, without money or kin, Nolop had had to rummage in garbage heaps for daily scraps of food. Lacking a blouse or bra, she had felt the powerful stigma of going bare-breasted in town and had scrounged for rags to cover herself. Despite these abasements, Nolop had cared for Kwelam until she recovered and they could both be flown back to Nomad, at government expense. Today, Kwelam walks with a limp but is otherwise healthy, and she seems to be one of the happiest girls in the village. Nolop's surviving son, Damya, is now married and has an infant daughter of his own. He is one of the most decent lay leaders in the Nomad Catholic Church and also a lead singer in the community's string band chorus.

As Nolop saw her children grow up successfully, she felt pressure to marry the widower Gono—the silent, wiry man who had been one of our carriers during our first foray into Gebusi territory. Perhaps she had found him a useful partner at the time. As he aged, however, Gono became crotchety, and he resented his wife's feisty wit and lack of deference. On more than one occasion in 1998, he beat Nolop. As an unusual stigma, Gono was criticized for his actions by both the men and the women of Gasumi Corners.

Quite her own person, Nolop went her own way; though she still lived in Gono's small house, she kept her affairs to herself. These included her earnings from the market, which she squirreled away without telling him. Although most wives try to keep their market money at least nominally to themselves, it tends to become part of the household economy and subject to the decisions of their husbands, especially if the proceeds accrue over time. Women earn money with painful slowness, but men typically decide how any larger sum will be spent. That said, women took pride in the knowledge that their hard-earned funds pay for prestigious tins of fish and bags of rice at community feasts—though their husbands presented these gifts and took credit for them. Even if they keep their own money, many Gebusi women were uncomfortable or embarrassed to make significant purchases by themselves at one of the Nomad stores.

By dint of personal will, however, Nolop had kept her small earnings to herself and for her own children. And she had wisely focused on raising and marketing peanuts, which were the one item that sold most widely and regularly at the market, even though it was not the splashiest or most prestigious thing to sell. Week after week, Nolop sold little piles of peanuts from her big bag. And over time, her 10-cent sales added up. After we were safely in her house, Nolop smiled wryly and carefully unwrapped several unobtrusive bundles. To my amazement, pile upon pile of coins poured out. She didn't know how much she had earned. When I counted up her earnings, they totaled more than 40 kina, or 20 dollars. This was equivalent to two hundred sales of 10 cents apiece at the market—approximately two years of market sales for the average woman of Gasumi Corners.

With easy trust, Nolop was delighted to give me the bulk of her coins in exchange for two of my crisp 20-kina bills. Everyone knew that the bright red pigs head money, as it was called, was the biggest and most important currency that circulated at Nomad. That Nolop now had two of these bills seemed to give her a great sense of satisfaction. As she carefully tucked them away, we both knew that she could use them however she wished. And they would be easier to conceal from others' prying eyes than her piles of coins had been. Perhaps Nolop would contribute unexpectedly to a major feast. Or give a gift to her children. Or buy something extraordinary at a special time. As for me, I now had all the coins I needed. As I walked home, I tried to carry my stash in my own net bag as unobtrusively as possible. I smiled at the thought that an economy of new money could, at least on rare occasions, benefit both a Gebusi woman and an outsider—without compromising the integrity of either. The economy of money in Gasumi Corners was paltry and in many ways unproductive, but its economy of culture was strong and important.

My experience with Nolop got me thinking about how women's relations with men were changing. If the Gebusi market underscored the hopeful and compromised role of women in a fledgling cash economy, it was complemented by their new role in other spheres. The Christian churches had given women a new sense of spiritual participation, even though men were ultimately in charge. Other institutions and activities at Nomad also reflected gendered change while simultaneously providing new forms of male dominance. These trends were particularly notable in education, in sports, and, perhaps surprisingly, in theft. But it was difficult for me to talk with women about these developments. For an unrelated man to talk with a Gebusi woman invariably implies sexual interest. Older women like Nolop and Bosap were easier for me to approach because they were no longer considered desirable as sexual partners or wives. But younger women were a different story. Even for married women in their thirties and forties, a personal interview was difficult to arrange and even more difficult to carry out. I could talk to a woman if her husband or brother was present. But then the man would reinterpret my questions and answer many of them himself.

The same was true of my attempt to talk to girls at the Nomad Community School; the boys took charge in responding. To be fair, part of the problem involved all the students. Repetitive drills and copying from the board took a toll on a class of forty, sixty, or even eighty pupils who sat cross-legged on the floor or on hardwood benches, hour upon hour. Students were not just Gebusi but came from several different language groups. Their language of instruction was that peculiar dialect of my own native tongue that is "Papua New Guinea English." After a year or two in school, students could understand this form of English fairly well. But the rote process of learning left them collectively passive and reluctant to speak. As in church, powerful outsiders controlled the expression of important knowledge. This problem was worst for the girls. To the teachers, however, the students were like the school's leaky water tank: when something new and good was imparted to them, like English language, they couldn't retain it but let it seep away.

I got my chance to break this mold when the teachers welcomed me to give guest presentations in their various classes. I tried to explore a more interactive form of teaching. Being demonstrative and something of a ham, I showed students glossy photo essays that my parents had sent me from *National Geographic*. Using the pictures as props, I talked about what it might be like to be a Tibetan pastoralist, sell crafts in Oaxaca, be a Navajo dancer, or raise ponies in the Shetland Islands. I showed them pictures of Atlanta and explained features of living in the United States. Closer to their own homes, I described my early experiences among the Gebusi, showed them photos from my first Gebusi fieldwork, and tried to get their sense of what had changed at Nomad since. The kids seemed to love my presentations. But when it came to saying much about themselves—indeed, when it came to saying much of anything that wasn't a collective repetition—they were tongue-tied. I remember asking a fifth-grade class to name pictures of things without my saying the names first. Although they knew all the words, this simple task was painfully difficult, especially for the girls. I gave one group of girls three photos of pretty flowers. I knew that they knew what they were. I coaxed them with antics and pleasantries to say the word "flowers." They wanted to say the name in the worst way; they beamed as they squirmed. But none of them could get it out. Finally, I gently leaned close so one of them could whisper very faintly in my ear, "Flowers."

Although girls from Gasumi Corners and other communities increasingly go to school, the gender gap between them and the boys is large, and girls drop out of school much more frequently than boys. In Gasumi Corners, only 12 percent of the women know *tok pisin*, the national language, as opposed to 60 percent of the men. And unlike a significant number of boys and young men, no girls from Gasumi Corners have completed elementary school.

Outside school, boys dominate in physical activity through sports. Although sports were hardly important to Gebusi in 1980–82—as opposed to ritual fighting and even warfare—competition on the ball field had since become a modern, more organized and disciplined, and less violent arena of collective male rivalry. Schoolboys from Gasumi Corners avidly play rugby and soccer. As they get older, they join community teams that play on the Nomad ball field for much of each weekend. The games are interethnic occasions at which several hundred spectators ring the field. But (as was also the case in ritual fighting and warfare display) women can rarely be found on the field. Indeed, they can seldom be found even on the sidelines. In contrast to the dozen or so men's matches each weekend, there is a single game of women's soccer, and this is played almost entirely by the wives and elder daughters of government officials. Women from Gasumi Corners told me quite earnestly that they would be glad for their daughters to learn how to play soccer. And they added that they would themselves be glad to go as spectators to see their daughters play. But athletic field sports have become a male province, beginning at school during recess. Few girls feel comfortable learning how to play or joining a team.

Ironically, men's dedication to sports was the ultimate solution to my difficulties in talking more earnestly with Gebusi women. After several sun-bleached weekends of watching game after game of rugby and soccer, I got bored. It wasn't that I disliked sports. When I was younger, I enjoyed playing and watching a wide range of sports, and I had even been a starter for my high school soccer team in the Connecticut state finals. But I didn't enjoy seeing game after game from the sidelines, and this didn't fit my notion of fieldwork with Gebusi. Since watching and playing sports were important to Gebusi men and boys, my hours of watching did yield insights. These concerned their style of gentlemanly competition on the field and the caliber of their play (which was surprisingly good, even in bare feet) and their dynamics of spectatorship. Men in the crowd interacted across community and ethnic lines without the expectations of hospitality, etiquette, or reciprocity that attended formal visits between settlements. Having uncovered these patterns, however, I still felt apathetic. So one fine Sunday afternoon, I just stayed home.

Predictably, the men and boys were all at the Nomad ballgames. But I quickly realized that this left the women alone back in the village for a few precious hours. Away from their husbands, brothers, and older male children, women's talk became freer and more relaxed. I found that I could interview women fairly easily as long as some of their female relatives were also present. It turned out that most of the women were eager to participate in my "talk-work" sessions. It helped that I had brought special trade goods for women that were otherwise hard to get—including dresses, bras, and costume jewelry. I had known that the bras and jewelry would be hard to find in bulk in Papua New Guinea, so I brought stocks of these with me from the United States. I can still remember the look on the saleswoman's face in the Dollar Store in Atlanta when I heaped fifteen inexpensive bras into my shopping basket along with mounds of cheap costume jewelry. Sensing that I should somehow "explain myself," I had said to her, without thinking carefully, that I was buying gifts for my many female friends in the rainforest. Aghast at the implications of my statement, I gulped as I guessed what she must be thinking. But it all turned out fine. The sales clerk was Malaysian, and she knew a good bit about rainforest peoples, the difficulty of obtaining trade goods in remote areas, and the politics of gift giving. In fact, she ended up advising me which bras were most likely to fit the short but sometimes well-endowed women of Gasumi Corners. I came away with a fresh understanding about crossing cultural boundaries with women—in Atlanta as well as in New Guinea.

Back in Gasumi Corners, the women greatly appreciated the goods I had brought. I talked with each individually as primary interviewees—listening to the woman's life history and getting her opinions and reflections on various subjects. Particularly with less articulate women, their female kin and friends chimed in with helpful promptings, clarifications, and elaborations. Young women and adolescent girls remained the toughest to talk with. Even when asked by a not-so-young and weirdly acceptable male such as myself, and even with other women there supporting them, their responses were often only shuffling feet, embarrassment, and blank looks. I tried to ask what kind of man would make a good husband. Or if they would like to see their own future daughters-to-be go to school. But their charged status as eligible young women overwhelmed their responses. Discussing positive characteristics of a potential husband implied a young woman's embarrassing preference for one or another young man in the village. Talking about unborn children awkwardly implied that she herself was almost mature enough to be a mother. Nonetheless, all the women, even the younger ones, maintained their desire to work with me. This was partly because the other women were also doing it, and perhaps partly because my interest and history in the community provoked a sense of obligation on their part. But mostly, I think, they wanted the trade goods that I gave them at the end of the sessions.

The final link in my investigation of gendered change—across developments in church, the market, school, sports, and domestic relations—concerned the heightened yearnings of women and men for modern goods and a modern way of life. During the latter part of my fieldwork, I sponsored a contest in which Nomad schoolchildren drew pictures of how they envisaged themselves in the future. I was amazed how eagerly and effectively they took up this task, not to mention the high quality of their drawings. Burgeoning on the pages were full-color pictures of the children in modern walks and ways of life. Boys drew themselves as heavy machine operators, pilots, doctors, and even as an actor or newsman. Girls drew themselves especially as nurses, teachers, or housewives in nice Western dresses. It was significant to me that girls as well as boys drew themselves in highly modern futures. A few actually drew themselves as living in a Christian heaven. By contrast, very few students—just 6 percent of the boys and 5 percent of the girls—drew their future selves conducting traditional livelihoods such as gardening, hunting, or fishing.

The optimism of the children notwithstanding, it seemed that many of their desires were unrealistic. It was very unlikely that many or perhaps any of them would be able to achieve the future lives they envisaged; the economy of Nomad is too paltry and education too limited. What will happen to the frustrated expectations of young people as their aspirations are dashed?

If gender does not divide the modern aspirations of young people at Nomad, one important contrast does emerge. Virtually half the boys envisaged their future as gun-wielding members of the Papua New Guinea Defense Force or the National Police. That boys gravitated to images and roles of forceful power is not surprising but does bear new implications in the modern context of Papua New Guinea. In a local world where manufactured goods and commodities are increasingly desired—and expected—frustrated aspirations can fuel the temptation to forcefully possess such items, especially for young men. Theft has been an increasing problem across much of Papua New Guinea. Back at Yibihilu in 1981, people had craved our Western commodities, but we had never feared having them stolen. Living so communally, Gebusi had made a virtue of necessity by respecting each other's property and sharing things with others. By my second fieldwork, however, things had changed. Villagers were more possessive with their Western goods, and money was increasingly important, and private. At the same time, activities at Nomad entailed interaction with many strangers—and potential thievery. Families became concerned about theft, and their desire mounted for chains, locks, and metal boxes. In the Nomad police register, theft was the most frequently reported offense—almost twice as common as any other crime. And most of these thefts were both made by and targeted against young men. Though theft at Nomad was only a small problem when compared to Papua New Guinea's larger towns and cities, it was still a focus of real concern.

During the months I was there, the biggest case involved the theft of two boom box radios from the Nomad Community School. Boom boxes had become a major icon of modern identity at Nomad, especially for young men. They referenced a prestigious world of commodities and accomplishment, of fluent speech in *tok pisin* or English, of rock music, and of sexual allure. The radios in question were also important signs of modernity for the school. In addition to playing music and tapes, the players broadcast national education programs in classrooms each morning. Throughout the country, students were presumed to listen in class at predetermined times to educational radio programs for their grade level.

Given their significance, the theft of the school boom boxes was a blow to the modern integrity and prestige of the Nomad community—and it highlighted young men's frustrated desire for prestigious commodities in and around the station. At a large public meeting, officials harangued villagers and criticized them for letting local boys get away with such an awful crime. If the trend continued, they warned, schoolteachers would not want to live and work at Nomad. They suggested that maybe the school itself would have to be shut down. Given a general shortage of teachers and funds, this was a very real threat, and many village schools in the Nomad Subdistrict are shut down due to lack of instructors or of money to pay them. If the central station at Nomad itself was going to be a "bad" place, a place of theft and "backsliding," officials continued, airplanes bringing supplies might stop landing at Nomad Station altogether. As the cause of this ominous scenario, villagers and young men in particular were disparaged as untrustworthy and deceitful, sinful and un-Christian. It was the villagers own fault that Nomad would continue as a place of economic and moral backwardness. As in church, some villagers hung their heads.

The theft of the radios reflected the difficulty of becoming modern in a place like Nomad. Institutions such as the churches, market, and school have brought people together in new ways and in the service of new endeavors. But they create an increasingly impersonal world. This world is marked by new inequalities and resentments, for instance, between government workers who can afford boom boxes and villagers who cannot. Particularly for young men who are unable to earn a modern living and achieve its way of life, pressure mounts to simply take what they can—to resort to force and to reject the slow, frustrating process of becoming modern through tedious and often fruitless effort. The problem of crime has become a major blight in the larger towns and cities of Papua New Guinea, as it has in urban areas of many countries. In 1998, this problem was small in comparative terms but important and revealing at Nomad.

These issues link us back to the role and significance of gender in culture change. If local men used to control indigenous means of violence, access to the spirit world, and the prestige of public festivity, their authority and sometimes their dignity can be undercut by modern status inequalities and impoverishment vis-à-vis powerful outsiders and authority figures. In some cases, these tensions are redirected by men back on local women—as was the case of Gono beating Nolop, his economically successful wife.

If local modern institutions afford women the potential for greater and more active participation than they had in the past, they can also threaten masculinity and increase the tensions that young men face in the pursuit of modern forms of prestige and success. At Nomad, men's preeminence and growing impatience—in school, athletics, church, and government activities—seem to contrast with the activities of most Gebusi women. In this regard, patient market women such as Nolop and Bosap form a counterpoint to younger and more restless desires, particularly among men, for quicker and more forceful routes to economic success.

※　　　※　　　※

BROADER CONNECTIONS: *Markets, Development, and Modern Aspirations*

- As is the case with many peoples, modern changes among the Gebusi include **increasing interaction with persons outside the area** as well as those from **other ethnic groups**.

- **Modern activities and institutions** that are common globally, including among Gebusi, include: **government schooling, going to church, sports leagues for men, and twice-weekly markets** (at which women are the primary sellers).

- In contrast to indigenous **gift-exchange**, modern **market exchange**—as reflected at the **Nomad market**—is relatively **impersonal**, involving the transaction of goods between people who are often **strangers**, through the vehicle of **money**.

- Like women in many world areas, **Gebusi women** were highly motivated to **invest time and effort in market activity.** Indeed, their **investment was more than what they received back in money.** This reflects **modern cultural values and prestige** influencing people's engagement with a modern cash economy.

- The **status of women** among Gebusi has **increased** in the sense that **women participate meaningfully** in modern institutions and activities such **as church, school, and the market. However, gender dominance takes on new dimensions;** women's education, church leadership, and economic control are significantly less than men's. In this sense, **modern development can be a double-edged sword for women's status.**

- As is often the case in developing countries, **education through formal schooling was important but compromised** at Nomad, with large classes and difficulty of educational advancement, **especially for girls.**

- As reflected in drawings of their anticipated adult selves, **children** at the Nomad School, like in many contexts cross-culturally, **desired to have successful modern futures.** However, most of these desires were **unrealistic** and unlikely to be fulfilled.

- As is the case for many peoples, Gebusi activities at school, market, the government, and even church reflected **a growing sense of national identification and nation-building.**

- The **theft of the school radios at Nomad** reflects much about **frustrated economic aspiration, marginality, and the stigmatizing of undeveloped peoples in the context of external authority, control, and power.**

- It is not uncommon for young men, such as those in the Nomad area, to **compensate for lack of economic success** through **theft and/or domination of women.** These trends are not yet strong among Gebusi, but they are significant.

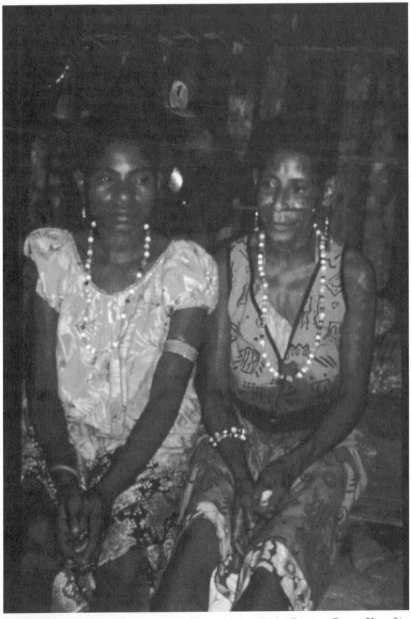

CHAPTER 9

Two women from Gasumi Corners at a village dance, 1998. (Photo: Bruce Knauft)

Mysterious Romance, Marital Choice

HE ALWAYS SEEMED TO ME as spare with his words as he was decent and direct in his actions. He was clearly troubled, so I asked him in. He came inside and hesitated, strong young man that he was, until the urgency of his question overcame his embarrassment. "Do you have any *adameni?* I would really like some." I had no idea what he was talking about, so I asked him what *adameni* was. He stammered and continued on: "*Adameni* is something special. It has to do with an unmarried woman and an unmarried man. When they really like each other and think of coming together." I still had no idea. Whatever adameni was, it related to sexual desire between young people. Wayabay was the oldest of the bachelors, and he was actively trying to find a wife. But what was *adameni?* I wracked my brain. Whatever *adameni* was, it was important to Wayabay. I was as concerned as I was curious.

Could Wayabay be asking me for a condom? I knew that he had worked for a trail-clearing crew a few years back and that he had been out to the town of Kiunga. He had a wider scope of knowledge and experience than many of the young men. Perhaps he was now in a romantic liaison and wanted to protect either himself or the girl. This would explain his embarrassment. Although Wayabay seemed too proper a young man to be involved in a casual sexual affair, I had certainly been surprised in the past by the public revelation of Gebusi sexual trysts. So I tried, gently, to describe a condom in the Gebusi vernacular: "There is this thing that men wear when they have sex. Is this like *adameni?*" Wayabay replied, "Well, maybe. I'm not sure." My unease was mounting, but I forged ahead: "This is something that a man puts over his 'thing,' his phallus. It stretches like rubber. He puts this rubber thing over his phallus before he has sex. He has sex with the woman but his 'thing' doesn't touch the woman's 'thing.'"

Now it was Wayabay's turn to be uncomprehending—and mine to be embarrassed. I tried to explain that men can use these rubber coverings when they don't want the woman to get pregnant or when they worry about getting sick from having sex. All of which sounded no better and, indeed, much worse when spoken in Gebusi. Wayabay shook his head vehemently; this was definitely NOT *adameni*.

131

In despair, we invited Sayu and Didiga into our conversation. Both of them spoke a smattering of English, and both had had more schooling than Wayabay. I mentally cursed myself for not knowing what *adameni* was—this term that was obviously so important in Gebusi sexual culture and that I hadn't uncovered during all my time with them. But Sayu and Didiga had no better luck finding a translation or an explanation. Yes, they said, *adameni* was something for a man. And, yes, it had to do with sex. It also had something do to with *oop*, the generic Gebusi word for "slippery, milky substance" that was especially associated with semen.

Sex. Men. Semen. I was stymied. Could they be referring to some custom or substance having to do with traditional practices of sex between men? This would certainly explain Wayabay's embarrassment. Perhaps he was having sexual relations with one or another young man before finding a wife. I took another deep breath. "Does this *adameni* have to do with Gebusi sex customs between men?" They looked puzzled, so I persisted: "Does it have to do with old-time Gebusi customs? You know, the sex custom in your initiations in which the adolescent boy strokes the phallus and swallows the semen of the man—so he can grow big and achieve more manhood."

Culturally speaking, I had dropped a bomb. Their mouths hung open in disbelief, and their faces grew ashen. Sayu finally broke their silence: "Did our fathers and boys really do that? In the olden times? Did they? Really?!"

Double ouch. I had been terribly rash. Although the three of them had all grown up in a world of male banter and horseplay, none of them, I now realized, had been initiated; the final initiation ceremony had been held before they would have been old enough. They had never been indoctrinated into sexual relations with other men. Given the community's conversion to Christianity, it was quite possible that they had never been told about the practice. Perhaps my companions had suspected or wondered about men's sexual customs. But perhaps not. Against their ignorance, I had asserted the reality of a strange sexual practice, a custom that was hard to believe and that seemed really distasteful to them. I had divulged a secret of my own generation and had shocked them. I felt awful. But I also felt that I had to answer them truthfully: "Yes, that is the custom that men and initiated teenagers followed at Yibihilu when I was first here."

After shaking their heads in disbelief, they stressed, as if it needed emphasis, that *adameni* had nothing whatsoever to do with sex between one man and another. *Adameni* was for use between men and women. This was the only sex that the three of them knew or cared about. What about *oop*? This wasn't semen. The *adameni* liquid was thick and viscous, but it smelled sweet and tasted good. It was something that a man would dab about his eyes. When a woman looked at him, she would find him irresistible. *Adameni* was evidently some kind of love potion. White people knew all about *adameni*, they continued. In fact, they said, it came from whites and not from Papua New Guineans. Wayabay had heard about *adameni* from men who had been with white people at a logging camp in another part of the province. The potion came in a bottle and was quite expensive. But the whites said that it really worked to attract women. The bottles of *adameni* had a picture of a naked man and woman on the label—just as described in the Bible.

White people. Nakedness. Bible. Irresistible sexual attraction. Eureka! *Adameni* wasn't a Gebusi word after all; no wonder I hadn't known it! Their accent and intonation had thrown me completely off. It was a Western sexual idea. *Adameni* was "Adam and Eve." It was a love potion that unscrupulous traders to the south had peddled at inflated prices in bottles featuring pictures of biblical sex and lovely sin. Wayabay wanted *adameni* to attract a woman. As a quiet and hard-working but traditional young man, he felt that he needed a modern love potion to gain a wife.

My companions persisted. Did I have any *adameni?* And if not, could I get any for them? Though I now understood their question, it still wasn't easy to answer. The three of them believed in this love magic, almost desperately in Wayabay's case. I had already deeply embarrassed both them and myself. I recalled the anthropological theory that holds magic to be an exercise in spiritual confidence boosting. The idea is that magic reduces uncertainty and instills faith in one's actions, like a baseball player who fingers a lucky charm as he steps up to the plate. For a moment, I thought of enhancing Wayabay's confidence with women by giving him some scented skin cream to dab some on his cheekbones. But I quickly dismissed this as a bad idea: I had already caused enough confusion for one day! So I said I didn't have any real *adameni*. Disappointed but at least in mutual comprehension, we finished our conversation, and they left.

If Gebusi culture had been hard for me to learn in 1980, I realized that its changes could still chew up my seasoned understandings and have plenty of spit left over. I was still challenged, surprised, and sometimes again at sea. During my absence of sixteen years, young Gebusi men had gone from actively and proudly having sex with one another to apparently not even knowing about the practice. Could this really be? Maybe my young friends had suspected or been vaguely aware of the custom from their boyhood years. But if they hadn't been directly exposed to or told about it, their knowledge would have been hazy. Compare it with our own knowledge of sexual practices among those who preceded us—for instance, our typically vague knowledge of the different types of sexual intimacy that our own parents may have had when we were young or before we were born. Like many peoples, the Gebusi distinguish carefully between things that they have witnessed or been told about directly and those that are only rumored and uncertain. In this sense, Wayabay, Sayu, and Didiga had probably not known about sex between Gebusi men. Until I had told them.

Although some cultures have a strong and deep sense of their past, the historical concern of other peoples can be shallow and weak—and Gebusi are decidedly in the latter camp. Gebusi life cycles are short. As a forty-four-year-old, I was one of the oldest men in the community. It was not uncommon for me to know more about Gebusi family ancestries, based on the genealogies and life histories that I collected in 1980–82, than it was for younger and middle-aged Gebusi. So in retrospect, the gap between my young companions' knowledge of traditional Gebusi sex practices and my own was not so surprising.

Beyond the shock and apparent unawareness of my three companions, the fact remained that their desire to attract women was now much more important than their concern with sex between men. In the past, insemination had itself been the introduction to marriage: a young man who had "become big" at the costumed initiation was attractive to women by his very presence. Within a few months, all the initiates had married. Typically, a woman would come to a new initiate of her own accord—or willingly allow herself to be claimed as his wife by his initiation sponsors. But now this custom was gone, along with the demise of initiations and much of men's social life. As I was finding out, the same was also true of women's obligations to marry through sister-exchange. Whereas more than half of women's first marriages had previously satisfied the demands of marital reciprocity, not one of the sixteen marriages in the community between 1982 and 1998 had been a sister-exchange. Although men still insisted rhetorically that their daughters and younger sisters would marry if the groom supplied a "sister" in return, the practice was moribund in fact. Correspondingly, men could no longer count on obligations of kinship and reciprocity to obtain a wife—any more than they could count on the splendor of ritual attraction. Increasingly, young men were on their own; they had to attract a wife through new and more modern forms of courtship.

Wayabay had not been successful in this regard. He was several years past the age of normal marriage and was increasingly concerned to find a wife. He was also among the small minority of young men who had not developed a keen interest in activities associated with the Nomad Station. He played soccer and rugby only intermittently and awkwardly, he would not dance to Papua New Guinea "disco music," he did not sing in the community's contemporary string band, and he had not been baptized and did not go to church. Instead, Wayabay honed his traditional skills and spent many days hunting in the forest and many hours building his house in the village. He was unusually devoted to indigenous dancing and was proud of his ability to travel to feasts and initiations in remote Gebusi villages and dance in traditional costume. In all, Wayabay was a good traditionalist born a generation too late. In this context, *adameni* was a hopeful substitute for the allure of the male initiation costume that Wayabay would never wear.

By contrast, the young Gebusi men who were most successful in attracting girlfriends and brides were those who were, for lack of a better word, more modern. They could joke with some facility in English or *tok pisin*, had been to school for at least a few years, and were more comfortable with the lifestyle associated with the Nomad Station. They managed to finagle a little money and to sport a jaunty baseball cap, sunglasses, or colorful shirt. Perhaps they even had a boom box on which they could play cassettes of rock music. They enjoyed playing rugby and soccer if not also dancing to disco music, and they appeared more at ease outside their own settlement. For Wayabay, however, being locally modern was difficult if not impossible. He could kill a wild boar in the forest but he could not shoot the modern breeze.

Even for bachelors who were relatively self-assured, modern courtship could be a stressful experience. On one occasion, Wayabay's two comrades worked up the courage to go to a disco dance on the far edge of the Nomad Station. (Wayabay himself was too reserved to go.) I decided to go with them to see what it was about. For them, it was an alluring adventure that held out the prospect of not just seeing marriageable women from another community but possibly dancing with them to disco music. This hoped-for attraction paralleled the modern romance that was sung about in cassettes and in the Gebusi's guitar-and-ukulele bands. The goal was to captivate a woman not by a display of traditional ritual but with modern confidence and aplomb—to talk to her directly and gyrate with her publicly in contemporary dance.

The risks of this endeavor stoked hesitation as well as desire. In fact, we never got to the disco. We approached it at night, stealthily, as if stalking a wild animal. We crept slowly and noiselessly down the path, the boldest in the lead. Whispered discussion ensued every few yards as to whether we should go forward with this chance for public display and humiliation. Flashlights were turned off so no one would know we were there. We strained to hear if there was any music in the distance. Eventually, however, we turned back, too nervous to proceed. During six months and despite several concerted attempts, I never did manage to attend a disco in a community on the far side of the Nomad Station.

The awkwardness of contemporary romance reflects not just new standards of courtship but also new material demands for young men—for colorful clothes, sunglasses, shoes, and boom boxes with cassettes. Failing these, men may crave a manufactured elixir with a naked man and woman on the bottle, a potion that, with just a magical splash about the eyes, could attract women. In many rural parts of the world, there is great demand for goods that convey a locally modern sense of sexual attraction. New commodities, clothes, cosmetics, and styles of using them frequently combine the allure of a modern way of life with emerging types of romantic desire. I remembered a story on National Public Radio about a Brazilian woman who canoed into the upper reaches of the Amazon and made quite a profit by selling Avon products like deodorant and makeup to Indians in the rainforest.

For young Gebusi men, the desire for modern commodities is further complicated by economic pressures to pay bride-price or bride-wealth. In the absence of sister-exchange, the brothers or fathers of young women say that they will be satisfied only with a large cash payment from the would-be groom. In some areas of the world—including parts of Africa and South Asia as well as the South Pacific—inflated demands for bride-wealth or dowry cause major problems for young people who want to get married. Fortunately for young Gebusi men, the amount of money they actually pay is comparatively low: of first marriages in Gasumi Corners between 1982 and 1998, the average bride payment was only 56 kina, or 28 dollars. But even this small amount was difficult for many young men to amass. And the demands of a prospective father-in-law or brother-in-law easily increases a groom's sense of inadequacy.

Gebusi courtship is now sandwiched between a rhetorical mandate for sister-exchange, inflated claims for bride-wealth, desire for commodities, and the demands of modern styles of social interaction. Bachelors in Gasumi Corners sometimes lamented that they would never get married. How do they find wives in fact? In large part through the idiosyncrasies of romantic attraction. In the present as in the past, a young woman and a man who are strongly attracted to each other may get married despite the objections of her father or her brothers. If romantic marriage had previously been a "minority option," it had now become the principal, if ever more stressful, way of getting married. Especially for a man, being locally modern had become an important part of this mix.

To review then, courtship and marital practices in Gasumi Corners had, by 1998, been impacted by the decline of previous customs such as initiations, sister-exchange, regular male dances, and other traditional displays of male splendor that attracted women. Young men now had a wider range of potential female partners, including at school and the Nomad station as well as other settlements and Gasumi Corners itself, but this circumstance was also stressful, especially for men such as Wayabay.

What about Gebusi women? How did they perceive the new potentials and challenges of romance and of finding a mate? In Gasumi Corners, the stresses that women are also under became poignant in the one attempt that was made to resuscitate older marriage patterns and forge a sister-exchange between two clans.

Guyul was a cheerful, strapping bachelor about twenty-one years old; his true sister was the comely and straightforward Kubwam, a mature sixteen years old and ready for marriage. On the other side was Mako, a slight young man about nineteen and his adopted "sister," the vivacious Gami, who was sixteen, full-bodied, and, if anything, readier for marriage than her elder "brother." Gami was to marry Guyul while her "brother," Mako, was to marry Guyul's sister, Kubwam.

After spicy rumors that spread throughout the village, the courtship of the two young couples became official. Following Gebusi custom, each young woman was "seized" by the wrist and led away by a male kinsman of her husband-to-be. Though this show of force conformed to the dictates of public display, neither woman resisted or tried to get away—which they could easily have done. Kubwam appeared a bit forlorn, which is considered proper etiquette for a woman taken in marriage. But Gami could hardly keep from smiling despite her presumed soberness. The four new spouses were made to sit together and were exhorted to keep their obligations to each other as husbands and wives. Much was made of the fact that the brother of Guyul's new wife was also the husband of Guyul's sister, and vice versa. It was not simply a double marriage but an exchange among the four of them. Everything was going according to plan.

The two women, Gami and Kubwam, then swapped residences across the four-minute walk that separated their husbands' respective households in Gasumi

Corners. Each extended family simultaneously gained a daughter-in-law while losing a daughter. The two mothers-in-law made special efforts to ensure that the incoming brides felt welcome and at home. I paid visits to both households and gave small gifts. With her typical pleasant reserve, Kubwam seemed comfortable in Mako's household. And Gami was practically ebullient with Guyul's family; she smiled broadly and engaged eagerly with his kin.

The first crack in the arrangement appeared after just a day and a half. Mako started spending time away from his new wife, going off with the remaining bachelors. Not yet twenty years old, Mako was still "young" to be a Gebusi husband. In sister-exchange marriages, the younger husbands sometimes took a while to settle fully into the new arrangement. In the present case, Mako's marriage was not yet consummated. But his new wife, Kubwam, continued to live in the household where he would also stay. By themselves Mako's actions represented only a small wrinkle and not a major cause for alarm.

On the other side of Gasumi Corners, Gami's relationship with Guyul got off to a rocketing start. She had been the village belle—friendly, easygoing, buxom, and with a bright, quick smile. Within a few days, Gami and her new husband "went off together" to the gardens. When they came back with moony dispositions and euphoric smiles, village gossip was ribald and irrepressible: Guyul and Gami had consummated their marriage. But this happiness did not last. Exactly what went wrong I never learned, least of all from Guyul or Gami themselves. But signals pointed to an abrupt U-turn in their sexual compatibility. Gami's disposition turned suddenly from sweetness to sourness. She wouldn't look at her husband, wouldn't work in his household, and wouldn't eat. She tried to go back to her adopted mother's home but was forced back to her husband's house. She tried again, but again she was forced back. Yet she refused to cooperate and returned yet again to her own family home. No entreaty made headway; no inquiry bore fruit. "Who knows what goes on in a young woman's heart or mind?!" "Gami is just stubborn and big-headed." "She just won't be married." "But why?" I would ask. "Just because," I was told repeatedly. "That's just the way she is."

As the hours passed, Gami's recalcitrance fueled increasing anger against her in the village. It is a very serious matter for a Gebusi woman to consummate her marriage and then to repudiate it. That a woman could have sex with a husband she had publicly accepted and then reject him after several days of romance struck at the heart of Gebusi morality. Not only was Gami's virtue on the line but also the manhood and self-esteem of her husband, Guyul. The stakes were yet higher because the marriage was a sister-exchange. Gami's rejection of Guyul also compromised the union between her "brother," Mako, and Guyul's sister, Kubwam. If her marriage dissolved, her brother's would also be forfeited.

In short order, everyone in Gasumi Corners turned against Gami. Her new husband disdained her, and her mother-in-law was incensed. Her adopted mother was even more furious, as was Mako. Her "mother" slapped her, her "brother" beat her, and she endured a barrage of verbal abuse. "What is WRONG with you?!" "You are good for NOTHING!" "Guyul is a fine man!" "You think you can 'open your skirt' to your husband and then just turn around and say you won't be married?! Huh? HUH?" "Don't you care about your 'brother'?" Don't you care about your 'mother'? No one in this village is going to protect you." "Where are you going to find a new husband? Do you think any man would want you now? Huh? HUH?" "You are alone, no one cares about you." "You can't stay here. You have no home here. You are finished."

Gami never once explained and never argued back. But she wouldn't budge, wouldn't go back to Guyul's household. As the hours mounted into a second day, the tension worsened. Women from other households took up the banner of village honor. Senior women badgered Gami in every way they could think of. Finally, Mako had had enough. He grabbed Gami and dragged her bodily out the door of his house. She shrieked and screamed, refusing to leave. Heavier and at least as strong as he, she held her ground. But as Mako grabbed one of her arms, his mother and another man took hold of the other. Gami was dragged screaming and crying, feet trailing and flailing. By the time they had hauled her fifteen feet from her house, she was covered in mud and bloody scrapes. Still she refused to cooperate. They pulled her by the hair, but she would not give in. Panting and screaming, they told her she could lie there and rot.

Then one of the senior women came over. She was a woman, here nameless, whom I otherwise liked and admired, but whom it was hard to forgive. She silently walked up to Gami, leaned down, and talked to her in low tones. Watching from my doorstep, some forty feet away, I had a sinking feeling that I knew what she was saying, and my suspicion was soon verified. It was terrible to have seen Gami being hit and dragged. But it is almost unimaginable for a young woman to be threatened with a public stripping. For Gebusi, this idea is so deeply shameful as to be a kind of social death—never forgotten, never expunged. And it is triply so for a nubile young woman. It was true that Gami had badly misjudged the game and the stakes of her marriage. Her girlish flirtation and mature body had led her to the four-sided vise of a sister-exchange. At first, she had complied willingly, even enthusiastically. But then she had come to realize that her actions were an appalling mistake that she would risk her reputation and even her life to repudiate. This new threat, however, made it too costly for her to resist any longer. A minute or two later, Gami calmly got up and walked lifelessly back to Guyul's household.

I assumed that would be the end of the story, that both unhappy marriages would remain intact. I was wrong. During the next few days, Gami stayed in Guyul's household, but she would not respond or cooperate in any meaningful way. She remained defiant, a living dead person. In exasperation, her relatives took the matter to a higher authority, the Nomad police. As chance would have it, I was in the police station studying the police register when they trooped in. The village men and a Nomad police officer sat Gami down in a chair, surrounded her, and began an inquisition. A uniformed constable took the lead: "Why won't you marry this man?" "Why did you have sex with him and then refuse him?" "Do you really want to reject your own family?" "What are you going to do if you don't stay married to Guyul?" "We can bring charges to put you in jail for immoral conduct." I thought for sure that Gami would crack.

Alone, she faced the most powerful men not just in the village but at the Nomad Station. But she refused, not just to comply but to speak. Her only words were "I don't know" and "I don't want to," as she hung her head and sobbed. Fortunately, the men did not touch or strike her. I don't know if my presence deterred them. But I was knotted up inside, frustrated at not being able to intervene. Ultimately, they gave up in desperation and returned Gami to our settlement. A public meeting was then held in Gasumi Corners. Again the invective started as people debated what steps to take next. They also aired their opinions of women's morality in the village more generally—how shameless and loose young women had become.

I had never made a formal speech at a public Gebusi meeting; I had never felt that it was my place to do so. And my mastery of the Gebusi language was never good enough for me to wrap myself in their rhetoric. But this time I felt I had no choice. I knew I couldn't change Gebusi customs, alter Gami's predicament, or impose my will on theirs. Still, these were people I had lived with, and they were my friends. I thought what they were doing to Gami was wrong. As I got up to speak, I started to tremble. It was like that first speech you make in your junior high school class, when you can't remember the words and you know your voice and your bearing betray that everything about you is awkward. But I had to continue. What I said, or at least what I tried to say, was that my Gebusi friends had to respect their own custom—the custom that no one can ultimately force a woman to be married. Even in the old days, I said, some women had refused to be married. No matter what anyone had done, and no matter even what the women themselves had done, they had simply refused. I alluded to some of the failed first marriages of the people sitting around me, including some of the older women who had berated Gami. They, too, I reminded them, ultimately had refused the men they had been pressured to stay with in marriage. The police, I said, respected the same custom, following the laws of Papua New Guinea. People could try to persuade a woman to marry, but they simply could not force her to do so. That was all.

I don't know if my words had any effect. I was too nervous to judge people's reactions or to recall things clearly afterwards. I wasn't saying anything radical but merely putting into words the reality that I hoped they would accept—and that they were grudgingly beginning to accept anyway. Then I did something else that I had never done before. After the meeting was over, I asked to talk with Gami. Alone. Of all the things I have intentionally done with the Gebusi before or since, this was the most awkward. An unrelated man simply does not talk with an unmarried woman alone—especially one like Gami, who bore the stigma of sexual immorality. In addition, Gami had been a flirtatious and endearing young woman. And anthropology is littered with tales of well-meaning white men who scheme to help attractive women of color, only to unwittingly leave them worse off in their own culture than they had been before. I had to be very clear about my motives.

My request, in fact, related to Gami's family situation. Gami's father had died, and her biological mother had remarried. This woman was now living near the town of Kiunga with her new husband; she was the only woman in the community to have left the Nomad area. Without money for another airfare, Gami had been left behind with her aunt. Now, however, Gami's true mother was the one person who might have cared enough to help her out. I knew Gami's mother from 1982 and thought she was a good person. Because Gami could not read or write, I thought she might like me to write a letter to her mother in Kiunga—to communicate with her and solicit help. This practice is not unusual in many parts of Papua New Guinea. For example, when I had previously visited male inmates at the national prison in Port Moresby, many of them had immediately accepted my offer to write letters on their behalf and to send them to their families back home. In some ways, I thought, Gami was now a prisoner in Gasumi Corners.

Apart from this, there was something else that I wanted to communicate. I wanted to tell Gami that I didn't think she was a bad or wicked person. Many young women struggle to find a man they can live with. I wanted to tell her that I thought she had courage to stand up for herself. I knew I was on cultural thin ice. I had no idea if these words would make sense or if they would backfire. But I had to try. And there was no way I could talk to her with other villagers intervening.

In the village clearing, I told Gami's adopted mother and the others gathered there that I needed to talk to Gami, alone. They looked at me, and I looked at them back. I told them not to worry, that I was only an "old man" and that we wouldn't be long. My excuse was that Gami had never shown me the abandoned spur settlement, just two hundred yards away, where her true mother had previously lived. (I also thought that this might be a good place for her to think of her mother and to tell me anything she wanted me to write in a letter.) I was touched that the villagers trusted me enough to let Gami go off with me. Gami herself had been through the wringer already, and who knows what she thought now. She had every reason to be scared of any new development, and she was, in culturally appropriate fashion, reluctant to go with me. To my distress, her relatives now *ordered* her to accompany me to her mother's old settlement. As I walked slowly out of our hamlet, Gami trailed a good fifteen feet behind. My first thought was to wait for her and say something innocuous. But when I slowed, so did she. It got worse when a twelve-year-old boy crossed paths with us. Gami and I were the spitting image of a married couple—adult man up front and younger wife coming behind. The boy was incredulous. I mumbled that Gami was going to show me her mother's house and that her "mother" had said it was okay. As we neared the site, a second boy, fourteen, appeared. I repeated the story. But he was too captivated by the sight of Gami with me to be easily deterred. Even as I told him to move along, I could see him scurry away only to hide and watch from the bushes.

My conversation with Gami took place close to the main path and was very short. We stood about a dozen feet apart—as close as we ever got. Both of us looked at the ground or anywhere except at each other. I said that I was sorry for her. I said that I thought she was not a bad person, but a person who had much inside that was good. I said, without repeating the obvious, that I knew she had "worries." Then I said that I had known her mother and that I knew she was now living near Kiunga. And I asked her if she wanted me to write a letter to her mother—to see if she or other members of her family could help. Nervously, Gami said simply, "No." I continued, "Is there anything else you would like to say? Is there anything that you would like to talk about or that I might do?" She replied again, "No." I responded, "That's fine. I just wanted to ask. We'll leave it go." Then we walked directly back to the village. Gami took the lead, walking much faster than she had before.

✿✿✿✿✿✿

I will never know if my awkward attempt to help Gami was an abject failure or merely a nominal one. Perhaps the thought of her mother finding out about Gami's predicament only added salt to her wounds. Perhaps the idea of telling one's long-lost mother about one's indiscretions wasn't that appealing. Perhaps I was guilty of cultural insensitivity or of taking license with Gebusi rules of gendered interaction. I could not know and could hope only that some part of Gami sensed, amid my ineptitude, that I was trying to help rather than hurt her. The best of intentions can sometimes have the worst of results. But I had to try.

What conclusions can we draw? On a personal level, my experiences, both with Wayabay and Gami, led me into the uncertain territory of trying to connect my own cultural understanding of the Gebusi with a desire to help some of them with their problems. In addition to being researchers, anthropologists are also people, and we sometimes feel compelled to act on behalf of those in our community. But we can't know the consequences of our actions or even if our good intentions will be recognized. It seems as important as it is difficult to balance our positive intent against our awareness of its unpredictable result. The interventions of Westerners among foreign peoples often have led to unfortunate consequences even when the intent was noble. This pattern continues to the present; some of the largest and most expensive international aid projects in Africa, Asia, Latin America, and the Pacific create little long-term benefit and sometimes do greater harm than good to local people. To correct for this possibility, a sense of humility and an awareness of our own limitations—as searchers, as advocates, and as human beings—is called for.

In topical terms, Gami's case and that of Wayabay illustrate the challenges of finding a marriage partner in a contemporary world of greater choices and also greater risks. In many parts of the world, personal options are expanding, including for women. Correspondingly, "marriage by choice" and/or "companionate marriage" is growing relative to unions arranged or pressured by kin and relatives. From female and male perspectives, Gami's plight and Wayabay's illustrate a similar pattern in Gasumi Corners. These new circumstances build on the spine of determination, physical attraction, and romance that women and men have probably always had while ratcheting up the stakes of choice from an expanding range of potential partners. Who can say if women or men are happier as a result? But in a modern world of many alternatives, the lives of young men and women are increasingly shaped by the intended or unintended consequences of their own actions rather than those of family members and kin.

Amid the clash of choice and constraint, some predicaments work out better than one might have guessed. This was ultimately the case for Gami and also for Wayabay. Despite their respective trials, each of them ended up finding an acceptable spouse after I left the field. In each case, their partner carried a history of difficult choices that complemented their own. And in each case, their partner had been living in the house next door. In December 2001, I received the following in a letter written on behalf of Sayu from Gasumi Corners: "Wayabay got married already to Gami. And ready to deliver baby."

Long live their lives together. Long live their resilience.

BROADER CONNECTIONS: *Youth, Modernity, "Companionate Marriage"*

- In many societies, **young people adopt modern customs** that include **greater individual agency in courtship and marriage.**

- Bruce's response to Wayabay's request for *ademini* reveals how: (a) **anthropologists may be surprised and ignorant even when they think they know a culture well,** (b) **good intentions in fieldwork can still lead to awkwardness or misunderstanding,** and (c) **local people are often forgiving of an anthropologist's unwitting mistakes.**

- As in the case in many societies, marriage among Gebusi **relies increasingly on personal attraction and modern means of courtship** rather than traditional male skills and formal ritual dancing.

- In many societies, the incidence of tightly prescriptive marriage is declining. Among Gebusi, the **rate of sister-exchange marriage** in Gasumi Corners **decreased to zero** between 1982 and 1998.

- Common with patterns in many societies, the attempted sister-exchange marriage between four Gebusi young people in 1998 revealed: (a) **the increasing difficulty of arranged marriages;** (b) **increasing choice and resilience of women against the will of others,** including their **marital choice;** (c) increased emphasis on mutually acceptable **"companionate marriage;"** and (d) the continuing **strength of moral principles against sexual misconduct.**

- Bruce's actions with Gami illustrate: (a) **anthropologists sometimes feel compelled to act as members of their field community;** (b) the importance of **caution and humility when intervening;** (c) the importance of **asking local people for their own opinion/s;** and (d) **creative local solutions**—such as the final marriage described in this chapter—**often exceed the ability of outsiders to address local problems.**

CHAPTER 10

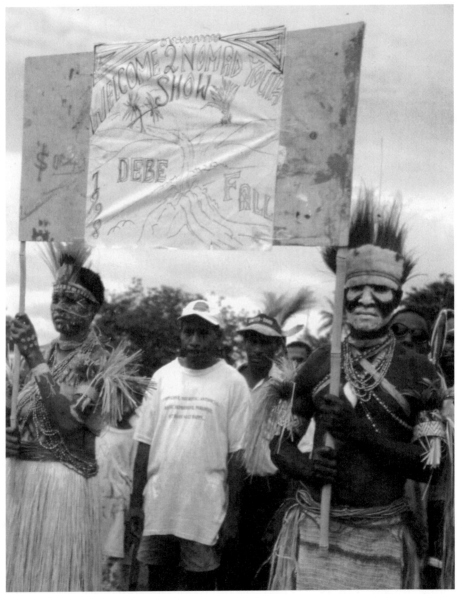

A man and woman in semitraditional costumes introducing their village dances on Independence Day. (Note: The T-shirt of the man standing in the middle reads, "Compulsive, Antisocial, Manic Depressive, Paranoid, but Basically Happy.") (PHOTO: Bruce Knauft)

Sayu's Dance and After

Sayu sidled ahead of me, down the trail and into the dawn. Daybreak bathed us in its softest light as we returned from our all-night ceremony. The previous evening, in a rare expression of a fading custom, Sayu had been the visiting dancer at the village of Kotiey-masam. In traditional costume, painted and plumed, he had enacted the spirits of old in their full splendor to the beat of his crocodile-skin drum. His jaw had been as firm as the pearl shell just beneath it, his eyes as bright as the red bird of paradise he had become. With a magnetic aura, he had been wonderfully transformed.

As we walked back to Gasumi Corners, I remembered Sayu from sixteen years before, when he had been five years old. His impish smile had lit his face like sunlight streaming through a crack in the forest canopy. His play had been as full of Gebusi tradition as it could be. He would wrap his small body in leaves, smear soot on his face, and put a feather in his hair. With supreme whimsy, he would take a length of bamboo as a make-believe drum and dance resplendently at an imaginary feast. He would lisp a fetching echo to the men's songs at night. Or pretend to marry a little girl in sister-exchange. Or cook some sago to divine and accuse a make-believe sorcerer. More than any other child, Sayu had been in our house and in our lives at Yibihilu. Now, this dancer of childhood returned home with me at a new dawn in this rainforest of memories.

Since my first departure from the Gebusi, Sayu's life had not been at all as I had thought it would have been. Just three years later, his young father, Silap, died. His mother, the fun-loving Boyl, perished suddenly just two years after that. Recently remarried, she had been foraging for sago grubs deep in the forest with Sayu and his younger brother, Huwa. Far from the settlement, before they could return, she had fallen suddenly and fatally ill. The two boys had cried and clutched their mother as she writhed in agony in the forest at night. A search party later found them and carried Boyl's body back to the village. Sayu was eleven or twelve years old; Huwa was about five. Sayu's new father-in-law, Doliay, was enraged by the death and pursued the sorcery inquest for Boyl with great intensity. Shortly

145

afterward, as described in Chapter 7, Doliay avenged her death by beheading Basowey.

When Doliay departed to serve his six-year term in prison, Sayu and Huwa were left back at Gasumi Corners. Five years later, following a dispute in the village, Sayu decided to leave the community and embark on a young man's adventure. At age seventeen, he and a friend walked eighty miles to the town of Kiunga—through lands he had never seen and groups he had never encountered. Kiunga was the district capital of three thousand people, a muddy gateway to the modern world and emerald city to those in the forest for hundreds of miles around. Quick and smart, Sayu finagled work in Kiunga as a domestic helper and "houseboy." He lived the life of a successful teenager in town: washing dishes, doing laundry, running errands—and learning to live in his employer's house, ride a bike, watch satellite TV, and dance disco. Two years later, he returned back to the outskirts of Nomad, where his treasured boom box broadcast music to everyone's delight. He had become a dandy, but he remained thoughtful and worked hard.

When I myself returned to the Gebusi, two and a half years later, Sayu quickly became my companion, helper, and confidant, along with Didiga, who was a good friend to both of us. I helped support them, and we shared many good times. On one occasion, Sayu delicately withdrew from a budding relationship with a flirtatious young woman in Gasumi Corners. Although their relationship had not turned serious or physical, the woman's father and brother suspected otherwise. The next day, while Sayu and I were doing chores, her male relatives charged out of nowhere, brandishing bows and arrows. Sayu and I stood side by side and turned to face them. I told myself to remain appropriately passive but defiant. Livid, the young woman's brother came at us in a dead run. As he closed to about twenty feet, he cocked his bow, drew back his arrow, and snapped his bowstring at us. Then he veered away. I knew well enough from my days at Yibihilu that this was merely a display of aggression, and I bore him no anger. We all laughed about it days later. But my spine had stiffened at the time. At a public meeting, the village councilor concluded that the woman's brother and father had been wrong to intimidate us; they had to pay a fine to Sayu for falsely accusing him of impropriety.

My many memories of Sayu linked back to the present as I walked back with him from his all-night dance at Kotiey-masam. He had danced until dawn for the first time, not to disco, as he had before, but in stately traditional costume. He had become an impressive and handsome young man, both in an indigenous and a modern sense. As his friend and part-parent, I felt a surge of pride and affection for him. I thought how deeply pleased Sayu's parents would have been to see him now. I told him what I felt: that my eyes had seen his traditional dancing with the happy heart-spirit of his dead father and his dead mother. Suddenly, I teared up. His lip quivered. I turned away so as not to cry.

The drama of the night receded slowly with the dark. Dawn approached as the trail took us back to Gasumi Corners, where traditional dancing is all but dead. On our way we walked by the Nomad Station, winding our way past its airstrip. The light was growing brighter. I could see that Sayu's pearl shell was crooked, his feathers skewed, and his red ocher paint smudged on his taut skin. Even on Saturday morning, he was concerned that someone from Nomad might see him in the grass skirts of a traditional dancer. Although he had been the center of ceremonial attention all night, this had been at an old forest village. Slipping behind a shrub, Sayu exchanged his grass skirt for a pair of shorts. Now hybrid, he left the signs of his dancing above his waist but kept the security of Western clothes below. Around his neck, he now hung the blue beads and cross of his Catholic baptism.

As Sayu had anticipated, we met others along the way. We snapped fingers firmly with them before finally reaching Gasumi Corners. There we were greeted by those who had not made the trek. They asked to hear the recordings I had made the previous night. As the tape played, we listened to the men's joking, Sayu's drumming and dance rattles, and the women's traditional singing. But there were other sounds that I had barely heard amid my focus on Sayu: the guitar and ukulele of the evening's string band, and the rock and roll of a Papua New Guinean band that one of the visitors played on a boom box. The clash of musical styles had mirrored the mix of celebrants in that old longhouse. Some had adorned themselves in leaves, body paint, and beautiful bird feathers. Others had sported a colorful shirt or hat, or even sunglasses in the night. Still others had mixed and matched cheerfully—a collage of body paint here, Western clothing there, a head-dress on a hat. They had drifted through shadows thrown alternately by tradi-tional resin torches and modern wick lanterns. All of them had paused apprecia-tively and even gratefully to pose for my flashing camera—as if my modern photography would validate their hybrid tradition.

Listening to the taped music, the men of Gasumi Corners talked of getting dressed up themselves in indigenous costumes—but not for a traditional ritual. Instead, they wondered if they could scrape together enough decorations to per-form in costume for the government-sponsored contest that would be held at the Nomad Station on Independence Day. Competing communities would stage reenactments of their indigenous dances. Officials would judge the performances and award a pittance of prize money to those whom they thought were best. The men of Gasumi Corners wanted to have at least some chance to be among the winners. They mused that maybe they would dress up Wayabay or one of their other bachelors in the full regalia of initiation—even though these men had not been initiated and never would be.

Listening to the tape recording and then to the men, I felt in a time warp between the past and the present. Partly this was from a lack of sleep. All-night feasts tend to make me a bit woozy the day after—as they do for many Gebusi. By traditional design, staying up all night mixes things up and turns them back to front; the spirits of the dark meld with the humans of the day; the performance of the present enacts the cosmos of the past. But now the spirits had not just vanished with the morning mist; they seemed to be gone forever from Gasumi Corners. It was now midday on Saturday. Only a few men from our village had gone to the feast; most of the men and boys were now preparing to leave for the ballgames at Nomad. Tomorrow, we would sing praises to God in the hot Sunday sun. Then there would be more rugby and soccer. When the men returned from the ball field on Sunday evening, their children would be going to bed—so they could get up and be off early Monday morning for a full day of school. As I drifted to sleep, I wondered if my memory of Sayu's dance was already fading. I realized that I was now immersed in the changing of Gebusi culture itself, beyond specific new activities or values derived from afar. I was confronting new meanings and emphases created by Gebusi themselves.

❧   ❧   ❧

The following day, my schedule returned to normal. But I didn't know what to expect over the next few weeks. Independence Day was coming up, and ceremonial life would be taking another turn. Would the festivities be traditional, modern, or somewhere in between? Everything now seemed geared to this next celebration. This was true even at Yulabi, a remote Gebusi settlement where a large initiation was being held. The arrangements were timed so their ceremonies would take place just one week before the national holiday. This would allow their new initiates to get dressed up again and parade in full regalia before officials at the Nomad Station on Independence Day.

In Gasumi Corners, preparations for the national celebration also intensified. Young men talked excitedly about their local genre of so-called string band singing. I became curious. A quartet of young men from Gasumi Corners had formed a singing group that featured two guitars, a ukulele, and a medley of original songs. The leader was Damya, Nolop's son, and one of the singers was Huwa, Sayu's brother. They performed one night in the village. And I was blown away. The songs were as stunning and soulful as those of the young boys I had heard earlier singing in the tree. And their tone was even crisper. The music soared with rich melodies, undulating rhythms, and resonating harmonies. Hard as it was for me to admit it, their new genre was more beautiful than the séance singing of old. The songs drew important threads from séance singing, including haunting nasal tones, falsetto harmonies, and surging refrains. But their quickened tempo, lighter lilt, and instrumental accompaniment rang clearly modern. The lyrics of the songs borrowed variously from Gebusi, English, tok pisin, the vernaculars of neighboring ethnic groups, and even phrases that had somehow been transmitted from distant New Guinean languages that very few Gebusi could translate. As in séance singing, the songs compressed poetic images that were evocative, longing, and nostalgic; they were short on content but lovingly repeated. Most of them involved contemporary contexts such as school, work, and romance. The following song was especially popular:

I go to school.
I look at my friend from before.
She looks at me and I look at her.
Her eyes fill with tears.
Why did you come to tease me?

Unlike séance singing, which had been spontaneous, string band songs were carefully rehearsed. When the people of Gasumi Corners gathered late in the evening to hear their singers, they were not communing with the spirits but listening to a musical performance. Men in the audience did not chime in with their own singing. There was no spirit medium, no dialogue with spirit women, and no divination for sickness or sorcery. Although some senior men might call out in emotional response, this was the exception rather than the rule. The audience was attentive and respectful, not ribald or raucous. [*To hear music clips, google "Bruce Knauft" and see under "Gebusi music."*]

As the Gasumi Corners string band intensified its practices, other men tried to locate or trade for items of indigenous costuming. How would they use them? Judging from their winks, nods, and smiles, it almost seemed as if each man had his own plan. As I slowly came to realize, there was going to be more to Independence Day planning than either the rehearsal of songs or the presentation of dances. Sports practices also increased, and there was talk of fierce competition on the ball field. So, too, there was reference to plans for disco dancing, "dramas," and a host of humorous as well as serious games.

If initiations had previously been the biggest and grandest spectacles of Gebusi culture, the celebrations of National Independence Day had since supplanted them. But the festivities at the Nomad Station would include more people than the Gebusi. Certainly, Gebusi dancing, athleticism, music, and who knew what else would be on display. But so would those of other ethnic groups that ringed the Nomad Station: Bedamini, Kubor, Samo, Oybae, Honibo, and even distant peoples such as the Pa and the Kabasi. Nomad is the administrative center for a subdistrict that includes some 9,000 people scattered across 3,500 square miles of rainforest. During the week prior to Independence Day, visitors and families from many settlements within several days' walk arrived and stayed in the "corner" of Nomad to which they were most closely affiliated. Gebusi culture was going to be presented as part of an interethnic and even regional festival that was linked, in turn, to celebrating the independence of the nation as a whole.

State employees at Nomad took a special role in organizing and planning the events—and finding government funds to pay for materials, organization, and prize money. Given that government programs at Nomad often underpay or fail to pay local workers, the thousands of kina obtained by the Nomad officials to host Independence Day festivities were important both as a message of local governmental support and as a kind of insurance against tribal reprisals against the government, especially by the larger ethnic groups, such as the Bedamini.

As a small part of this larger mix, Gebusi culture was now thoroughly enmeshed with the activities and institutions of the Nomad subdistrict, its various ethnic groups, and the national and provincial government, which controlled the schools, police, and local administration. In terms of religion, Gebusi now identified with Christian denominations that spanned the district, the nation, and, indeed, the globe. All this would be on display at the local Independence Day celebrations on September 16. For my part, I realized that my conception of

Gebusi culture was expanding to include a much broader range of identifications, meanings, and institutions. Anthropologists often look to rituals of display and tradition as key expressions of a culture's values and history. As cultures interconnect, these associations increase—and the lines that distinguish them easily blur. The meanings, identities, and values of "local culture" are at the same time regional, national, and international in scale.

Independence Day at Nomad ultimately featured almost a week of festivities and celebrations. More than 1,000 people attended. The ceremonies began with two days of team sports on the Nomad ball field, with competitions escalating through several rounds and climaxing in all-star games that pitted the best players from different ethnic groups against each other. For the Gebusi, their key matches were against the Bedamini. Of course, the Bedamini of the past had raided and decimated Gebusi villages. Numerically, the Bedamini population remained seven or eight times larger than that of the Gebusi—and they kept a reputation for fierceness. But the Gebusi had important new advantages. Most Bedamini settlements were distant from Nomad, whereas those in Gasumi Corners lived in close proximity to the government ball field. Without regular practice and league competition, it was difficult for Bedamini to hone their athletic skills—and Bedamini fighting tactics don't work so well on a closely refereed playing field! Finally, the Gebusi—especially those from Gasumi Corners—had a home field advantage; they played on the same pitch, with the same referees, and with much of the same crowd that they encountered every weekend.

At the end of the competition, the headline could have read, "David beats Goliath!" In an amazing coup, the Gebusi won all except one of their matches against the Bedamini. Their defeated rivals were so frustrated and angry that they accused the Gebusi of using magic to sabotage them. But government officials upheld the Gebusi victories. What was the Gebusi response? From an American perspective, I expected a big celebration and at least a little gloating. But Gebusi were subdued and circumspect. They worried that their Bedamini adversaries might take revenge by breaking into the little store that we had started in Gasumi Corners, or even that they would break into my house and loot it while I was attending festivities at Nomad. This lack of boastful or gleeful behavior fit with Gebusi reactions after their victories during the regular season; they remained even-keeled and sportsmanlike.

As "Independence Day" unfolded in other dimensions, I struggled to keep up. There was excited talk of "dramas." I had little idea what this meant. As dusk turned into night, a large performance area was roped off next to the government station. Gradually, hundreds of people amassed to watch the performances. When they started, what a shock! The bulk of the performances were spoofs, farces, and parodies of local traditions. These were acted out by villagers themselves dressed in elaborate indigenous costumes. In one skit, for instance, a man in black paint, wearing a cassowary headdress and an old loincloth, groaned buffoonishly as he tried with clumsy and exaggerated effort to hack down a tiny tree using a traditional stone ax. Every few swings, the stone would fall from the ax handle and the man would stumble and grunt stupidly, looking for it in the grass. Then he would try to sharpen his ax with a traditional grinding stone, while cursing in the coarsest traditional manner. His slapstick antics and rudeness were really quite funny, and the audience laughed loudly. Meanwhile, the man's sardonic companion smoked a traditional pipe and refused to help cut the tree until they almost got into a fight. Again, the audience erupted in laughter. At the end of the skit, the performers explained its "meaning" to the audience in *tok pisin* over a battery-operated bullhorn: "In the old days, we were ignorant. We didn't know about steel axes, and we tried to chop down trees using stone axes. This didn't work, and we got angry and fought with each other."

In skit after skit, one or another traditional practice or belief was skewered for the audience's delight. Many of the customs were ones that I had seen practiced quite genuinely back in 1980–82. Rites that had once been performed with dignity and grace—including magic spells, origin myths, fish poisoning rituals, spirit séances, divinations, and dances—were turned into farce. What bittersweet comedy! As an anthropologist, it was sad to see such a mockery of rich local traditions—and by the very people who used to practice them. And yet, the skits *were* very funny, sometimes uproariously so. I fought back tears of laughter even as I felt pangs of nostalgia for customs that I had seen "for real" just sixteen years before.

For me, the most dramatic skit was performed by some of my friends from Gasumi Corners. It was a spoof of sickness, death, and sorcery divination. The opening performer was Mora—the teenager who had sought to be my romantic partner in 1981 and who was now a senior man with several children. He was caked with mud and wore a large fake phallus strapped around his waist. Smoking continually from a traditional tobacco pipe, he wheezed and coughed in exaggerated fashion until, in a spasm of sickness, he toppled over with a loud thud. This attracted the attention of a spirit medium, played by Damya, the son of Nolop. Damya's costume was absurdly traditional, including an upside-down cassowary headdress and a bark belt that was so oversized that it slid down whenever he got up. Mora proceeded to cry that he was going to die. This prompted Damya to lean over him and screech directly into his ear. This parodied the traditional Gebusi custom of yelling to keep a person's spirit from leaving his body when he or she was near death. Damya's efforts were ineffectual, and Mora quickly "died."

After energetic and farcical wailing, a sorcery suspect was paraded up to Mora's corpse. The suspect was Kawuk, a senior man of Gasumi Corners and staunch supporter of the Catholic Church. (During the early years of colonial influence, Kawuk had, in fact, killed a family of three—a husband and wife accused of sorcery plus their son.) In the skit, Kawuk was brilliantly made up with black paint, white body markings, leaf strips, and feathers. Now it was his turn to be the "victim." He was forced to wail over Mora's corpse in an attempt to prove his innocence. As he did so, the corpse gave a dramatic "sign." A fishing line that had been tied to the tip of Mata's fake phallus was surreptitiously pulled. As the corpse dramatically arched its back and moaned, this large organ raised up suddenly as a monumental erection. Audience members could scarcely contain themselves in laughter. Needless to say, the corpse had indicated that Kawuk was "guilty" as the sorcerer responsible.

Now judged, Kawuk was taken by Damya and farcically interrogated. Kawuk cried like a baby as villagers "hit" him. He initially denied but finally admitted that he had killed Mora with sorcery. His captors then untied him and beat him until he fell down. Then Bulobey—who is Mora's real-life cousin and a former spirit medium who was himself implicated in sorcery killings—took up a large piece of wood. Winding up with histrionic ferocity, he finished Kawuk off with a great wallop (striking the ground right next to where he lay). With Kawuk now "dead," his kin in the skit became incensed and took up their bows and arrows. With great buffoonery, the two sides squared off for a mock bow-and-arrow fight—until they all ran off. That was the end of the skit. To conclude the act, however, the performers now distanced themselves clearly from the roles they had been playing. They marched solemnly back into the performance area, lined up in a neat row, and stood at attention in front of the judges. Formally and soberly, they bowed in unison to each side of the audience that encircled them— to the left, to the right, to the rear, and to the front. Finally, with military precision, they marched out, to the cheers of the crowd.

What was I to think? On the one hand, the richness of Gebusi spirit beliefs, the poetry and aesthetics of their spirit mediumship, and even their concern for the sick and dying had been turned into a joke. On the other hand, the skit represented a stinging critique of the sorcery beliefs, inquests, and fights that had killed many Gebusi in the past. That persons such as Kawuk and Bulobey could play lead characters in this mocking retort—having themselves abetted violence against sorcerers in years gone by—underscored this rejection. The skit was funny, smart, and very well performed. I was left with much to ponder.

During two nights, a total of forty-two dramas were performed. Most, like that just described, were spoofs of tradition. But these were thrown into relief by the remaining acts. Some of these were Christian morality plays, with large posters upon which verses from the Bible were written. Others were skits of first contact. In these, local villagers were portrayed as stupid, violent, and clumsy until they were shown the fruits of modern civilization—peace, trade goods, and store-bought food—by benevolent Australian patrol officers (played by villagers). It was hard to watch these without thinking that a core tenet of anthropology—that indigenous ways of life should be respected—was being turned upside down by local people themselves. Certainly, there were features of Gebusi tradition that I was glad to see disappear. But much that was beautiful was lost in the bargain. And the new inequalities that Gebusi now experienced—in church, school, and at the market—were not always preferable to the features they replaced.

The final skits, though few in number, suggested a more balanced view between extremes. These enacted the traumas and foibles of living a modern life. Some skits portrayed the problems of trying to earn a living in Kiunga, of scrounging medicine for a sick child from a pompous official, and of coping with children who drift into trouble after school. In one poignant little play, an impoverished city youth stole and ran off with a suitcase full of money. The owner then returned, pulled out a gun, and shot dead the two security guards who had failed to guard his wealth. Here, the hungry boy had escaped as a criminal, but even worse, the powerful boss had become a murderer. Obviously, modern life was not all that it was cracked up to be. Indeed, the skit echoed the life of the provincial premier, who had recently been charged with attempted murder. Despite the seriousness of such themes, the skits maintained a humorous tone. In this way, they provided a sense of alternative outcomes rather than foregone conclusions.

Taken together, the dramas were so rich and varied that I could probably write a whole book about them. But even so, they represented just one slice of the larger festivities surrounding Independence Day—and these continued day and night for several more days! The remaining events supplied yet more missing pieces to the puzzle of contemporary culture in and around Nomad. It was all coming together, but only gradually in my awareness.

Although local traditions had been lampooned at night, they were honored the following day. Troops of villagers in gorgeous, meticulously arrayed costumes danced in full customary fashion. The throngs of people who watched the performances were even larger than they had been at the evening "dramas"—more than 1,000 strong. A wide range of ethnic groups displayed their dance and initiation rites: Bedamini, Kubor, Samo, and even the Pa from across the Strickland River. Their costumes were spectacular, a photographer's dream. Gasumi Corners was represented by Halowa, Yuway's married brother and an Evangelical Christian, who drum-danced in stately costume accompanied by a traditionally dressed Gebusi woman from another settlement. But the performance that stole the heart of the audience—and of the judges—was by a group of dancers from the distant Kabasi peoples, who lived three days' hard walk southeast of Nomad. Dancing in a slow and dignified manner while singing haunting songs, they performed both standing and sitting for over half an hour. Many in the audience were visibly enthralled and appeared to never have seen their style of performance.

I couldn't help but think that Independence Day was expanding indigenous practices at the same time that it transformed them. Rather than being performed at night in a darkened longhouse for kin and friends, rituals were now reenacted on the official grounds of Nomad Station for a thousand strangers in the hot light of day. Even a member of the national parliament was present. The instrumental purpose of the performances was not to initiate a young man, cure a sick person, celebrate a local accomplishment, or reenact the spirits. Rather, it was to celebrate the nation of Papua New Guinea and to provide a secular display of body art and dancing. This was underscored by the rating and judging of the performances by officials, who both enjoyed the proceedings and grumbled about the extra hours of work that it took to organize and orchestrate them. As those from Gasumi Corners had emphasized, the small prizes of money that were given to winning performers were a major motivation for many participants. Some villages dressed up practically anyone they could regardless of whether the person was qualified to wear the costume. For many and perhaps most of the performers, the displays did not reflect current practices, beliefs, or rituals in their own villages. Indigenous culture was increasingly reenacted as historical folklore for regional and even national consumption.

If the Independence Day festivities alternately spoofed and then celebrated traditional dances as a kind of secular folklore, they also played with features of contemporary life. Toward the end of the week, more and different events were held. These included such playful competitions as drinking quantities of hot tea, pillow fighting while sitting on a beam, having blindfolded women try to split papayas with bush knives, and climbing a greased pole. The atmosphere was similar to that of a country fair. Hundreds of people milled about. Scattered along the walkways were stalls of blaring boom boxes where villagers sold cooked food. Tables of ring toss and even rudimentary gambling were set up for those willing to risk 5 or 10 cents in a game of skill or chance. In the afternoon, an avidly attended "disco contest" was held. The dance ground was thronged with bodies gyrating to the throb of Papua New Guinea rock music broadcast over speakers. Although a few brave women were there, including mothers dancing with their daughters, the dance ground was dominated by the older boys. The dancing appeared to be entirely same-sex: guys with guys, and girls with girls. The dancers' outfits presented a mélange of styles ranging from spiffy modern shirts and jeans to hip-hop clothes or traditional costumes. Some young men dressed up and danced buffoonishly as women.

What sense can be made of this hodgepodge? Ultimately, the festivities were a smorgasbord in which diverse cultural practices—traditional and modern, nearby and distant—were put on display for performance, reflection, and playful combination. Within this potpourri, indigenous customs were alternately taken out of context, parodied or debunked, or reperformed with praise and honor. And this was also the case with many modern customs and practices. If rituals reflect and symbolize the structure of people's social life, as Émile Durkheim suggested long ago, then the Independence Day celebrations reflected the fact that life in and around the Nomad Station had become diverse and multifaceted across a range of indigenous and modern affiliations, practices, and beliefs. For Gebusi, the festivities of Independence Day symbolized the challenge of new and competing ways of living. Those from Gasumi Corners have actively pursued these new combinations by moving from the deep rainforest to the edge of the Nomad Station. Reciprocally, the multifaceted culture expressed at Independence Day both reflected and reinforced their alternative possibilities of social life and culture.

🌿   🌿   🌿

In the aftermath of Independence Day, the Nomad area seemed to relax. Having worked and played so hard, people unwound in a kind of collective morning after. Like a series of happy aftershocks following a marvelous large quake, a few settlements held subsidiary feasts and celebrations. In Gasumi Corners, the period of respite lasted several weeks before gradually giving way to planning for another festivity. This occasion was especially poignant for me: the feast to commemorate my own departure. As my time to leave inched gradually closer, my days became increasingly bittersweet. My friendships had been so deeply rekindled, and new ones had taken root. How could I go?

It ended up being an incredible finale, and I can't claim to be the reason for its success. Village celebrations have always served multiple purposes. And the Gebusi are the first to keep anyone from getting a big head. But it was hard not to cry when I first heard the song that the Gasumi string band composed to thank me for having come back to them.

With their typical casual gusto, the village started to buzz with preparations. Firewood and cooking leaves were stockpiled, sago was processed, and game was hunted deep in the forest. As a contemporary twist, profits were pooled from our local store to buy a large stock of tinned fish and rice. Added to these were my own gifts to the community, both to individuals and for our collective feast. The latter included further cartons of store-bought food and a score of coveted shotgun cartridges, which Wayabay and other young men used to hunt a stunning array of wild pigs and cassowaries.

During the several weeks of preparation, everyone was so busy gathering food and materials in the forest that I started to feel lonely in the village. I longed to be with them in their timbered hideaways, and I was nostalgic for the rainforest. So Sayu, Didiga, and I set off to visit some who had traveled from Gasumi Corners to their makeshift forest camp at Harfolobi. To get there, we traveled up the Kum River under the stately canopy of the towering trees that lined the banks. We climbed up the bluff at Yibihilu. My lip quivered to see our former village and even the site of my first house. It was all overgrown, not just with weeds but with good-sized trees turning into forest. Gone as well were so many of my friends from my first fieldwork, reclaimed by nature in graves that ranged around the former settlement. Up at Harfolobi, I visited the grave of Sayu's wondrous mother, Boyl, and it was hard not to weep. I sat in the crystal waters of the little waterfall where I had bathed. And I enjoyed for the last time the easy rhythm of rainforest living—husbands, wives, and children relaxed and peaceful, and I at home among them.

After several days, obligations drew us reluctantly back to Gasumi Corners, where the buildup for the celebration continued. Although I knew the general contours of the event to come, both from planning and from precedent, what my friends were devising by way of entertainment remained a mystery. I sensed that it would be a vintage Gebusi mix of joy, sadness, and bittersweet remembrance of the past.

On the day of reckoning, visitors came from near and far—all of those still living whom I had known so well, many others whom I had seen occasionally, and a few who knew of me only by reputation. For several days ahead of time, the piles of coconuts, a ton or more of sago starch, mounds of dried game, and stashes of rice and fish spawned a veritable village industry of cutting, cleaning, wrapping, and cooking. Now it was time to pull it all from the cooking fires, divide it up, and give it away. Hundreds of visitors had come. Amid our shouts of laughter and whoops of celebration, the gift-giving continued long after dusk turned into night. I was no longer a bystander but a primary host. I tried to make sure that my friends and acquaintances, the government officials, and even the hangers-on each got an appropriate share.

Then came the entertainment. Would this be a traditional dance, linked to my widely known appreciation of historical customs? Or would it be modern? Instead of choosing a single course of action, my friends had opted, as it were, to let all the flowers bloom. On one side of my hamlet, in the dim light of a darkened house, a visiting performer danced in the full dignity of indigenous costuming. Older men and women were especially drawn to this proud display of days gone by. Mothers held their smallest children, some of whom were possibly seeing a fully traditional Gebusi dance for the first time. From the other side of the village came the strains of a visiting string band, replete with guitar and ukulele, playing wonderful songs that I had never heard. In the middle of the settlement, its central clearing, was the festive pièce de résistance: a modern disco. My friends had finagled a really nice boom box and a set of speakers from work-ers at the Nomad station and had lugged them all the way to Gasumi Corners. A bright lantern illuminated the area, and the music poured forth. As older folks looked on, youngsters picked up the beat. Within minutes, they were moving and grooving in ways that would have passed quite tolerably in most dance clubs in the United States.

In the moonlight and gentle breeze, the joy and sadness of nostalgia blurred together. For me, it was the modern Gebusi equivalent of old *fafadagim-da*—the wistful enjoyment of intense and indescribable longing, of being together while thinking of loneliness and loss. Swaying to different beats from one end to the other, the village became a three-ring circus of bittersweet pleasure. I shuttled back and forth between the traditional dance, the string band, and the disco in the middle, delighting in each for their part. Together, they formed a fugue of contemporary cadences that were at once discordant and yet strangely harmonious. No one seemed to mind this jumble of aesthetics and experiences, and neither did I. Perhaps I had learned something new after all—not just to accept the fragmentary nature of Gebusi culture as it now expressed itself, but to enjoy and be part of it. I thought back to Sayu's dance and all the years of ritual splendor that had preceded it. Was Gebusi ritual life now a past tradition, or a spirit of new things to come? I realized that the answer could not be one or the other; it was both at the same time. I was partial to many Gebusi customs I knew from sixteen years earlier. But now I truly appreciated their relaxed ability to mix old and new, to fear neither the past nor the future, and to combine their possibilities in the present. Outpacing my understanding, the people of Gasumi Corners had become modern in their own unique way. On the eve of my departure, I contem-plated again what had they given me. Their truest gift had gone beyond the past or the present of their lives. They had shown me the continuing surprise of dis-covery in the unfolding of human cultural connection.

BROADER CONNECTIONS: *Nationhood, Ethnicity, and Folklore*

- Features of **expressive culture** or **popular culture**—including **dance, music, public display, and major celebrations and festivities**—reveal much about **contemporary conditions of culture and culture change**.

- The traditional dance of **Sayu**, childhood friend to Bruce during his first fieldwork, illustrates the **discordance between waning indigenous customs and the advent of modern practices**.

- Many peoples feel conflicted or ambivalent about some of their indigenous cultural beliefs or practices. At the **National Independence Day celebrations, old-time customs** such as sorcery divinations, spirit séances, warfare, and even indigenous material culture **were spoofed and mocked**, though there was also great **nostalgia for indigenous costuming and dancing**.

- In many societies, including the Gebusi, some indigenous practices are **taken out of cultural context** and enacted as **performances of historic folklore**.

- Independence Day revealed and symbolized how **Gebusi, like many peoples, are increasingly now becoming part of a regional and national culture**, including **increased inter-ethnic activities** and **regional and national identity as citizens of a modern nation-state**.

- Like events of **public culture** in many developing societies, Independence Day festivities **reflect and symbolize diverse alternatives and values** that confront Gebusi society and culture.

- Following the theories of sociologist **Émile Durkheim**, the **rituals and festivities** of Independence Day at Nomad **reflect patterns of social life** for contemporary Gebusi.

- The cultures of many peoples now combine or mix and match **modern or contemporary practices** with **long-standing or indigenous orientations or customs**. This is evident among Gebusi in the combination of traditional dancing with modern sports, games, and plays or "dramas" at the Nomad Independence Day festivities.

- **Anthropologists over time frequently become closely associated with the people they study**, including the forming of strong personal relationships and friendships. For Bruce, this is reflected in his continuing ties with the Gebusi. At the final feasts that commemorate his departures from the Gebusi, he is increasingly a primary participant and host in addition to being an observer.

- A final lesson of Gebusi for Bruce was that **older and newer patterns of culture do not need to oppose each other**. This fuels **our continuing surprise and discovery in the unfolding of human cultural connections**.

Three Decades of Cultural Change

CHAPTER **11**

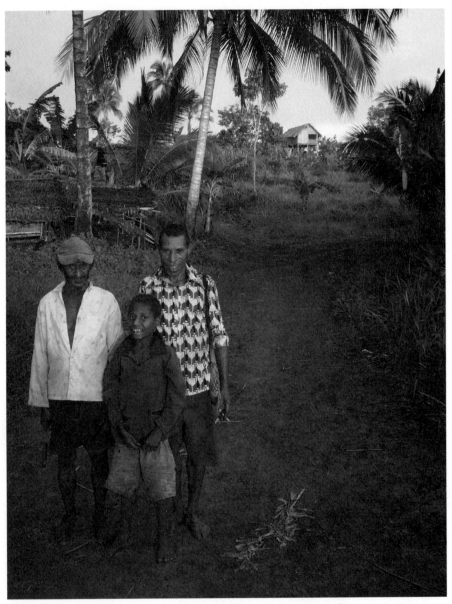

Villagers on the Gasumi Corners path, 2008. (PHOTO: Bruce Knauft)

Revival 2008

I HAD TRIED TO SEND WORD to my Gebusi friends ahead of time. I was coming back. This would be a briefer visit, to be sure, but no less important for that. Ten years later, what had changed? Would my Gebusi friends be yet more engaged in an outside world, the old customs further gone, the Gebusi's rush to be modern, albeit in their own way, yet more intense than before?

My first inkling was the challenge of getting there. Flights were no longer going to Nomad Station at all. I looked in amazement at my computer screen to see the e-mail from the Mission Aviation Fellowship (MAF): the Nomad airstrip was closed. How could this be? For forty-four years that airstrip has been the lifeline to the outside world for Gebusi and their neighbors. Since Nomad still has no roads to anywhere, what did this new isolation mean? Had it made Gebusi yet more remote than they had been in 1998? How had they responded, given all their new aspirations and the changes they had undergone?

These questions filled my mind as I made my plans. My sinking fear was that I would not see my Gebusi friends at all. With no air transport, what would I do? The overland trip to Nomad from Kiunga still takes up to a week to complete on foot, including across swamps and the dangerous Strickland River. I was almost tempted to try this route, but thought better of it. Fortunately, the MAF agent had another idea. He suggested that I fly north of Nomad and land at a tiny mission airstrip that was still open—and then hike with my gear from there to Nomad and on to Gasumi Corners. If I was lucky, the Nomad strip might be fixed and reopened by the time I arrived in Kiunga. If all else failed, I would simply remain in Kiunga and make contact with whichever Gebusi happened to be residing in the corners of the town.

When I left Atlanta, I didn't know which of these options would come to pass. My best guess was that I would land north of Nomad and trek south to the Gebusi. But twenty-eight years after my first trip, I was to be surprised yet again—and I was not disappointed.

After the grueling trip from Atlanta to Los Angeles to Australia to Papua New Guinea's capital of Port Moresby, and then to Kiunga, I finally got some word about Gebusi. Though none of my advance communications had gotten through, Father Eddy at the Kiunga Catholic mission recognized my photo of Sayu. He said that Sayu was now married, that he had several children, and that he had previously been working with Father Aloi at the Catholic Church at Nomad. My appetite whetted, I was all the more eager to see my Gebusi friends. But first I had to get there.

🌿   🌿   🌿

The logistics that surround key features of infrastructure such as airstrips are socially and even culturally important in developing countries such as Papua New Guinea. In the case of Nomad, the local government had run out of funds to pay Gebusi and other workers for cutting and clearing grass on the airstrip. Laborers had continued for several months but eventually gave up and stopped working.

As the grass shot up, the airstrip deteriorated and incoming planes could barely land. Nomad's government officials, most of whom hailed from other towns and cities in Papua New Guinea, reacted by leaving altogether and flying out on the last planes. Amazing as it may seem, politics and networks allowed them to reside in Kiunga or elsewhere and continue collecting their government salaries while not living or working at Nomad at all. Officials themselves viewed this arrangement as a kind of extended or semi-permanent official trip, paid at government expense, because they did not consider their job postings at Nomad to be viable. Government presence at Nomad hence declined to almost nothing. The grass on the strip continued to grow, and the airfield was eventually closed.

In Papua New Guinea and many other developing countries, decline or closure of rural infrastructure is a great problem. Even for Papua New Guinea's extensive Western Province, however, the closure of the large Nomad airstrip was a worst-case scenario, and one which had great impact on the various ethnic groups and thousands of people who live in the Nomad Subdistrict.

Back at the Nomad Station, one lower-level government worker from the area and another who had married a local woman continued to stay on. After months of persuasion, cajoling, and diligence, they managed to get some money and pay part of what was owed to local airfield laborers, who then started to re-clear the airstrip. Even when their work was finished, however, the landing area was soft and easily saturated by rain. By the time I had hoped to arrive, the airstrip had been closed for nine months.

In Papua New Guinea's Western Province, the only regular flight service to outstations is provided by MAF. By early 2008, officials there wanted to know if and how the Nomad airstrip could be reopened. Their test case turned out to be me. When I arrived in Kiunga, Nick Swaim, an accomplished young MAF bush pilot, said that he would try to fly me to Nomad if I would pay full charter fare—almost 3,000 kina—for a flight of less than ninety minutes. I could take only a few supplies, so the plane would not be too heavy when landing on the soft airstrip. Before touching down, Nick would fly over the Nomad strip and inspect it. If it looked okay, we would land; otherwise, we would fly north to

Honinabi and I would walk from there to Nomad and then Gasumi Corners. If it was raining or had rained the day before, the strip would be wet and we wouldn't fly.

Luckily, the weather cleared. I loaded my few things and we were finally bound for Nomad. As the plane lifted off, I marveled as if for the first time again at the full magnificence of the rainforest, from horizon to horizon. A rush of awe and also sorrow swept over me as I realized how rare such an unbroken vista of rainforest has become—one of the most endangered sights on our shrinking planet.

Almost before I was ready, the Strickland River passed beneath us and we approached Nomad Station. Nick circled and we careened down to just six or eight feet above the airstrip—so he could inspect it carefully. As I looked across anxiously, he pulled up suddenly to get us back over the treetops. Then he gave me the thumbs up; we were going to land. My pulse continued to race as we circled again. On finally touching down, we caught a rut and the plane skidded to the right and then to the left. But Nick calmly got us straightened out and brought the plane to a gentle stop. It was only later that he told me the greater risk—that if the plane had hit a deeper rut, it could have been catapulted sideways or forward. If the lone propeller hits the ground, it typically flips the fuselage to disaster.

But, oh, to be safely back! I gazed out eagerly as we taxied, remembering how I had done the same thing in 1980 and again in 1998. Who would be there? What would I find? Each time was a new beginning.

As I later found out, word of my arrival had gotten to Nomad only that same morning. Many of my friends had been out in their gardens, but Sayu and Didiga had heard the news and rushed to the airstrip; there they were to greet me! I could hardly believe it. We hugged and hugged and snapped fingers. At first we could barely say anything, overcome by the joy of simply being together once again. Their faces were now middle aged, but their smiles were bright and deep as ever.

As I got my bearings, I realized that most of the clothes on those gathered around me were plainly ragged. This caught me off guard, as the Nomad airstrip is quite a public place. I then looked up and across to the Nomad Station. It, too, was ragged. Most houses were deteriorated and boarded up. The Nomad schoolyard, which had been full of pupils running to meet the plane ten years ago, was devoid of life; even its grass was burned and charred black. Turning to the right, I saw the remains of the Nomad ball field that had seen so many rivalries and triumphs played out—now grown over with two feet of grass. Gebusi themselves were smiles all over. But what had circumstances done to them?

Not wanting to linger at Nomad, we gathered my few supplies and prepared to go. I shook hands and exchanged warm greetings with Father Aloi, the Gebusi's Catholic priest. News of him had been encouraging when I had passed through Kiunga—that he loved the Gebusi, was actively learning their language, supported their customs, and was shaping the church to meet local needs. I was sorry to see him go so quickly. But after waiting months to leave Nomad for a much-needed break, he was eager to board the plane that had brought me. Departing the airstrip, we ourselves trotted off in high gear to Gasumi Corners. I explained to everyone with apologies that I had not been able to bring as many supplies and gifts as I would have liked; the weight limit on the plane was the price of my ability to arrive at all. To my surprise, my friends not only understood but hardly seemed to care. My wonder and curiosity grew at how Gebusi had been dealing with the fact that their material circumstances had so obviously declined. My questions deepened when I got to the village and saw that my friends' possessions were indeed fewer, their clothes more torn, their pots more battered, and their knives and axes more worn than before.

My first priority, though, was simply to find out who was still alive. To my huge relief, most of my closest friends had survived. A surge of welcomes came from Kilasui, Mosomiay, Hogaya, Wayabay, Agiwa, Yokwa, and my great old friends Yuway, Keda, Uwok, and Hawi. Among the women, Mus, Dohayn, Dasom, Tabway, Kuni, To'ofun, Towe, Hahap, Oip, and many others were still living. Along with the adults was a bounding gaggle of new children who had been born since my last visit. I struggled to record and remember their many names. As my tabulation finally showed, the work of time has been kind to the population of Gasumi Corners, which grew 38 percent in the ten years between 1998 and 2008—from 122 to 168. Among the additions is one new "Knauft" in the world: Didiga's first son, to whom he gave my last name. I was deeply touched.

Among many peoples across the developing world, growing numbers of children pose a major challenge. High rates of fertility mean more mouths to feed—and can easily increase and intensify poverty. But Gebusi have extensive tracts of land. Given their history of being preyed upon and depopulated by Bedamini raiders, the Gebusi's current surge in numbers is more a healthy replenishment than a crisis condition. The total number of Gebusi is still under 1,000. The main stress caused by their population growth is competition for land in and around settlements such as Gasumi Corners itself. But as developments at Nomad Station have become moribund or been scaled back, the people of Gasumi Corners have oriented increasingly to their forest gardens, to foraging, and to other activities in the rainforest, where land remains plentiful.

This trend has influenced their basic pattern of subsistence. In 2008, those in Gasumi Corners were not raising anywhere near as many sweet potatoes or other root crops as they had ten years earlier. This was not surprising, since the local market for these foods had been supported by the purchases of now-absent government workers and their families. With their departure, Gebusi in Gasumi Corners relied more firmly on their traditional starch staples, especially bananas and sago, and they no longer worked to keep pigs away from root crop gardens.

※   ※   ※

How else had the community changed? As I strolled along with a throng of friends that first day, the biggest change was also the most obvious—a great new longhouse in the middle of Gasumi Corners! I knew right away what this meant:

a whole new generation of Gebusi had been initiated since the last time I had been there. Their transmission of core cultural features across generations has been resuscitated and maintained. What a joy! Given this, I strongly suspected I might soon learn of other traditions that were also being reasserted.

As I entered the house, as if there were any doubt, I was besieged by a full flurry of traditional welcoming. My fingers were snapped again and again, my gift exchange names called out, and the floor swept clean. After being begged to sit down, I was offered water, bananas, and, most importantly, round upon round of strong sweet tobacco from traditional bamboo pipes. In short order, the festivities were punctuated by waves of good-natured sexual joking, just like I had remembered from 1980. In marked contrast to 1998, the men were delighted almost to tears that I was able to joke back with them in their own traditional terms.

As our conversations started in earnest, I found that my own interest in long-standing customs of Gebusi culture was no longer marginal to my friends in Gasumi Corners as it had been a decade before. Alongside a resurgence of older traditions was a surprising new curiosity about details from the past, including the historical records and old genealogies that I had photocopied and brought with me. In 1998, this information elicited scant attention from Gebusi. Now, however, men in the community took interest and pleasure in my tabulations and charts of kinship connections, residence histories, and genealogies, including who had been married to whom, the names of their children, and where they had lived in days gone by. Enough time had passed that much of what I had recorded from those early days was unknown to a number of the men gathered around. They seemed to marvel at my ability to resurrect facts and to punctuate them with accounts of my personal experience from almost three decades before. They heartily supported the idea that I give a complete copy of my Gebusi clan gene-alogies to my friend Didiga Imba, who could read and recite the information as a kind of community history. That night, I stumbled to bed amazed: the Gebusi were reclaiming their past.

When I got up the next morning, I found my friend Keda, now more usu-ally called Joseph, reading one of my books about the Gebusi that I had brought. I had given copies of these especially to Sayu and Didiga, and they had already started circulating in the community. My first surprise was that Keda could read. I had known that he could speak and understand the national pidgin-English language, *tok pisin*. But I hadn't known that he could read English. In fact, he had just finished reading my story of Doliay—how as a young man he had beheaded Basowey as a sorcerer and how he later became a staunch Christian. Unfortunately, Doliay had died since my last visit. He had been one of those whom we had helped initiate in 1981, but now only two of those six young men were still alive.

Putting down the book, Keda told me how interested he was in the story and how glad he was that I had written it down. But it was especially Didiga who liked to read my writings on the Gebusi. If Gebusi are recreating their traditions, they are certainly doing so with all the tools they have at their disposal, including modern literacy as well as traditional memory and experience.

I am at pains to convey how meaningful and satisfying the Gebusi's cultural re-naissance is to me. In 1998 I had tried hard to respect and document their desires for change and the forces that were so strongly affecting my friends and their local world. At the time, I wondered how they would be able to benefit from greater interaction with the outside world without losing what was distinctly theirs. What I observed this time was a greater sense of self-determination by Gebusi, who now seemed to be seeking a balance between their desire to be modern and an appreciation of their cultural past.

To my surprise and delight, this balance now includes the performance of traditional dances. Within three days of my arrival, a dance in full regalia was held in a large house just a ten-minute walk from the center of Gasumi Corners. In good classic style, the dancer was from a distant village; he came to help cure a man who was starting to emerge from illness. In style, form, and costume, the dance was just what I had witnessed so many times twenty-eight years earlier. In fact, the custom of men drinking kava, the local root intoxicant, was even more prevalent than it had been during that earlier period. The young men were the most active drinkers.

Thankfully, some traditional beliefs that had become moribund by 1998 remained absent. For instance, sorcery inquests were still no longer practiced. When I asked why, my Gebusi friends noted the continuing absence of spirit mediums; the last ones had died or given up the practice, and no new ones had been indoctrinated. As in 1998, they said: "If we could talk with the spirits through our traditional spirit mediums, we could find out who sent the sorcery and per-haps take action. But without our spiritual go-betweens, we just cannot know. So we leave it up to God, if he wants to take action."

Instead of spirit séances, the lovely string-band singing that had come to the fore during the 1990s persisted and expanded. Rather than singing to traditional spirits via a spirit medium, Gebusi continue to enjoy nonspiritual plaintive songs of longing, sexual attraction, and allure accompanied by guitar and ukulele—and now accompanied as well by bouts of active sexual humor and joking.

Figures bear out the link between Gebusi's changed forms of cultural expres-sion, spiritual belief, and violence. Of the various deaths that occurred in Gasumi Corners since 1998, not one was a homicide. There have been no killings of those who might have been suspected as sorcerers; the community homicide rate has been zero from 1989 to 2008—for almost two decades. Given that previously almost one of every three adult Gebusi had been violently killed, this is a major, and, to my mind, wonderfully positive change. Among other things, it testifies to and underscores the human ability for aggression and violence to be effectively managed and reduced through social and cultural change.

Influencing if not underlying the reduction of violence in Gasumi Corners is the St. Paul Catholic Church. As I quickly found, the Nomad Catholic Church is one nontraditional institution that has grown and intensified rather than dimin-ished for the people of Gasumi Corners. Its influence has persisted despite decline of government services, wages, and the small cash economy—and despite the relative decline of many other Christian churches in the Nomad area, including Evangelical and Seventh Day Adventist congregations. Gebusi have grown more closely associated with their local church, and especially with its resident priest, the smart and compassionate Father Aloi, who is a native of Indonesia. As explained to me later in Kiunga by Bishop Gilles Coté, a dearth of new priests from Western countries forced the Catholic Church of Papua New Guinea to look farther afield in finding young priests—and especially to South and Southeast Asia. He reported that this experiment was a great success and said with a laugh that he wished he had thought of it years earlier. In the case of Father Aloi, who I later came to know well, I agreed heartily. An engaging and energetic polyglot, Father Aloi spoke a half-dozen or more languages, including Indonesian, English, *tok pisin*, a vernacular from interior Borneo, and, more recently, a strong complement of Gebusi and other tongues from the Nomad area.

More importantly, he understood and respected the intricacies of Gebusi's spirit beliefs, disputes, social mores, general ethos—more than I could have imagined of a young Catholic priest. Perhaps this was due to his own background and rigorous service in Indonesia, including in a Jakarta slum and with a Borneo hill tribe. Whatever the reason, he cared about Gebusi on their own terms—and had gained their strong affection as well as their respect.

From his main residence on the fringe of Gasumi Corners, Father Aloi has kept his mission materially supplied from Kiunga, which was no mean feat in an environment of declining or defunct government services. He had further taken responsibility to spread church outreach by visiting a broad range of settlements, including in the deep bush. These long excursions to distant areas had little real precedent in the Nomad area since the patrols of the intrepid Australian colonial officers and a few white missionaries some thirty-five years before. Often gone for weeks at a time, Father Aloi traveled on foot and canoe or motorboat, accepting local food and trying to appreciate local customs wherever he went. He recounted with a laugh having unwittingly smoked a large amount of marijuana that was "innocently" put in a traditional tobacco pipe by a mischievous welcoming villager in a distant Bedamini settlement. As it turned out, the raising and selling of marijuana has become a major problem in the general Nomad area, especially to the east of Gebusi. This problem has intensified as the local cash economy based on garden produce and other forest products has largely collapsed.

During his travels and activism, Father Aloi has both entrusted and encouraged those from Gasumi Corners to take charge of the Catholic mission church in his absence, including the running of the Sunday service. This was the case during my own time at Gasumi Corners. On one occasion, for instance, Yamdaw (now "Luke") led the church service and Anagi (now "John") read the scripture and Keda (now "Joseph") gave the sermon—while Sayu and others played guitar and ukulele to lead the singing.

Amid the strength and compassion of Catholic leadership, many Gebusi in Gasumi Corners have taken new responsibility and expanded their role in their church. In the process, they have also mixed and combined ritual practices of Christianity with those of traditional custom. Father Aloi has been in favor of

Gebusi in traditional costuming for a Catholic welcoming ceremony, 2008; Sayu is on the far right. (PHOTO: Father Aloi, smm)

these developments, just as he supported the building of a new longhouse and the holding of Gebusi initiations. Now, the people of Gasumi Corners actively cooperate in creating indigenous-style costumes and performances that help celebrate Christian events, activities, and special occasions. As a result, the separation and the inequity between Catholic leadership and Gebusi culture seemed less than before. This illustrates how Gebusi, like other peoples, do not simply reproduce their past even as they draw upon it as a renewable resource—the resource of culture. They extend and develop their culture as they confront new realities, explore new ways to express themselves, and find new avenues to create meaning and find value in their lives and livelihood.

Considering their other changes, what has happened to the external factors and forces that loomed so large in Gasumi Corners during the 1990s? At that time, of course, the Nomad school, police, government officials, development projects, health clinic, sports league, and twice-weekly market were all not just strong but powerful magnets of interest and activity. Now all of these institutions and activities are dormant or defunct. The elementary school is closed, the health clinic is all but shut, the police are gone, the central government station has no officers or radio, the Nomad market is desultory, and the sports leagues are no more. Maybe they will come back again someday, but for now, they are gone.

Gebusi themselves say simply, "The government has died" (*gamani golom-da*). But to my surprise, they say this with a glint in their eye, almost with a sense of "good riddance" rather than pining for lost advancement or opportunities. True, their material standing is less than it used to be as judged on the basis of income, manufactured goods, or employment. And yet, though they earn less than one U.S. dollar per day—the international standard of extreme poverty—Gebusi reliance on their traditional economy and customs is stronger and prouder in 2008 than it was a decade before.

Gebusi do lament and criticize the inefficiency and waste of the Papua New Guinea government, including the continued payment of Nomad's civil servants when they live elsewhere. But those from Gasumi Corners do not sit by and degrade themselves as a result. They do not agree with the opinion of government officials that the people of Nomad are undeserving of government presence, programs, and support. Instead, they have taken it upon themselves to develop and reassert their own customs and beliefs and their integrity as an indigenous people. In the process, they have taken responsibility and initiative, and drawn on their cultural and environmental resources to shape their own destiny.

What Gebusi illustrate is the ability of peoples across the world to create dignity and meaning amid conditions of change and challenge in their individual and communal lives.

Before I left my Gebusi friends, I went up once more to my old village site of Yibihilu. It was almost unrecognizable, just another part of the forest. On the way in the canoe, Didiga clubbed a low-perching bird. Keda deftly grabbed it, and Sayu roasted it carefully for lunch. To commemorate our last meal together in the forest, we stuck the bird's feathers in the rafters of the tiny lean-to that is now the only structure in the general vicinity of Yibihilu. We talked and laughed and sighed about days and people gone by, the passage of time. On our way back to the village, we brought food to a party of men from Gasumi Corners who were carving a canoe from a big tree along the river. We stopped and joked, smoked tobacco, cursed the mosquitoes, and danced around in horseplay. The canoe was being built for Father Aloi, and he would pay them in cash. But the power of traditional practices, and especially of good company, was as strong as ever.

Regardless of how many times I return to the Gebusi, their story will never be predictable. Each time, my own expectations of what Gebusi were, or could be, have been wonderfully recast. In the process, not just my understanding but my life has become richer through the power of human connection. What my times with the Gebusi have taught me is that our understanding of other peoples and cultures—across the world or around the corner—is never finished. Today's new finding could be either reinforced or overturned tomorrow. This does not mean that our efforts as cultural anthropologists are either random or doomed to obsolescence. It simply means that our work, like our lives, thrives on new cycles of experience that freshly engage both our hearts and our minds.

So, too, my Gebusi friends, their families, and their future will always be meaningfully growing and changing. As long as I live, I hope to keep contact with Sayu, Didiga, and my other Gebusi friends. Since 1980, their culture has been transformed for me from an alien world to one of powerful value and then to one of friendship and deep connection.

Across the miles and the years, what more can one ask?

BROADER CONNECTIONS: *Cultural Survival, Economic Decline, and the Reinvention of Culture*

- **Problems of infrastructure** and **poor government services** are a **common problem** in **rural areas** of developing countries.

- Like people in many world areas, Gebusi responded to their marginality by **rejuvenating some older cultural practices—rediscovering and reinventing their traditions.**

- Gebusi were **poor in economic terms**—earning less than a dollar a day—but were arguably **richer than they had been in cultural meaning and social quality of life.**

- With passage of time, like many peoples, Gebusi took **increasing interest in their own cultural past,** including **ethnographic documentation, books, and other information given to them by Bruce.**

- Peoples undergoing cultural loss do not recoup the full range of their previous beliefs and practices even during periods of cultural rejuvenation. Gebusi **have not reestablished spirit mediumship or shamanism, séances, sorcery divinations, or practices that lead to violence. The homicide rate among the people of Gasumi Corners has continued to be zero since the late 1980s.**

- The reduction of Gebusi homicide illustrates generally (a) that **violence is not innate or inevitable but is strongly shaped by social and cultural changes,** and (b) that **culture change on its own terms can have positive results.**

- Gebusi illustrate the importance of **complementing** our understanding of **large-scale changes, including globalization, chronic poverty, and challenges of development,** with **a human appreciation of how people adapt and find meaning and value in their own culture.**

- Gebusi reveal both that **culture change can be surprising and unpredictable over time,** and that **human cultural connections have the potential to transcend these changes,** both within societies and, potentially, for the anthropologist as well.

CHAPTER 12

A young girl of contemporary Gasumi Corners, wearing a ragged dress
(PHOTO: Bruce Knauft)

2012 and Beyond

YUWAY HAS DIED. And with him, virtually the whole generation of Gebusi whom I first knew as young adults. But Gebusi culture has not died, neither its energy, its persistence, nor its ability to survive major changes. These changes did not begin with the arrival of Australians in 1963. Indeed, Gebusi had probably dealt with greater change, especially the violent raids against them by the Bedamini people during the decades prior to Western contact. In some ways, it was this preceding stress that made Gebusi so accepting and appreciative of Australian colonial arrival—and, even after they left, so welcoming of modern institutions such as the church, school, market, and government administration. More recently, Gebusi have again had the relative independence, and necessity, to chart their own local future.

Around the world, traditions fade. But important parts of them are rediscovered, reinvented, and expressed in new ways. This pattern continues for the Gebusi and their neighbors. On the one hand, they continue to be challenged by their geographic and economic isolation. As of late 2011, the Nomad airstrip continues to be closed much of the time, as local workers are often unpaid and the grass grows too high for planes to land. Government presence and administration at Nomad continue to be vestigial or absent. No Gebusi have yet graduated from high school, and though the Nomad elementary school has reopened, it is poorly and inconsistently staffed. Father Aloi has left Gasumi Corners for another posting elsewhere, and his absence is sorely missed. Gebusi still have no roads to anywhere. And with the airstrip undependable, it is increasingly difficult for me to dependably return again, though I still plan to do so. I have little doubt, however, that Gebusi are doing quite fine, thank you very much, on their own.

There is some irony in this. In our 21st century, the human globe is more connected than ever. But Gebusi are no more accessible from the outside world—and in some ways less so—than they were when I was first with them in 1980. Yet, just two weeks ago as I write this, I received an email from a young man from another ethnic group in the Nomad area who is now studying for a teaching degree at the University of Goroka in the eastern highlands of Papua New Guinea. It is a delight for me not only to get updated information from him about the Nomad area but to know that at least a few persons from the region are establishing greater connections with a broader world, including through higher education. At the same time, the breadth and speed of modern communication, which links people and places instantly across the world, also masks the uneven nature of global development. Some people get richly "developed" while others do not or get poorer.

In the Gebusi's regional context, this is evident from the impact of a large and technologically sophisticated mine, the Ok Tedi gold and copper mine, that lies 100 miles to their northwest. In 2010, this mine supplied 18 percent of the Gross Domestic Product of the entire country of Papua New Guinea as well as 32 percent of the nation's export earnings. A few landowners near the mine site got very rich from large royalty payments to compensate them for the use of their land. Beyond this, a portion of the mine's revenue supports the substantial cost of developing and maintaining at least a skeleton of infrastructure across the expansive rainforest of the country's Western Province, including the Nomad Station. The large province constitutes 20 percent of the nation's landmass but harbors only 3 percent of its population. Within it, the large bulk of government and mining revenue is spent for developments in and near towns and major areas of resource infrastructure—not in places like Nomad Station, much less Gasumi Corners.

Even so, the Gebusi's larger fate in coming years is still tied significantly to the Ok Tedi mine. The existing deposits of the mine are nearing depletion, and the whole operation is slated for either closure or drastically reduced operation in coming years. The national and regional desire to keep the mine running—for the sake of the economy—directly confronts the fact that the mine has produced, and continues to produce, one of the largest riverine ecological disasters in the world. The rock-born toxic waste from the Ok Tedi mine, including heavy metals, has profoundly and lastingly polluted one of the world's few remaining large pristine river systems. As I write this chapter, the mine was recently shut down after an unknown design flaw caused at least four ruptures in an outlet pipeline, spewing out large quantities of pyrite concentrate. As engineers scrambled to find the cause, the mine was closed—at a cost of five-and-a-half million U.S. dollars per day. As one expert told me, the spilled pyrite turns to sulfuric acid when exposed to the air. If not permanently corrected, this spill and others like it will make heavy metals bioavailable and poison the ecosystem for centuries. This is exponentially worse than the ecocide that has already occurred—like the difference between a major earthquake or tsunami (horrifying) and a nuclear meltdown (beyond horrifying).

Even more recently as I write, the Ok Tedi mine has now been reopened—after a revenue loss of 200 million dollars. Though the mine does not affect the Gebusi's own ecology directly, there remain questions about whether the problem has been "fixed"—and the premier of the Western Province is livid that he and other Province officials were not consulted or involved in the decision to reopen the mine despite its ecological danger. To offset more than one-third of its recent losses, the Ok Tedi mine has quickly slashed more than 150 million kina that it had already allocated for important development projects in the Western Province, including funding for hospitals, health clinics, schools, and airstrip maintenance and upgrades. Given that the Ok Tedi mine is now owned by the PNG government along with the PNG

Sustainable Development Program, there is a direct conflict and very difficult trade-off between the government's need for infrastructure and services—and hence for mining revenue—and its mandate to protect the environment. Even when the pipeline of money is flowing "normally," people like the Gebusi barely get a trickle at the end of the line—and this trickle easily dries up.

In significant parts of the world, the problems as well as the opportunities caused by globalization are significantly greater than what the Gebusi themselves have directly experienced. For the last several years, I have complemented my interest in the Gebusi and in Melanesia by directing a project of engaged anthropology that has taken me to challenged parts of the developing world such as Liberia in West Africa, the Congo (DRC), Ecuador, Mongolia, and the Himalayan areas of Tibet (China), Nepal, Bhutan, and northern India. In each case, my goal has been to identify and put together networks of influence that combine expert anthropologists, leaders of civil society organizations, and policy-makers—including high-ranking government officials and administrators from the United Nations. All too often, these groups communicate and operate separately, in self-contained worlds. Against this, our States at Regional Risk Project (SARR) develops conferences and workshops that bring together members of these different constituencies for engaged dialogue within the country or region itself. We have mounted such gatherings in places such as Monrovia, Liberia; three cities in East Congo; Bujumbura, Burundi; Quito, Ecuador; Ulaanbaaatar, Mongolia; and Lumbini, Nepal. In each case, the great benefit of constructive dialogue and robust connection between scholars, civil society activists, and practical policy makers within countries and regions is powerfully evident (see *www.sarr.emory.edu*).

In the course of this project, I have realized how important it is for regions of the developing world to manage natural wealth for the public good lest it become a curse of political or military conflict. Whether it be diamonds in West Africa, precious minerals in East Congo or in Tibet, cocoa or natural gas in the Andes, or copper and gold in Mongolia, the material resources of developing countries—which developed countries crave—can be a source not just of inequality but of depredation, oppression, and violence. The conflict in East Congo, fueled by greed for enormous mineral wealth, has claimed more than 5 million lives—the greatest human-caused loss of life since World War Two and the Holocaust. At the other end of the spectrum, rapidly developing countries in significant parts of East Asia, South and Southeast Asia, and South America experience a significant increase in living standards (though this wealth is not spread evenly and may not confer personal or political freedom).

As these trends suggest, it is difficult to generalize about the impact of globalization on society and culture apart from the world area and local context being considered; the range of variation is enormous. For cultural anthropology, this underscores the importance of avoiding either rosy assumptions that the world's peoples benefit from global development, or pessimistic ones that they are going "down the tubes" of human disenfranchisement or degradation. Rather, a combination of scholarly and engaged anthropology is needed to determine exactly what kinds of social inequity and exploitation occur in which contexts and regions, why this is so, and how these issues can be practically addressed—including by facilitating dialogue among people in their own local, national, and regional situation. Within this process, culture is not simply a passive bystander to processes of economic development, political control, or manipulation. Rather, cultural identity—including ethnic identity, national identity, or religious affiliation—is very often at the heart of the matter, including why resources do not get distributed equitably. As such, it is increasingly important for cultural anthropologists to communicate with those outside a scholarly world, not just to learn about but to help address and mitigate major human problems both at home and abroad. In their own small part of the world, Gebusi don't and can't provide full purchase on all these issues. But in their larger regional, national, and international context, Gebusi do provide one illustration of how culture, political economy, and the human and physical environment are interconnected in the world today, even in its most seemingly remote regions.

Through culture, the paths of the past continue to fertilize those of the present, even if the latter seem increasingly large and well-trodden. People like the Gebusi experiment continually with this mix. As an ethnographer and as a person, engaging this process has been an intellectual challenge and also an emotional one. Addressing the dynamics of culture change requires a balance and sometimes a healthy tension between the larger analysis of our minds and the ethical principles and humanitarianism of our hearts. Where would we be without both of these in our lives and in our work?

Over the years, as I have felt and thought about changes in Gebusi culture, I have traveled increasingly beyond a view of Gebusi as either fundamentally indigenous or as orphaned from their rich past. Instead, I view Gebusi as simply vibrant in their present. I have realized that Gebusi themselves negotiate their tensions better than I could have imagined. The same is true of peoples in many parts of the world today. For Gebusi, I think they have managed well in part because of their abiding flexibility, on one hand, and their sense of playfulness, on the other. My Gebusi friends might embrace new events and activities as if they were separate from their past, or they may rediscover older customs in a new light. But in either case, they convey strong awareness—through humor and irony, play and performance—that developments are neither as fixed nor as serious as they might appear to an outsider. Even as some of their beliefs or practices are left aside and in some cases actively abandoned, others are rediscovered or reinvented.

Gebusi still desire money, modern goods, and more contemporary styles of life. But they are no longer as subordinate to outside authority figures—pastors, teachers, government officials, and buyers at market—as they were during the 1990s. Their lives then more fully embraced a larger and more complicated social universe at the Nomad Station. Gebusi at that time seemed fully committed to, and practically dependent on, the local market for their economy, the school for their education, the aid post for their health, the government offices for political development, the interethnic league for sports, the police station for social control, and Independence Day as their largest ritual celebration. But since the 1990s, the people of Gasumi Corners have reasserted their own social world and have emphasized greater social integrity in their own community, including in relation to the rainforest.

Like other peoples in the contemporary world, Gebusi are becoming more contemporary or modern in their own distinct way. Gebusi still value quiet moments in the rainforest, the bonds between kin and friends, and the aesthetic splendor of their traditional costuming and performance. They also engage and aspire to features of so-called modern life, including long-standing reliance on steel tools and manufactured implements, clothes, a desire for money, strong involvement with their local church, and interest in new cultural forms of aesthetics and music. The resulting combinations are distinctive to Gebusi and not the same as in other countries or even in other parts of Papua New Guinea. Like the mixed vocabularies that pervade their string band songs, contemporary life for Gebusi cannot be framed solely in terms of either external influences or indigenous dispositions; it is rather a product of both. This has become their culture.

In Western perception and scholarship, it is sometimes said that social and economic developments converge globally to make peoples increasingly alike around the world. In selected ways this is true. For instance, widely shared modern institutions of schooling, health care, government projects, local markets, and churches have had a deep-seated impact on Gebusi in recent decades—even if, as is also true in other rural areas, some of these developments may not be especially active at the present time. In complementary fashion, it is often said that those left behind in the process of global development are becoming relatively poorer and more disempowered. This is also true of Gebusi. But Gebusi also put such assertions in deeper and more human perspective. As their recent developments illustrate, the resurgence of local cultures should not be discounted in our twenty-first century. In some ways, in fact, the explicit assertion of cultural diversity across the world is now becoming as great as and sometimes even stronger than it was before.

In the context of their own local conditions, Gebusi are especially fortunate to have the continuing bounty of their land. They own not only their own settlement sites but the gardens and pristine forests that provide them with their food, and a surplus to boot. Many peoples who experience so-called modernization are not so lucky. By contrast, Gebusi have not had to endure violent subjugation, land alienation, heavy taxation, exploitative wage labor, slavery, depletion of natural resources, or degradation of their immediate natural environment. The inhabitants of Gasumi Corners are additionally fortunate that part of their land lays within a few minutes' walk of what remains the largest outpost for many miles in any direction—the Nomad Station. This provides them the flexibility, depending on conditions and their disposition, to orient to a greater or a lesser extent to the events and activities of the government, on the one hand, or the primary rainforest, on the other.

I have been fortunate as well. I have had the rare opportunity to know the Gebusi, to be part of their lives, and to share in their customs across a rich spectrum of traditional, modern, and combined practices and orientations. That these have spanned such great cultural distance during just three decades makes my fortune all the greater. The Gebusi in 1980 were neither pristine nor fully "traditional," but their history gave them a special opportunity to develop their culture, in significant part, on their own terms. By 1998, the Gebusi's path of cultural development had not just taken off but run circles around its previous scope and scale, including changes in subsistence, economy, religion, marriage, politics, aesthetic life, and even their sense of time. Due to these changes, Gebusi will never be as independent or remote from outside influence as they once were. More recently, a negative turn of their regional economic wheel has impacted Gebusi, and withdrawal of outside resources and services persists. In the mix, Gebusi traditions are both more fully reasserted and more fully combined with newer developments. Gebusi traditions are resurgent not as simple replicas of the past, but in new ways that draw on longstanding customs as deep and powerful resources.

As part of their openness, the Gebusi warmly welcomed me from the start. They have given me the greatest gift that people can give and that we can all appreciate: the sharing of life across differences of culture.

FAREWELL

On the day of departure, I had no shame. The morning started rainy, and I hoped it would continue so the plane wouldn't come. I didn't care that my few boxes were already sealed and that everything else had been given away. Eventually, though, the rain let up, and I trudged in sorrow with everyone else to the airstrip.

I started choking up well before the plane emerged on the horizon. I knew it would happen, just as it had before. I fought back the tears, but they kept coming. I had known the people of Yibihilu and then of Gasumi Corners so well before and now again through many years—first when they were children or young adults and now with their own children in their place. It always remains a question whether I can return to the Gebusi yet again. Nomad is so remote, and the logistics of getting there are difficult. The tropics grind hard on my middle-aged body, and my obligations back home remain packed in a whole other life. My Gebusi friends know this. Those who are older know that I may never see them again; each time, more of them are dead by the time I can return. Despite other changes, their lives remain short.

Instead of using my camera on the last day, I took mental pictures that are more indelible. As I moved down the sorrowful line of those gathered to say their good-byes, I forced myself to peer in the face and gaze in the eyes of each man and woman, each boy and girl from Gasumi Corners. Snapping their fingers in the best and most forthright manner, I burned into my mind the living image of each of these unique persons so as never to forget their exquisite humanity. Their tear-streaked faces mirrored my own as they fought the impulse to turn away. I cried along with them, oblivious to onlookers, a six-foot white guy bawling with a crowd of villagers.

I lost it when I came to Sayu and Didiga. I have become so close to them over the years, since they were very small. They have shared much about their lives with me, and I with them. It is hard to think that I don't know when I will see them again, and that in the interim I will have but fleeting contact.

Then there was Yuway. Yuway helped lead me on my very first patrol to the Gebusi. He was my most sensitive and caring helper when I was first learning the language, and was my best friend. I saw him fall in love and get married, and I know his five children, who are now mostly grown. Throughout, Yuway has been one of the nicest and most decent people I have ever met. When I left him, I looked into his eyes and blurted out, "Friend. Oh friend. When will I ever see you again?!" His wisdom was greater than mine. With a weepy and yet dignified smile, he told me, "I'll see you later, in heaven."

My last sight of Yuway then was at the end of the airstrip. He had walked down the path to its conclusion. He waved me a final goodbye as the plane soared off. Then I sailed up toward the heavens, and Yuway awaited his own.

As Didiga told me in a letter, Yuway died on June 16, 2009. This book is dedicated to his memory, to his family, and to the future of the Gebusi.

Who can deny the world of change in cultures? Or the richness of humanity that persists despite all that would suppress it?

BROADER CONNECTIONS: *Globalization, Political Economy, and Engaged Anthropology*

- As Gebusi illustrate, **globalization affects all societies and cultures** but is also **highly uneven** in its impact and affects. Changes may **increase poverty and disenfranchisement—or increase standards of living.**

- Patterns of economic development do not always move "forward." **In *some* ways, Gebusi are more remote going into 2012 than they were in 1980.** The airstrip stays intermittently closed, schooling and healthcare are minimal, and police and government presence are vestigial or absent.

- As is true of most peoples today, the larger political and economic factors that the Gebusi are subject to inform their **regional political economy.**

- **Culture—including ethnic, racial, national, and religious identity—is a key dimension of the impact of regional and global political economy.**

- Amid globalization, **some cultural traditions fade while others are rediscovered, reinvented, and expressed in new ways.**

- Many **developing peoples are impacted by forces outside their direct experience or control.** Among Gebusi, this is illustrated by the Ok Tedi gold and copper mine in the Western Province of Papua New Guinea.

- The **Ok Tedi mine** also illustrates how **exploitation of natural resources can be at once an economic benefit, an environmental disaster, and a cause of competition and conflict.**

- Bruce's States at Regional Risk Project, which addresses issues of sociocultural and cultural recovery in different world areas, provides an example of **applied anthropology or "engaged anthropology."**

- It is increasingly important and useful for **cultural anthropologists to engage in practical dialogues with policy makers and members of civil society to facilitate positive social change.** It is equally important that **local and national constituencies be strongly involved to influence outcomes.**

- As Gebusi illustrate, including with respect to historic patterns of violence, **local initiatives are often better at instituting positive change than those envisaged or directed primarily by outsiders.**

- **Many peripheral peoples in the world today have a history of having been subject to coerced labor or slavery, tribute or taxation, land alienation, out-migration, or indebtedness due to reliance on cash crops or commodities. Geubsi are fortunate to have not suffered directly from such negative impacts.**

- Like other peoples, Gebusi are becoming **contemporary or modern in their own distinct way.** In this regard, Gebusi **flexibility** and **creative playfulness** are especially useful and effective.

- Both personally and professionally, **cultural anthropologists** such as Bruce are **fortunate** that the people they live with in the field **share their lives across differences of culture.**

- **Cultural anthropologists and the people they study may become closely connected personally as well as professionally over time.**

- Fortunately, **the world of vibrant and creative change in cultures cannot easily be either denied or suppressed.**

List of Persons

Bosap: 1998 — older woman, never married, mother of Kuma, regular market seller; **2008** — deceased

Basowey: 1989 — adult man, killed by Doliay for the sickness death of Boyl

Boyl: 1982 — mother of Sayu, wife of Silap; friend of Eileen; **1998** — deceased

Bulobey: 1982 — active spirit medium, newly married; **1998** — Evangelical Church member, married with five children; **2008** — deceased

Damya: 1982 — young boy, son of Nolop and Wosip; **1998** — married with children, lead Gasumi string band singer, devoted member of the Catholic Church; **2008** — Catholic prayer and service leader, father of three children

Didiga: 1982 — young boy, son of Imba; **1998** — grade six graduate, good friend and helper of Bruce; **2008** — son had been named "Knauft"

Doliay: 1982 — initiate, friend of Hawi, transient tryst partner of Nolop; **1989** — widower of Boyl, killer of Sabowey, begins prison term in Port Moresby; **1998** — married with three children, devoted member of the Catholic Church; **2008** — deceased

Dugawe: 1980 — husband of Sialim, committed suicide by drinking fish poison, died childless

Gami: 1982 — born in Yibihilu very shortly after Bruce and Eileen's departure; **1998** — temporary wife of Guyul; **2001** — wife of Wayabay; **2008** — mother of three children with Wayabay

Gono: 1980 — carrier for Bruce and Eileen on first expedition, forwent initiation to marry early; **1998** — husband of Nolop, father of teenage girl; **2008** — deceased

Guyul: 1982 — young boy; **1998** — temporary husband of Gami

Gwabi: 1982 — young boy; **1998** — builder and owner of Bruce's house, married with one son

Halowa: 1982 — young boy, younger brother of Yuway; **1998** — member of Evangelical Church, married with four children; **2008** — father of six children

Hawi: 1980–82 — carrier for Bruce and Eileen on first expedition, initiate, friend of Doliay; **1998** — married with four children, lived at Nomad Station, devoted member of the Evangelical Church, helped keep track of aircraft cargo; **2008** — still alive

Haymp: 1982 — initiate; **c. 1983** — father of Kubwam; **1998** — deceased

Hiali: 1981 — younger brother of Silap, died of sickness eleven days after being initiated

181

Howe: 1982 — young boy, son of Kawuk; 1998 — young man; member of Catholic Church, singer in the Gasumi Corners string band

Huwa: 1998 — orphaned teenage younger brother of Sayu, Gasumi string band singer

Imba: 1982 — senior man of Yibihilu, father of Didiga; 1998 — deceased

Kawuk: 1982 — cofounder of Yibihilu longhouse, married man with two small children; 1998 — senior man of Gasumi Corners, devoted member of the Catholic Church, married with five children; 2008 — security guard for the Catholic Church, five children and six grandchildren

Keda: 1982 — teenage younger brother of Yuway; 1998 — married with children, active Catholic Church member; 2008 — Catholic church lay leader; father of three children

Kubwam: 1982 — born in Yibihilu shortly after Bruce and Eileen's departure; 1998 — temporary wife of Mako; 2008 — divorced Gebusi husband, married Bedamini man, moved to Bedamini territory

Kuma: 1982 — young boy, son of Bosap; 1998 — marriageable bachelor

Kwelam: 1998 — teenage daughter of Nolop

Mai: 1982 — young daughter of Tewo; 1998 — adult woman, living with Tewo outside of Kiunga

Mako: 1982 — young boy; 1998 — young man, temporary husband of Kubwam

Marbwi: 1998 — young girl, adopted daughter of Gwabi; 2008 — outmarried to a Sirigubi settlement

Mokoyl: 1979 — mother of Sialim, killed by Swamin for the sickness death of his wife

Momiay: 1982 — initiate; 1998 — deceased

Mora: 1982 — teenage boy, solicitor of Bruce; 1998 — married with three children; 2008 — deceased

Nolop: 1982 — mother of Damya and Korlis, wife of Wosip, transient tryst partner of Doliay; c. 1983 — mother of Kwelam; 1998 — older woman, market seller, wife of Gono

Sialim: 1982 — widow of Dugawe, mother of one daughter, wife of Swamin; 1998 — deceased

Silap: 1982 — cofounder of Yibihilu longhouse, husband of Boyl, father of Sayu; 1998 — deceased

Sagawa: 1982 — forwent initiation to establish a temporary relationship with Sialim; 1998 — deceased from a death adder bite

Sayu: 1982 — young boy, son of Boyl and Silap, friend of Bruce and Eileen; c.1994 — lived in Kiunga; 1998 — bachelor, friend, helper, and confidant of Bruce; 2008 — father of four children by two wives in sequence

Swamin: 1980–82 — carrier for Bruce and Eileen on first expedition, main spirit medium of Yibihilu community, widower, father of Wayabay, married Sialim; 1998 — deceased

Tewo: c. 1983 — mother of Gami; 1998 — living with husband and family outside Kiunga

Uwano: 1982 — Young adult man, "breadfruit" exchange partner of Bruce; 1998 — deceased October 9, 1998

Warbwi: 1982 — new wife of Yuway; 1998 — wife of Yuway and mother of five children; 2008 — still alive

Wayabay: 1982 — young boy, son of Swamin; **1998** — bachelor, hunter, and house builder; **2001** — husband of Gami; **2008** — father of three children

Willy: 1998 — boy, son of Doliay

Wosip: 1982 — husband of Nolop, father of Damya and Korlis; **1998** — deceased

Yaba: 1982 — widower, jokester in Yibihilu; **1998** — deceased

Yuway: 1980–82 — initiate, carrier for Bruce and Eileen on first expedition, language helper and friend of Bruce; **1998** — husband of Warbwi, father of four children, member of the Seventh Day Adventist Church; **2008** — member of the Catholic Church, father of five children; **June 2009** — deceased

Index